D1330396

Psychology of the Media

WITHDRAWN FROM
THE LIBRARY

UNIVERSITY OF
WINCHESTER

KA 0362128 6

AIM HIGHER WITH *PALGRAVE INSIGHTS IN PSYCHOLOGY*
Also available in this series:

978-0-230-24988-2

978-0-230-24986-8

978-0-230-27222-4

978-0-230-24944-8

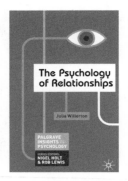

978-0-230-24941-7

978-0-230-25265-3

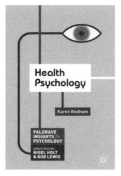

978-0-230-24945-5

978-0-230-24987-5

978-0-230-24942-4

To find out more visit
www.palgrave.com/insights

Psychology of the Media

David Giles

PALGRAVE INSIGHTS IN PSYCHOLOGY

SERIES EDITORS:
NIGEL HOLT
& ROB LEWIS

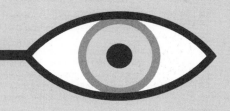
palgrave
macmillan

UNIVERSITY OF WINCHESTER
LIBRARY

© David Giles 2010

All rights reserved. No reproduction, copy or transmission of this publication may be made without written permission.

No portion of this publication may be reproduced, copied or transmitted save with written permission or in accordance with the provisions of the Copyright, Designs and Patents Act 1988, or under the terms of any licence permitting limited copying issued by the Copyright Licensing Agency, Saffron House, 6–10 Kirby Street, London EC1N 8TS.

Any person who does any unauthorized act in relation to this publication may be liable to criminal prosecution and civil claims for damages.

The author has asserted his right to be identified as the author of this work in accordance with the Copyright, Designs and Patents Act 1988.

First published 2010 by
PALGRAVE MACMILLAN

Palgrave Macmillan in the UK is an imprint of Macmillan Publishers Limited, registered in England, company number 785998, of Houndmills, Basingstoke, Hampshire RG21 6XS.

Palgrave Macmillan in the US is a division of St Martin's Press LLC, 175 Fifth Avenue, New York, NY 10010.

Palgrave Macmillan is the global academic imprint of the above companies and has companies and representatives throughout the world.

Palgrave® and Macmillan® are registered trademarks in the United States, the United Kingdom, Europe and other countries.

ISBN: 978–0–230–24986–8

This book is printed on paper suitable for recycling and made from fully managed and sustained forest sources. Logging, pulping and manufacturing processes are expected to conform to the environmental regulations of the country of origin.

A catalogue record for this book is available from the British Library.

A catalog record for this book is available from the Library of Congress.

10 9 8 7 6 5 4 3 2 1
19 18 17 16 15 14 13 12 11 10

Printed and bound in Great Britain by
CPI Antony Rowe, Chippenham and Eastbourne

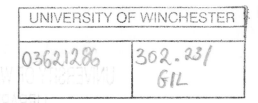

UNIVERSITY OF WINCHESTER

03621286   302.23/
            GIL

Contents

List of figures and tables

Figures

Tables

Note from series editors

Wherever we find people, we find psychology. Nowhere is this more evident than in the media, where we find people reported upon for the interest and satisfaction of people like us who read about them. The media play an important role and can be hugely influential, and it is not surprising that we find psychologists, such as David Giles, specializing in this important area.

David Giles is a leading media psychologist and we were delighted that he agreed to contribute a book to this series. He has written extensively in the area and is known for his often light, always rigorous, sometimes journalistic style. This is not surprising really, given his background in journalism, which gives him a unique insight into the psychology of the media.

- *Those of you reading this book as preparation for your university studies* should know that media psychology is rising hugely in popularity. Books you will read during your university studies will, no doubt, be influenced by David Giles or written by him. This book gives you a strong introduction to media psychology that will be more than adequate for many of you during your time at university.
- *Those reading the book while at university* may already have studied the media from an academic perspective, perhaps in media studies or as part of a pre-university qualification. David's approach is open and engaging. This book offers a psychological perspective to add to your knowledge.
- *Those reading the book in preparation for pre-university courses, such as A-level* will know from your course textbooks that the psychology

of the media is more prominent now than it has ever been in the past. The Reading Guide at the end of the book tells you where different A-level specifications appear.

When we commissioned and edited these books, we spoke to psychologists, sociologists, media studies lecturers and many others, including journalists, and know that the material David Giles has addressed here is relevant to these areas also. Whatever your area of study or whether you are reading the book for interest, we are certain you will find it to be a useful addition to your bookshelf.

NIGEL HOLT AND ROB LEWIS
Series Editors

Introduction to Media Psychology

1 History of the mass media

2 Ways of thinking about psychology and the media

Section summary

We live in an age in which media are everywhere. We consume media constantly: radio, television, Internet, electronic games, multiple sources of advertising. We *use* media constantly: mobile phones, social networking and various communication devices. So prolific have the media become, we sometimes exist in a state of 'media blindness', where we fail to acknowledge the presence, much less the influence, of media in our decision-making, beliefs and attitudes. And with the arrival of the Internet – it's easy to forget how recent it is – the distinction between traditional ('passive') media and communication ('active') media has become blurred. It's not surprising therefore, when we talk about media, that the term means different things to different people. And very often, people use 'the media' in a lazy, shorthand way for newspapers and TV shows they don't like.

So that's really my starting point for this book. In order to understand how media and psychology interact, first of all we need to work out what media are, and where they come from. As a matter of fact, psychology has neatly avoided saying much about the media until fairly recently, probably because psychologists have tended to be more interested in universal phenomena, disconnected from time and space. As each new medium appeared – radio, television and so on – it was hoped they would eventually go away and stop bothering us. Maybe it is only with the Internet, a medium now used by all academics, everywhere, that the media have become impossible for psychologists to ignore. Nevertheless, we still hear claims that the Internet is special, something above and beyond the media.

Partly, this is because the media have earned themselves a dreadful reputation over the decades. Sensationalist news reporting, unethical advertising, 'trash' television, pornography and violence are all charges that have been levelled at different media over the years. We hear all manner of dreadful things being blamed on the media, often, ironically, by people on television and in newspapers, and psychology has played its part by producing what seems to be extensive evidence for the ill effects of media on human behaviour. But along came a medium that psychologists rather liked. When you've been accusing the media for years for their part in the decline of civilization, how do you face up to the fact that some media might actually be good?

Well, the fact of the matter is that no medium – from the humble newspaper to the cyberspace paradise of *Second Life* – can ever be evaluated in purely moral terms. There are bad people, who sometimes own media, and use them for their own self-promotion or power. Other bad people, such as political extremists and paedophiles, create a market for certain types of media content. But these things are the fault of bad people, not the media they use to communicate with one another and to express themselves.

When thinking about media, one of the most important things to acknowledge is the date. With media, we can't wish time and space away. A study conducted in 1962 can tell us very little about the psychology of media in 2010. It can begin to point the way, but one of the fundamental considerations of media psychology research is that humans have very different media experiences in different historical periods. When television first appeared, it seemed like magic. How would people from the first half of the 20th century deal with the Internet?

That's why it's important never to lose sight of the history of the media. In Chapter 1 we'll consider how remarkably new many of the media that we use every day are, and at the same time, how many of the same issues crop up each time a new medium arrives on the scene. Perhaps there may be something 'universal' about human responses to media after all.

One medium, several media

The word 'media' is a plural noun. You can't have 'a media'. If you're just talking about one form of media – television, say – you have to call it 'a medium'. Just don't get it confused with palm readings and seances, that's all.

Chapter 1

History of the mass media

👁 Introduction

This opening chapter aims to introduce you to the concept of media in general. It is actually quite a difficult concept to define, so I begin by discussing what qualifies something for it to be considered a medium, the definition of 'mass medium', and, in particular, the work of Marshall McLuhan, one of the most important thinkers about the media in history. I go on to explain why McLuhan's ideas are vitally important to media psychology, even though they have been ignored by a good deal of the research that is covered in this book.

👁 What is a medium?

Any history needs a starting point, and the obvious place to begin here would be the appearance of the first medium. But we can't kick this story off without defining the term 'medium'. We might use the term 'medium' to refer to literally anything that humans use in order to communicate some kind of message – a cave wall, perhaps, in the Stone Age, or a Post-it note today. However, the kinds of messages discovered in prehistoric caves, the subject of much historical debate, are likely to differ markedly from those stuck on desks and doors, which solely convey a short-lived, soon-to-be-redundant piece of information: 'Back at 9.30', 'Charlie rang' or 'Don't forget the onions.' Whatever Palaeolithic humans were daubing down in their subterranean chambers, it probably wasn't 'Don't forget the onions.'

If all media were essentially the same type of communication system, it would be easy to identify the key moments in media history. But we have to fit in something like the telephone, which as a communication system has been so popular that we cannot imagine life without it, yet – until the advent of text or SMS – it has never been capable of broadcasting messages to more than one listener.

And what do we define as a **message**, anyway? Should we all be able to agree on its content and meaning? Should it have a clear, unambiguous sender, and a clear, unambiguous hearer or reader? These questions might appear abstract and philosophical, but, as you will see as you think more and more about media, they are fundamentally important, particularly if you are studying their psychological impact.

Media or mass media?

According to McQuail (2005), there are four elements that determine the emergence of a mass medium:

1 Purpose of, or need for, communication
2 Technology for public communication
3 Social organization for production and distribution
4 Governance in 'the public interest'.

The first two elements may be independent of one another: the emergence of a medium may, or may not, arise out of a need for communication (although it could be argued that this basic human need underpins the success of all media), but it could simply reflect technological progress and the availability of the new technology. Even then, the latter two elements are essential for mass take-up: a company, or several companies, producing the hardware and software, and some kind of state or multinational body to oversee the medium's evolution and monitor its uses. In effect, though, the term 'mass media' has become almost obsolete in recent years, probably because when people refer to media, it is almost always the mass media they are talking about. The 'mass' bit has simply dropped off.

Marshall McLuhan: media visionary

The most famous writer on media in history is undoubtedly **Marshall McLuhan** (1911–80). McLuhan grew up in Canada but studied at

Cambridge University and various US colleges and published a series of ground-breaking books in the 1960s that were picked up by the media and other communication theorists. His most famous work is probably *Understanding Media: The Extensions of Man* (1964/2001), and it is worth reading for its seductive blend of philosophy, history and literature. McLuhan is sometimes criticized, like Freud, for not having tested any of his theories (McQuail, 2005), but this is no reason to discount them.

McLuhan is best known for coining the phrase 'the medium is the message'. He was trying to say that media and their messages cannot simply be separated and studied as separate entities. Let's take music broadcasting as an example. Since the birth of radio, music has dominated the airwaves: being an aural medium, it is not surprising that music should have proved its most successful type of programming. And it's easy to present music on the radio: whether you are a classical presenter or an urban DJ, it's simply a matter of cueing up the recording and announcing the details.

Music on television has turned out to be quite a different matter. An orchestra sitting on a stage is only of interest to serious musicians. Only a DJ would really be interested in the sight of another DJ working the decks. Until promotional videos appeared in the mid-1970s (Queen's 'Bohemian Rhapsody' being one of the first), TV producers had to fill studios full of dancing teenagers in order to provide some visual appeal for the audience, even at the height of glam rock. Increasingly, with the advent of MTV and other round-the-clock, non-stop video channels in the 1980s, the message seemed to be less about the music and more about what was happening in the video. The 'message' provided by music on TV, then, is fundamentally different from that communicated by radio.

Another important concept developed by McLuhan was the idea of media as 'extensions of man'. He argued that a medium could be defined as any phenomenon that changed the way we go about the world. Two objects he defined as media were the electric light and the car. Before the electric light, night-time had a different meaning than it does today. Take a walk through the city at night and try to imagine the experience without any artificial light. You'd probably want to turn back home very quickly! Then think of all the human activities, particularly in the winter, that are illuminated by electric lighting, from everyday things like cooking the evening meal, shopping and travelling, to entertainment, social life and playing floodlit sport.

For McLuhan, the electric light acted as a medium because it opened up new possibilities for human activity. Before it arrived, the difficult business of struggling with oil and gas lamps, and simple candles, made it hard to do more than a few essential activities at night. With electric lighting, the dark half of life became full of possibilities. Today, there are people making a living from the entertainment industry who practically live a nocturnal existence – all because of the power of this particular medium.

For the electric light, substitute the car. Think of life in the late 19th century, when the railways were the only real option for long-distance travel, and private transport consisted of nothing much faster than a horse-driven carriage. People's life choices were severely limited. You couldn't live far from your work, unless you could travel by train. Shopping had to be done locally. Visiting people and places was dependent on distance or, if possible, the railway timetable. But the car has opened up innumerable options for people to plan busy lives, commute many miles to work, and travel to far-flung parts of the country for leisure or business, often on a daily basis. Prior to the car, there was the wheel: McLuhan saw the wheel as an even more fundamental medium, which speeded travel up, and paved the way for all the means of transportation that followed.

What have these things got to do, you may be wondering, with radio, television, the Internet – all the conventional media you expect to read about in a book on media psychology? Well, McLuhan encouraged us to consider these devices in exactly the same way. Just as no one envisaged what changes in society the electric light, or car, might eventually bring about, no one really imagined the effect that television or, indeed, the Internet would eventually have on society. The world-changing success of sites such as *Google*, *eBay* and *Amazon*, and the explosion of online social networking, dating and blogging, was not predicted by even the most fanciful of early Internet enthusiasts. The point is that humans are creative and adaptable, and will exploit all the technological features of any medium, however limited.

McLuhan and media psychology

McLuhan's ideas are vitally important to media psychology, because psychology has always had a rather *functional* perspective on media. If we see radios, TV screens and computers as technological devices presenting 'stimuli' to research participants, then we are not studying them as media, just as technical apparatus. Here, the 'message' is composed of abstract information, carefully composed by the researcher, and the medium is merely the latest piece of kit for displaying it. Sadly, much psychological research on media has taken precisely this approach.

Let's think of violence as an example of a mediated message. A chemistry-style scientific approach might be to try and isolate violence in the laboratory as an experimental stimulus in order to channel it through the latest medium, say, an interactive video game. The whole idea would be to study a participant's reaction to it as a piece of universal behaviour, in which media are simply the latest manifestation of earlier media – different screens, but the same, fundamental, chemically reduced, message. Of course, though, we aren't dealing with abstract, value-free chemicals. Violence is an extremely complex human phenomenon that becomes even more complex when considered as a media phenomenon. It is interesting how much of the research on video games repeats previous experiments conducted on television and film. But anyone who has ever played a video game knows that the user's *experience* of violence is completely incompatible with the experience of watching a gangster film, a Bugs Bunny cartoon, a boxing match, or any of the dozens of different media materials that have been lumped together in media violence studies – never mind the experience of *actual* violence.

McLuhan's theory of media forces us to treat each new medium that emerges as an entirely new cultural phenomenon. So the interactive video game cannot automatically be studied as just a glorified TV. It might be more instructive to return to research conducted on games per se – toy soldiers even, or Monopoly. Other researchers prefer to think of video games as texts, or narratives, rather than just stimuli. Either way, it's essential for us as psychologists to be as adaptable to the medium as the people who use it.

◉ History of media: from early newspapers to *Twitter*

Pre-twentieth century

Leaving aside electric lights and cars for now, the history of conventional mass media can probably be said to begin in the 17th century. The invention of the printing press, and the emergence of the book, takes us back to the medieval era, but in terms of mass circulation, and instant communication, we should start with the earliest commercial newspapers. Handbills and other publications had been circulating for some time, with private adverts and announcements of local events like fairs and markets, while the first recorded newspaper appeared in Germany in 1609. The first daily British newspaper, the *Daily Courier*, appeared in 1702, consisting mainly of advertising. Before long, it had become essential for any developed country to have at least one national newspaper.

In addition to newspapers, magazines (also known as 'periodicals') began to be published in the 18th century. These were aimed initially at middle-class households, but later became more specialized, dealing with all manner of leisure interests and also with current affairs and politics. Eventually, newspapers – especially at weekends – began publishing their own glossy magazines as they began to incorporate more and more advertising space.

It is a frequent criticism of newspapers that they appear to be full of advertising, that the news at times seems almost incidental, with the implication that the 'classic' newspaper was once a lovingly crafted, ad-free collection of news stories and erudite feature articles. In reality, the history of newspapers and magazines is – even more than other media – indistinguishable from the history of advertising. News has never really been more than attractive filler material, wedged between the adverts that pay for its existence. Indeed, no new publication has ever appeared on the market without an eager market of advertisers and a clear advertising strategy.

Twentieth century to the present day

We have to wait until the 1920s for the next truly mass medium to emerge – radio –which overlooks a period of intense economic, industrial and technological development, and also the emergence of visual media such as photography and film. While these are undoubtedly media, we might regard them more as art forms, as with the book, and various recording formats such as vinyl records, CDs and DVDs. We should also note the appearance of the telephone during this period.

Although we tend to think of radio and television in Britain as initially state-run public services, the original BBC (the British Broadcasting Company, begun in 1922) was actually a commercial organization, and it was only after several years that it was taken over by the Post Office and licensed to the government. In 1927, it was renamed the British Broad-casting Corporation, and thanks to laws restricting the use of UK airtime, it had little commercial competition until the 1960s, when 'pirate' radio stations, broadcasting from offshore locations, started to pick up a large audience, particularly composed of young listeners. These stations were outlawed by the British government, but by 1967 the BBC had its own pop music station, Radio 1, presented by some of the DJs who had previously worked on the pirate stations (notably Tony Black-burn and John Peel).

BBC television followed in 1936, as did television in the US and a number of European countries, although the Second World War hampered progress, and it was not really until the 1950s that significant numbers of households began to acquire television sets. In the UK, commercial competition arrived in the shape of ITV in 1954, and during the 1980s cable and satellite technologies opened up a plethora of different channels that were available to viewers, many of them requiring separate payment. Despite the changing landscape of British television, TV owners are still required to pay a licence fee to fund the BBC.

In the past 20 years, the mass media picture has become increasingly complicated. Most of the media that have emerged during this period have become known as 'new media', although as some commentators have pointed out, this is ironic since much of the technology appeared as long ago as the 1980s (Lister et al., 2009). But essentially 'new media' distinguishes computer-based media from broadcast media like radio and television.

Above all other new media sits the **Internet**, the basic communication network that links together all (enabled) computers in the world. The Internet is now so vast that it has become common to talk of media that sit within the network, so email is a communication medium as distinct from the Web, even though both operate using the same basic technology. New media experts also distinguish two clear phases of Web technology, **Web 1.0** and **Web 2.0**, the latter term describing media that have appeared in the mid- to late 2000s, such as *Second Life*, social networking sites and blogs.

To complicate the picture yet further, the evolution of devices that interact with the Internet – notably mobile phones and digital music players such as iPods – has forced us to expand our criteria for mass media to encompass the contemporary equivalents of devices that were neglected in the study of old media, such as the humble telephone and portable music players like the 'Walkman' from the early 1980s.

To bring us full circle, we have to acknowledge the fact that old media have established their own presence within the new media. So, newspapers, radio and TV stations have evolved online equivalents that have become almost as important as their offline selves. You can't fold up the online Guardian and read it on the train like an old-style commuter, but you could access www.guardian.co.uk through a handheld device. Then again, as McLuhan might have said, perhaps the advent of handheld devices means we'll do other things to pass the time while travelling rather than read the paper.

Media are everywhere, all the time

One of the most important insights that McLuhan has brought us is that media are not, as we often talk about them, simply convenient technologies for communicating the same content from one generation to the next. The newspaper owners who feared for their future with the arrival of radio misunderstood this point, as do the many social commentators who see the Internet as replacing and rendering redundant the old media.

Indeed, one of the characteristics of contemporary society is the overwhelming quantity of mediated information. Social commentator Alvin Toffler (1970) has spoken of 'information overload', whereby we encounter so much verbal and visual material in everyday life that it leads to a state of disorientation. Sorting out reliable, or useful, information from junk, marketing and downright lies requires a level of **media literacy** that is not always within our capabilities. The upshot may well be a state of 'media blindness', where we are unable to locate the source of the information we acquire, and confuse our actual experiences with mediated experiences. For instance, advertising works because we can't always see it. We are often media blind to advertising. Try looking at yourself in the mirror. It is quite likely that somewhere on your person you are advertising something. It might be on a T-shirt or pair of trainers, or a plastic bag you're carrying, but unconsciously, every day, many of us are marketing products without even being aware of it, simply through wearing a designer shirt or carrying a cheap store carrier bag.

One of the aims of media psychology is to try and make all of us that little bit more aware of the way that media infiltrate everyday life and, indeed, how media have now *become* everyday life to an extent that we frequently fail to realize. I have lost count of the number of intelligent people who watch television avidly every night, or who chatter on about celebrities, and then claim that the media have no influence on their lives.

We may never really know the true extent of that influence: it may not be something we can ever ascertain, much less measure. But media psychology is about at least *trying* to understand how the way we behave in 2010, or whenever you're reading this, is a combination of the contemporary media age and deep-rooted, enduring human characteristics.

Further reading

Giles, D.C. (2003). *Media psychology*. Mahwah, NJ: Lawrence Erlbaum.

Lister, M., Dovey, J., Giddings, S. et al. (2009). *New media: A critical introduction* (2nd edn). Abingdon: Routledge.

McLuhan, M.D. (1964/2001). *Understanding media: The extensions of man*. London: Routledge Classics.

Chapter 2

Ways of thinking about psychology and the media

👁 Introduction

Having introduced the concept of media itself in Chapter 1, it is time to bring in psychology. In this chapter, I will outline some of the different positions we can adopt when studying the influence of media on human behaviour. Some of these ideas come straight from communication science, which as a discipline has worked on the problem longer than psychology, although it has incorporated many ideas from psychology along the way. Others come from fields like media studies. And then there are insights from psychology itself.

👁 Studying the media

In Europe, and particularly in the UK, there has been a long-established tension between the disciplines of media studies and psychology. Britain is unusual in global terms because it has never fully embraced the academic discipline of communication, from which derives much of the research cited in this book. Communication has traditionally attracted many social psychologists, along with sociologists and other social scientists interested in the media.

In the UK, a different discipline altogether emerged – cultural studies – which was broadened to include media studies in the 1980s. It is this discipline which has tended to attract British academics interested in studying the media. However, cultural scholars tend to be fiercely critical of psychology as a discipline, attacking it for its focus on the individual, and its reliance on quantitative and experimental methodology. Many of their criticisms are valid. However, psychology is a diverse discipline that embraces many different methodological and theoretical approaches, not all of them preoccupied with measuring the individual.

In this book, I will try to navigate a path between these different disciplines and approaches, drawing from the most relevant research to try and answer some of the most pressing questions about psychology and media. I will begin here by outlining some of the major research traditions that have dominated thinking around media over the years.

The 'media effects' approach

The media effects approach is the most intuitive one for psychologists interested in the media, because it fits most comfortably with typical psychological research questions. 'What is the effect of watching violent films on human behaviour?' is a question asked repeatedly over the past few decades by politicians, journalists, teachers and parents. 'What is the effect of reading magazines full of images of thin celebrities?' 'What is the effect of looking at pornographic images?' These appear to be simple questions, but it has proved notoriously difficult to provide simple answers to them. For a start, it is almost impossible to isolate the target 'stimulus' (e.g. violence) from all the other cultural baggage that surrounds media and the way we use them. It is even harder, however, to isolate, or produce, the 'effect' we are interested in.

Most of the research carried out in the **media effects tradition** tended to be experimental in nature, which gives researchers a chance to claim that the media cause a particular effect, but in very few cases have the media and the effects resembled the real-life media and effects that inspired the research in the first place. For 'violence', researchers have often had to make do with short, unrepresentative and decontextualized clips from films; for 'effects', ethical considerations have meant simulating aggression, such as delivering loud blasts of noise to rival participants, or inferring it from 'hostile' questionnaire responses.

The Taylor Competitive Reaction Time Test (TCRTT) is a frequently used means of simulating aggression in the laboratory. Participants complete a pre-test phase during which they play a video game (either violent or non-violent), or watch a film, and then take part in what appears to be a game where the participant and a fictitious opponent have to respond as soon as they hear a tone. The 'loser' in this game receives a blast of noise whose volume level can be set either by the participant or automatically. The participant's settings for the blasts of noise are taken as a measure of aggression (see, for example, Anderson and Murphy, 2003).

Media scholars are hostile towards effects research because they see it as removing all context from media, reducing them to mere stimuli, and because they argue that the laboratory setting, and the tasks used to measure aggressive behaviour, are so divorced from real-life media experience that the results cannot be used to make meaningful statements about the everyday relationship between media use and behaviour (Barker and Petley, 2001; Gauntlett, 2005).

This rift in understanding stems as much as anything from the different perspectives of psychologists and media scholars. A psychologist is primarily interested in understanding why human beings behave as they do, and media constitute just one of several influences that contribute to the overall picture. A media scholar, however, is primarily interested in media and their products as cultural objects. So chopping them into 10-minute clips of violence (with the narrative context edited out) makes little sense. It turns cultural material into meaningless chunks of information (or stimuli).

However, the psychologist is unlikely to have the time or resources to screen an entire film to their participants. It would also be far too complicated, and indeed ethically questionable, to examine the effect of the film by tracking their participants' every move in the hours following the screening. So the psychologist settles for a compromise: a segment of film, followed by a laboratory simulation exercise. The result is a tightly controlled study, but one that has low **ecological validity**. To what degree can we sacrifice ecological validity? What is more important: experimental rigour, or meaningful results?

One solution to the ethical problems of generating aggression, or something similar, in the laboratory has been provided by advances in neuroscience. The increased availability of brain–imaging technology has enabled researchers to study neural activity in response to experimental stimuli, which neatly avoids the problem of devising ingenious tasks for simulating behavioural effects. It does, of course, mean that one can only study thought patterns, and, even then, one has assume that activation in a particular region of the brain directly corresponds to certain types of thought process. It is also a challenge for researchers to have to sift through lots of random electrical activity in order to clearly identify patterns of firing in selected areas.

Nevertheless, brain imaging offers at least some evidence that the presentation of certain media is associated with certain neuropsychological responses. For work carried out in this area, see Anderson et al. (2006a).

Theoretical background to effects research

Another objection to effects research is that the theoretical rationale for many of the studies is often not fully developed: some of the findings can be explained as pure imitation (a kind of 'monkey see, monkey do' explanation); others require some physiological changes (excitation); others require some form of cognitive transformation, such that exposure to media brings about changes in thinking.

The direct transmission approach actually dates from early work on media influence, known as the **hypodermic needle theory** (Lasswell, 1935). This was an analogy that was created to describe the effects of radio propaganda on early audiences: the suggestion was that Hitler (or even just someone advertising toothpaste) makes a statement on the radio and this inserts itself in the listener's brain like the injection of a needle, thereby brainwashing the hapless victim. Lasswell's research was based on the use of radio in the First World War, some while before its take up as a mass medium. However, more recent research has suggested that, in a society heavily dependent on radio as a medium, propaganda can still produce spectacular effects.

Rwanda in the early 1990s was one such society. Radio Rwanda was broadcast from a station next to the presidential palace and even used the palace's generator during power cuts, while President Habyarimana provided cheap transistor radios to the whole of the country so they could listen to it (Kellow and Steeves, 1998). Foreign journalists reported that everyone in the country seemed constantly to have an ear pressed to a transistor. During the ethnic uprising of 1994, the same airwaves were used to broadcast ethnic hate propaganda, provoking Hutus by recounting alleged atrocities committed by their Tutsi neighbours. The upshot was a disastrous civil war that claimed the lives of nearly a million Rwandans.

The image of a country glued to its radios is similar to other descriptions of strong media dependencies. There are plenty of accounts of

Latin American cities that practically grind to a halt while the residents follow the latest broadcast of a popular *telenovela*. Some European soaps have had this effect too: in the Flanders region of Belgium, the streets would empty while residents watched *Schipper naast Mathilde* in the 1950s (Dhoest, 2006).

There was also a remarkable incident that took place in the US in 1938, the early days of radio. Listeners to a dance music programme suddenly had their entertainment interrupted by a newsflash informing them that the Martians had landed and were making preparations for an invasion of Earth. It was nothing more than Hollywood actor Orson Welles dramatizing a scene from H.G. Wells's novel *War of the Worlds*, but it sparked mass panic throughout America, with people taking to the streets to find out what was going on (Cantril, 1940). A Spanish re-enactment provoked a riot in Quito, Ecuador, several years later (Gosling, 2009).

Today, you might argue, listeners would simply have turned on the television or logged on to the Internet in order to find corroborating evidence of the Martian invasion. It would have to be a very slick operation indeed, involving the collaboration of many radio and TV channels and their websites, in order for it to have the same effect. And then wouldn't we all be a little suspicious? One thing frequently ignored by researchers is that, over time, audiences become increasingly **media literate** and sophisticated. We remember this kind of thing.

Lasswell's hypodermic needle theory was, of course, somewhat crude compared to later social psychological accounts of media effects. One theory that became popular in the 1970s, was **excitation transfer**. The act of watching violent films, or aggressive sports, raises levels of adrenaline in the viewer, without them recognizing the source of their heightened excitement, and leads them to overreact in certain social situations (Zillmann, 1971). For instance, after watching an exhilarating fight scene, a young man is jostled in the street and reacts by violently lashing out at the person who knocked him.

Later theorists have extended the effects research to examine the way that media violence might 'prime', or activate, aggressive thoughts (Berkowitz, 1984). Here, the young man still reacts the same way when jostled, but rather than explaining this by way of physiological arousal, he is said to have been primed with a violent 'script' that becomes active in a potentially aggressive situation. Of course, the more violent films he has seen in his lifetime, the more accessible the violent script will be. Bushman (1995) and others argue for the inclusion of personality variables in any theory of media effects: the impact of the violent film will vary according to viewers' different predispositions to violence.

However, media effects research is by no means confined to the study of violence. Increasingly, researchers have studied a wide range of psychological and physiological effects produced by an equally wide range of media. For example, Joanne Cantor and colleagues have run innumerable studies on the negative effects of various media on children (Cantor and Sparks, 1984; Wilson et al., 2002). Cantor's approach is largely driven by her concern that media frighten children, rather than encouraging them to become aggressive, and may put them at risk of developing psychological problems in later life. Other researchers have measured physiological responses to media, such as the electrical activity of facial muscles to measure emotional response (Bolls et al., 2001), or heart rate and skin conductance to measure changes in cognitive or emotional state (Lang, 1994).

More recently, media effects researchers have adopted the neurological approach to studying responses to media by measuring brain activity (Anderson et al., 2006a). This approach has inevitably been applied to violent media (see Chapter 3), but has also generated some interesting data that demonstrate the complexity of cognitive activity that takes place when people view television in an apparently 'mindless' way: this complexity entails the coordination of 17 separate cortical areas (Anderson et al., 2006b). The same researchers also present evidence for language-like processing of visual media, perhaps supporting the argument that narrative is an essential consideration for understanding how media are processed by their users.

The Bobo doll and its arguable relevance to media effects

Perhaps the most famous and most controversial research in the effects tradition was the series of 'Bobo doll' studies conducted by social psychologist Albert Bandura and his colleagues in the 1950s and 60s. The Bobo doll was a giant inflatable object shaped in such a way that, after a blow to its head, it would simply bounce back up into its original position – ideal, then, for kicking and generally duffing up. Bandura was primarily interested in the transmission of human aggression – particularly from adults to children – and was interested to see to what extent children would copy adult 'models' (Bandura et al., 1961).

In the experimental condition, children watched an adult model bashing around poor old Bobo and in the control condition, they watched an adult playing quietly with other toys; then, both groups of children were observed during a set time in the playroom. Unsurprisingly, the experimental children spent significantly more time bashing Bobo than did the controls. Indeed, some authors (e.g. Gauntlett, 2005) have argued that, given Bobo's properties, it was unlikely that children would have been unable to resist having a pop at him once they had seen what the effect would be.

What's all this got to do with media, you might wonder? Well, the connection is tenuous and yet, for decades, the Bobo doll studies have been cited, by developmental psychologists in particular, as hard evidence for the negative effect of cartoon violence. This is because, in addition to variations of the basic experiment where children watched the adult 'models' bashing Bobo on video, there was a variant that Bandura, perhaps mistakenly, called the 'cartoon' condition, in which the adult model wore a cat costume, intending to resemble the appearance of a cartoon. That the cartoon cat also encouraged significantly more of the experimental group to bash Bobo has been upheld, for decades, as evidence that *Tom and Jerry* can be held responsible for sowing the seeds of homicide.

Perhaps the biggest criticism of all those levelled at media effects research is that it reduces the media user to a state of complete passivity. Ecologically, these experiments could only be valid if participants' actual experience of media consisted of brief, controlled exposure to media whose content was dictated by either the hardware or its operator, for example a parent selecting viewing for a child. In reality, though, it is the viewer who decides what channel to select, down to the specific show itself, and the viewer is usually well aware of the possibility that the content will be violent or sexual, or whatever effect is under investigation.

Returning to the ideas discussed in Chapter 1, we might argue that the media effects tradition works in direct contrast to McLuhan's theory of media. It assumes that media through the ages are simply different technological vehicles for broadcasting the same material to their audiences, and that violence, as a 'message', has the same meaning in any context, whether it is CCTV footage of a pub fight, or a slapstick sequence in a *Tom and Jerry* cartoon.

👁 The individual as a media user

In the 1970s, communication theorists responded to the criticisms of effects research by developing research traditions that took a different approach to the relationship between media and audiences. The most influential of these is the **uses and gratifications (U&G) theory** of media, in which the individual is treated as a media user rather than a passive observer (Katz et al., 1974).

Like the media effects approach, U&G research is rooted in psychological theory, in this case the idea that human beings have basic psychological needs that can be satisfied by media. The crucial difference between the two approaches is that in U&G the media user is an active agent: they actively seek out and select certain media for gratification purposes, while rejecting other media. Intuitively, this approach is closer to real life, where we are free to change channels and skip websites that displease us; at the same time, it offers an alternative explanation for the fascination of violent (and other controversial) media based on individual curiosity rather than random 'exposure'.

Psychologically, we can trace U&G theory to the work of humanists such as Abraham Maslow (1943), who envisaged the individual as an active agent driven by the desire to satisfy certain needs. In an affluent society such as America in the 1970s, the basic needs such as hunger and shelter had been long fulfilled for the majority of the population, and media appealed to more sophisticated needs, such as the need for amusement or entertainment, as well as some fairly basic ones such as the need for information. Based on this concept, McGuire (1974) identified 16 different types of motivation for media use.

Seen in this light, media have an evolutionary basis too, for instance we might regard the use of news as an instinctual response to monitor the environment. Our fascination with crime media may indeed have its roots in the need to keep watch for potential predators, referred to as the 'surveillance function' of news (Shoemaker, 1996). A story on the local news bulletin about a series of attacks in the neighbourhood serves as a useful warning to be on guard when out and about.

Here, the media serve a dependency function (Ball–Rokeach and DeFleur, 1976). In our eagerness to seek out gratifications using media, we come to trust certain sources and distrust others. Perhaps the best example of **media dependency** is the weather forecast. If you are planning a day outdoors and you want to know what the weather will be like, where do you go to find out? Chances are you have a favourite TV channel, teletext service or website that you trust more than others, for a variety of reasons. Eventually this becomes a media dependency. If you are unable, for some reason, to access your preferred forecast, you are less confident about the information, and more inclined to take along an umbrella even if the prediction is for a sunny afternoon.

Until recently, people were fairly consistent in the source they used to obtain information about current affairs, with people preferring newspapers for surveillance needs and television for escapist needs (Vincent and Basil, 1997). However, the emergence of online news seems to have complicated the picture, with many younger people becoming 'news grazers', flitting between different media with less loyalty to specific sources, like a preferred newspaper (Diddi and LaRose, 2006).

Some U&G theorists have tried to explain our use of media on the basis of expectancy–value models, which are complicated formulae for calculating how much our expectancy that a certain medium will satisfy our needs matches the value we gain from it (Palmgreen and Rayburn, 1985). Suppose you see a trailer for a new comedy show. You watch the show, expecting to have a good laugh, but you don't get the jokes, you don't like the characters; the whole thing falls a bit flat. The value has not matched the expectancy.

In practice, these models have limited predictive ability (McQuail, 2005). Clearly, there are too many other factors that influence media use above and beyond the expectancies of individuals and the values derived from media. For one thing, much of the time we consume media as a social group, even if it's just you and a friend watching a programme or logging on to a website. The individual needs and gratifications often give way to group demands, so formulae based on individual preferences are not always likely to fit actual media use.

Uses and gratifications methodology

This brings us to a key feature of U&G research – the use of **psycho-metric scales** as research tools. Whereas effects researchers have predominantly used experimental studies to test their hypotheses, U&G researchers have typically correlated scores obtained on various scales and questionnaires. A standard scale presents the participant with a series of statements, such as 'I regard the mobile phone as a necessity' and then asks them to rate each statement on a Likert-type scale, an ordinal sequence of numbers, such as 1–7, which correspond to degrees of agreement, such as 'strongly agree', or 'disagree somewhat'.

A typical U&G study will examine scores on more than two scales to see which variables best predict a target measure, using a statistical technique known as 'multiple regression'. For example, a researcher might be interested in the psychological factors that predict the use of social networking websites, so they collect measures of personality, self-esteem, need for social interaction and so on, and enter these into a statistical equation that can predict the extent of participants' use of sites like *Facebook*.

One of the big advantages of U&G research, then, is that it can take previous media use into account, something which has generally been ignored in effects research. While it might be spectacular to produce a short-term effect from laboratory exposure of a short media clip, what really interests psychologists is the cumulative effect of media consumed over a lifetime. We may not always be entirely trustworthy witnesses of our own media consumption, but at least it makes sense to ask the question, and to assess the preferences for certain types of media.

Cultivation theory

The cumulative effect of media is sometimes referred to as the 'drip drip' hypothesis of media influence. This approach is known as 'cultivation theory', because it argues that media gradually cultivate certain views and values in their audiences over time. Cultivation theory is rooted in the work of George Gerbner and colleagues, who have been tirelessly collecting data since the 1970s to illustrate the type of influences that TV audiences are exposed to in America.

Gerbner's methodological approach is called **content analysis**, and has been extremely influential in communication and media studies. It involves the analysis of hours and hours of television material, recording each instance of a particular phenomenon (e.g. violence) following an elaborate coding scheme. At the end, the researchers can conclude things like '89% of programmes between 9 and 10 p.m. contain at least one violent scene' from the evidence of weeks and weeks of painstaking records (e.g. Gerbner et al., 1978).

Cultivation theory has been applied at a global level to try and account for the popularity of certain media across the world. The gradual convergence of world views among different cultures is called 'mainstreaming', and has often been cited as an explanation for the way that American values seem to have been absorbed by different cultures in the world due to the transmission of US programmes on various overseas TV networks.

These effects can be intensified through the process of 'resonance'. Audiences do not simply take on trust everything they encounter in the media; it needs to 'resonate' with them in order to have a serious effect on their beliefs. If we live in a crime-free area, repeated viewing of crime shows is unlikely to contribute to our level of fear when we step outside the front door. If, on the other hand, we have experienced one or two unsavoury incidents in the local area, frequent viewing of crime drama should make us more anxious still about the potential of becoming a victim.

The 'drip drip' effect of media violence, according to cultivation theorists, has not necessarily made us more aggressive, but instead has made us more fearful about the world. Signorielli (1990) calculated a 'mean world index' based on various factors such as 'heavy' viewing of violence and level of education. However, it has produced inconsistent results across different cultures, and may be useful only for explaining the effects of US media.

On the surface, cultivation theory seems to have addressed some of the criticisms levelled at effects research, particularly its low ecological validity. Certainly, cultivation theory takes into account individual media histories and does not assume that media have a direct transmission of its messages to subsequent behaviour. However, it has been criticized for treating the audience as passive recipients of media – fundamentally it is the same dose–response logic in operation, only on a grander scale – and also for making assumptions based on content rather than on actual behaviour. Gerbner et al. (1978) may have done a thorough job of cataloguing what viewers *can* watch at any given time, but have provided rather less information about what and, crucially, *how* they've watched.

Nor would McLuhan have much time for the Gerbner approach. In the 1960s, he was already scoffing at communication researchers' fondness for content analysis. After all, if the medium is the message, then its content is largely accidental. Cultivation theory assumes, like effects research, that TV – and it is largely TV that has been studied in this tradition – is a convenient, though sadly inadequate, means of representing reality to audiences, and is therefore constantly guilty of misrepresenting reality.

Active audience theory

One final approach I will discuss in this chapter is the notion of the 'active audience' that has proved popular in European cultural and media studies in recent decades, particularly with the advent of 'new media', which inevitably places the user in pole position.

Active audience theory has always contended that audiences are much smarter and more inventive than traditional communication theory has given them credit for, and they can be highly creative in their responses to media. Because many theorists in this tradition come from a humanities or arts background, they have spent much time focusing on media 'texts' – a far cry from the artificial clips beloved of effects researchers. The key concept behind active audience theory is that audiences 'read' media texts in different ways, and not always in the way intended or expected by media producers. One well-known example of this is the 1970s BBC sitcom *Till Death Us Do Part*, in which writer Johnny Speight made the central character a racist bigot called Alf Garnett (played by Warren Mitchell), largely with the aim of satirizing his right-wing views about women, ethnic minorities and other social groups. However, while educated audiences 'read' the show this way, many other viewers interpreted Garnett as a hero, championing their own prejudices.

At their most extreme, cultural theorists have argued that we should do away with notions of audience and text altogether: 'There is no text, there is no audience, there are only the processes of viewing' (Fiske, 1989, p. 57). Audiences are free to do as they wish with the cultural material on offer. Henry Jenkins (1992) has conducted some fascinating studies into the creative responses of fans to media texts such as *Star Trek*, generating new stories and other related artwork, and using original footage to create alternative endings to episodes.

Of course, the advent of the Internet has given active audience theorists plenty of encouragement, since here the user is placed at the centre of the action, and is very much a generator of material or text, unlike the more passive recipient of radio and TV. Some cultural theorists have almost lost interest in traditional media as a result, talking about the evolution of 'Media Studies 2.0', with reference to the concept of Web 2.0, a marketing concept that is now common currency in media studies for describing online innovations during the latter half of the 2000s (Gauntlett, 2007).

In some ways, active audience theory is more in keeping with McLuhan's conception of media than the other approaches discussed here, except that they are sometimes in danger of allowing the media to disappear from view. If all media can be reduced to abstract text, then we may as well do away with media psychology and treat everything in this book within the context of cultural psychology. This would, however, ignore the practice of media use, and the important issue of context.

◉ Further reading

Giles, D.C. (2003). *Media psychology*. Mahwah, NJ: Lawrence Erlbaum.
Littlejohn, S.W. (2002). *Theories of human communication* (7th edn).
Belmont, CA: Wadsworth.

Section Two

Media
Influences
on Social
Behaviour

Section summary

This section of the book focuses on the topics that have traditionally preoccupied psychologists interested in the media – sex and violence, advertising and body image. Most of the research on these topics has dwelt on the negative effects of such material, particularly violence, which has generated a vast literature in the social psychology and communication fields. Advertising has spawned its own, equally vast literature, becoming an academic discipline in its own right. Body image is a relatively late arrival on the scene, but here too the focus has been on the effects of viewing images of thin models.

Needless to say, much of the research on these topics has been conducted within the media effects tradition, with experiments designed to isolate the media phenomenon of concern in order to examine its effect on a second task, usually performed in a psychology laboratory. But there is plenty of survey data too, and increasingly qualitative research, particularly from the media studies field, that adds important findings to the literature.

Chapter 3

Media influences on prosocial and antisocial behaviour

👁 Introduction

Probably the biggest area of research in media psychology, the effects of media on antisocial and prosocial behaviour, has been studied using experiments, surveys and interviews. In this chapter, the evidence from this vast literature is weighed up. Is the media violence link with aggressive behaviour quite as strong as some authors claim? What reasons might there be for taking a slightly sceptical stand on the findings of laboratory research? The nature of media violence itself, and what exactly constitutes antisocial and prosocial behaviour, is also explored. The chapter ends with a consideration of some of the findings relating to the positive effects of media, a much smaller research literature. Are prosocial effects caused by the same psychological processes as antisocial ones? And if not, what might this tell us about media influence?

👁 Awash in a violent tide? Media and aggression

How can media make us behave badly? How can they make us behave well? These questions have preoccupied researchers for decades. Since the early days of Hollywood, there have been concerns about the themes of crime and violence in films (Gunter, 2008). Millions of dollars have been spent researching the effects of viewing violence in the laboratory, and cataloguing the incidence of violence on US television. One leading figure has claimed that '[the US public is] awash in a tide of violent representations unlike any the world has ever seen' (Gerbner, 1994, p. 133).

There is now a wealth of research that, on the face of it, suggests that viewing violence is linked to aggressive behaviour, or even causes viewers to behave more aggressively. The findings are fiercely defended by some psychologists, particularly in the face of apparent US news media indifference (Bushman and Anderson, 2001). Indeed, some researchers believe that the research evidence is so conclusive that they have claimed that 'the debate is over': the link between media violence and aggressive behaviour is as strong as that between smoking and lung cancer (Eron, 1993).

It seems remarkable, therefore, that other authors have so often discredited this entire body of evidence. For many years, there have been serious methodological and theoretical criticisms levelled at the media violence research literature (Barker and Petley, 2001; Fowles, 1999; Freedman, 2002; Grimes and Bergen, 2008). In a paper considering a multitude of factors influencing aggression, Twemlow and Bennett (2008, p. 1172) argued that:

> studies regarding the influence of violent media are ... inconclusive. The question ... is intrinsically problematic, and no direct general causality is likely to be found.

At the same time, there has been an increasing amount of research exploring the ability of media to encourage 'prosocial' behaviour, either in the form of 'entertainment-education', such as children's programmes like *Sesame Street*, or through public service announcements promoting healthy behaviour or other desirable outcomes. If viewing violence really does cause aggression – and we'll weigh up some of the evidence shortly – then are the same psychological processes responsible for the positive effects of prosocial media?

Naturally, one of the difficulties with all this research is that what constitutes 'antisocial' or 'prosocial' behaviour will differ from one society to another. If one person hits another in self-defence, this might be recorded in a content analysis as 'antisocial', regardless of the context. For this reason, the media violence debate needs to be understood partly as a moral debate about the way people in a society conduct their lives. Most of the concern over viewing violence has been levelled at fictional portrayals of violence, rather than the real, and often graphic, violence viewed nightly in news bulletins. Yet, apart from a brief suggestion by a

British broadcaster in the 1990s (Lewis, 1994), nobody has called for any kind of restriction on news coverage.

Hill (2001) has suggested that the entertainment media are heavily criticized because they are seen to have lower moral standards and appeal to the masses, who are therefore felt to be more impressionable. This is known as the **third person effect** – the belief that other people are more influenced by the media than you are, especially if they're younger, less educated, of a lower socioeconomic status, female, and from an ethnic minority (Perloff, 1999). Third person effects occur with just about all media, and they are deeply embedded in academic attitudes. After all, if just viewing violence really does cause all viewers to be more aggressive, we would have to be very careful when talking to a psychologist who studies it, or, worse still, a film censor who has sat through hours and hours of footage that is too shocking to even merit a certificate.

👁 What is media violence? What effects does it really have?

The long history of popular fears about media violence is well documented, and there have always been moral guardians – from Mary Whitehouse's National Viewers' and Listeners' Association in Britain in the 1960s to the American Psychological Association this century – who issue frequent warnings about the negative impact of screen images on impressionable minds. The media violence/aggression link has been reinforced in popular culture by occasional news stories that generate an outcry, propelled by the media themselves, about the threat of viewing violence.

Media violence in the news

Two such stories from the UK will serve as examples. The first concerns the Stanley Kubrick film *A Clockwork Orange*, which went on general release in British cinemas in 1971. This film, in which the leader of a teenage gang is arrested and then subjected to aversion therapy, became notorious for its violent scenes of rape and murder, although in fact these are condensed into the first 15 minutes of what is a long, and actually quite hard-going, movie. Well before this, the press had broadcast the coming threat: 'The shocker to end them all' read the headline in one newspaper, and a Labour MP warned that it would 'magnify teenage violence'.

It was almost inevitable, then, that when the film did go on show, a number of 'copycat' incidents were widely reported in the press: the murder of a homeless man by a youngster who had allegedly watched the film, and, in direct imitation of one particularly controversial scene, the rape of a Dutch tourist in London by a group of teenagers singing 'Singing in the Rain'. Other defendants, in search of more lenient sentences for their crimes, tried to use the film as a convenient excuse for their behaviour. Stanley Kubrick, the director, eventually became so fed up with having the blame laid at his door for these incidents that he demanded that the film be withdrawn from general release. It remained on the censor's shelf until after his death, when it was reclassified in 2000 and went on general release again. In the 10 years it has been available, there have been no reports of copycat crimes.

What happened in those 30 years? The media violence critics would argue that, as a society, we have become 'desensitized' to violence as more and more graphic and technologically sophisticated films have entered the market. Now, perhaps, *A Clockwork Orange* looks rather tame, in contrast to decades of violent cop films and Quentin Tarantino movies. The violence is certainly highly stylized, in that realism is sacrificed for artistic impression. Many of the initial concerns surrounded the glamorization of Alex's gang, with their cultish uniform of bowler hats and white overalls. Once the immediacy of the film had passed, the feared 'Clockwork cult' disappeared, and the remaining violence made little apparent impact.

The second big media scare involving violence occurred in the early 1990s, after the murder on Merseyside in 1993 of 2-year-old James Bulger by two 10-year-old boys. The older boys had kidnapped the toddler from a shopping centre and killed him in a remote railway siding. The case was particularly notable for the extent of media outcry and public disbelief, the apparent loss of childhood innocence, and the general impression of moral decline in society.

The media were itching for a scapegoat, and when the trial judge mentioned 'violent videos' in relation to the kind of culture in which the boys had been raised, they found one. A reporter discovered a video in one of the boys' homes that had been rented by the father – *Child's Play 3*, a low-quality sequel to two earlier films featuring a toy doll serial killer called Chucky. In one scene in the film, the doll splashes blue paint on one of its victims, and blue paint had been found on James Bulger's body. This was a tenuous link at best, but the connection had been made and the British media were only too keen to follow it through. An explosion of headlines ensued, reigniting an earlier moral panic around 'video nasties'. A child psychologist emerged on the scene, Elisabeth Newson, who had never published any research involving media, but who was happy to cobble together a review of the extensive media violence research at the request of a Christian organization and a Liberal Democrat MP, who subsequently used it as evidence to amend a government bill on video rental (Hill, 2001).

Eventually, it transpired that neither boy had actually seen *Child's Play 3*. The link between the film scene and the murder was so tenuous that one commentator claimed that you might as well blame *The Railway Children* for inciting the crime. Nevertheless, the damage has been done: routinely, the Bulger murder is trotted out as irrefutable evidence for the effects of media violence. As with the MMR controversy, the facts have never got in the way of a good story: released slowly, at long intervals, after the furore has died down, and usually on the inside pages, they make little impression on the public consciousness. Ironically, two copycat incidents were subsequently blamed on *Child's Play 3*, but only in the days after the media outcry. As Elisabeth Newson (1994) herself pointed out, the film had been on release, and the video on sale, long before the Bulger murder.

In the case of both *A Clockwork Orange* and *Child's Play 3*, it seems that it was not the media violence itself that influenced subsequent antisocial behaviour, but the publicity generated by the news coverage, and the aura of 'forbidden fruit' surrounding both films. Nevertheless, most researchers would argue that it is the *cumulative* effect of media violence that is of concern, not a couple of scenes from the odd video nasty.

Media violence in the laboratory

Since the 1950s, researchers have been devising increasingly ingenious experiments in the laboratory to test the effects of violent media. Overwhelmingly, they have tested the hypothesis that viewing violence results in increased aggression. Much evidence has accumulated that seems to indicate support, particularly a number of meta-analyses that accumulate the findings of previous studies and carry out an overall statistical test of significance (Paik and Comstock, 1994; Wood et al., 1991).

Various theories have been used to provide a rationale for the aggression hypothesis. Bandura's Bobo doll studies (see Chapter 2) suggest the role of **modelling**, or imitation, of adult behaviour. Clearly, this would explain copycat incidents modelled on film scenes. Excitation transfer is another theory (Zillmann, 1971), by which increased adrenaline generated by the film then leads viewers to react inappropriately in subsequent situations. This might explain aggression in the immediate post-viewing period, but there are few accounts of trouble in and around cinemas screening violent films. Nevertheless, it is argued that repeated exposure to violence might raise levels of adrenaline more generally.

Cognitive priming has also been identified as an important factor (Berkowitz, 1984), whereby violent films provide 'scripts' that viewers might later act out in ambiguous social encounters, or even just the generation of aggressive thoughts (Bushman and Geen, 1990). Here again, we could see how viewers might imitate scenes from films, or patterns of behaviour frequently depicted when hostile characters confront one another.

Finally, one frequently cited effect of media violence is the **desensitization** of viewers towards violence in general. While little supporting evidence has been produced in the laboratory, Murray (2008, p. 1223) has suggested that the repeated viewing of violence over time results in lowered emotional arousal and produces a 'drugging' effect similar to addiction. A more plausible account comes from the literature on sexual violence, where male viewers of filmed rape scenes adopt more lenient attitudes towards rapists and less sympathy with victims (Donnerstein, 1984).

Laboratory research on media violence is frequently criticized for lacking theoretical coherence, and it is true that the desensitization theory is not fully compatible with excitation transfer: indeed, before expounding his 'drugging' hypothesis, Murray (2008) presents a long list of evidence that even violent cartoons result in *greater* arousal in children. Furthermore, if desensitization effects occur due to repeated viewing of violence on television, then we should not see highly aggressive children displaying higher arousal, and greater aggression, in the laboratory following a short violent clip. But this is what seems to happen in most of the published experimental studies on media violence.

In their polemic against the 'massive dose of violent media' in modern society, Bushman and Anderson (2001) use as their primary evidence a number of meta-analytic reviews that pool evidence across a number of separate experiments to test their combined effect. The two most prominent meta-analyses are those by Paik and Comstock (1994) and Wood et al. (1991). The former study looks impressive, in that it combines 217 studies testing over 1,000 separate hypotheses: the authors found a 0.41 correlation between televised violence and antisocial behaviour in the laboratory. The Wood et al. (1991) study is less convincing, because only 23 studies were included, several of which only tested effects on 'emotionally disturbed' children, a population that seems to be unusually vulnerable to the effects of media violence (Grimes and Bergen, 2008). However, it could be argued that this analysis is more reliable, since a sample of 217 studies contains too much variety for the results to be meaningful. The 'outcome measures' – antisocial behaviour – comprised a huge assortment of different behaviours, and the 'violence' – the stimulus materials – were similarly varied.

One of the other problems with meta-analyses is that they tend to rely for their sample on published findings. It is well known that academic publications have a bias towards significant findings (Peters and Ceci, 1982), which means that meta-analytic results are inevitably inflated, since they consist largely of accumulated significant test statistics (Paik and Comstock, 1994, do offer some counter-evidence in their paper, but it is not particularly convincing).

The publication bias effect is further exacerbated by the tendency of experimental studies to test explicitly the hypothesis that media violence causes aggression. In another meta-analysis, Hearold (1986) compared studies with an 'aggression' hypothesis with those testing a neutral hypothesis and those testing explicitly non-aggression hypotheses. The correlation between media violence and aggression for the 'aggression' studies was 0.41, compared with 0.17 for the neutral studies and –0.01 for the non-aggression studies. In other words, it appears that experimental researchers – at least those who get their work published – largely obtain the findings they expect.

As an example of how this works, let's consider one of the higher quality studies in the Wood et al. (1991) meta-analysis. Josephson (1987) compared the responses to a violent clip of boys who were either already high or low in a measure of aggression. In order to induce aggression in a hockey-style game, she designed the violent clip 'in such a way as to preserve certain features of the violent action that are thought to make viewers' subsequent aggression more likely' (Josephson, 1987, p. 884). Sure enough, the boys in the violence condition did display more aggression in the hockey game, but *only* if they were highly aggressive at the start of the study. On this occasion, the carefully designed clip consisted of 17 minutes spliced together from a police drama that contained the most violent scenes from the show. The artificial treatment of media stimuli has led to many criticisms of the laboratory research, although researchers generally do not claim that their methods resemble real-life viewing conditions and materials. The argument is usually that anything observed under tightly controlled experimental conditions is likely to be, if anything, an *underestimate* of the real-world experience of viewing violence.

Video game violence

A research literature still somewhat in its infancy has grown up in the past decade around violent video games (VVGs). This is not surprising, since the video game industry has demonstrated enormous worldwide growth during the same period, overtaking both the movie industry and the music industry in terms of revenue (Gentile et al., 2009). The same authors report figures that claim that 99% of boys and 94% of girls – in the US at least – play video games at least some of the time.

While a substantial literature has grown up around the study of game playing per se (game studies has now become an academic discipline in its own right), most psychological research has tended, as ever, to dwell on the negative features of the activity. Naturally, many researchers have treated violent games as simply an extension of violent film and television, applying the same theoretical models and methodologies. However, intuitively, we would expect psychological processing to be different in each case.

The actual experience of playing a video game is quite different from that of watching a film or TV show. You get to control the action directly: even if you are being shot at, you still make the decision to shoot. The concept of 'exposure', controversial enough in the laboratory research on television and film, is even more inappropriate when applied to video games, although one could always be coerced into playing them in childhood. Undoubtedly, the experience of video game playing, apart from Internet-based games (to be discussed in Chapter 11), is as a social activity, whereas in most of the media violence research, viewers have been treated as isolated individuals stumbling across disturbing scenes.

In the experimental tradition, Craig Anderson and colleagues at the Center for the Study of Violence at Iowa University in the US have studied the behaviour of school children and university students after taking part in violent and non-violent games (Anderson et al., 2004, 2007). They have found that, in a subsequent learning task, aggression could increase by as much as 40% in participants in the 'violent' condition, and that violent thoughts could be more easily accessed by this group.

Other studies using similar methods have produced mixed results, such as the study by Ivory and Kalyanaraman (2007), which also explored the impact of technological advancement on game playing. They anticipated that the more realistic the portrayal of violence in the game, the stronger the effect, but although players reported feeling more excited, had higher skin conductance (a measure of physiological arousal), and greater involvement in the game, there was little or no effect on any of the aggression measures. One explanation for this discrepancy is that the measure of aggression used by Anderson and colleagues was derived from the Taylor Competitive Reaction Time Test described in Chapter 2, where blasts of loud noise are delivered at imaginary opponents during the course of a response time task. Whether blasting an opponent with loud noise in a laboratory exercise can really be regarded as an act of aggression remains open to question. It does seem rather fun, not unlike something you might get to do in the course of a video game.

More convincing, at least from a methodological perspective, are neuroimaging studies of video game play and electrical activity in the brain. The work of René Weber and colleagues (Weber et al., 2006, 2009) is particularly interesting, where brain activity is recorded in relation to the specific events in the game. They claim to have identified different patterns of neural activity for defensive violence (where a player shoots to avoid being killed) and lustful aggression (indiscriminate killing of opponents), the latter being more closely related to brain activity known to be related to aggression.

Sophisticated as this methodology might be, it tells us very little about the actual longer term effects of game playing. A study of focus groups comprising adolescent boys (Olson et al., 2008) produced some interesting data that seem to support a catharsis explanation. Boys frequently spoke of VVGs as a means of releasing pent-up frustration and resentment towards school, bullies and other daily stressors. As one participant expressed it: 'Say some kid wants to fight you, and he talks trash about you. When you go home and play you're like, "this is the kid that I hate" and you beat him up and stuff' (Olson et al., 2008, p. 65). It could be argued, therefore, that video game violence might actually *reduce* real-world aggression.

A word of caution → **How to exaggerate your claims with statistics**

Research on media violence is awash with scare statistics. By the time the average American child reaches the age of 10, they will have seen X murders on television, X% of primetime TV features violence and so on. One of the most ludicrous claims, by Centerwall (1993), is that every year, media violence is responsible for 10,000 homicides. Where *do* they get these figures from?

Well, it really doesn't matter, since it seems that, even in highly respected scientific journals, any figure will do so long as the editors trust your claims. But, whether or not one agrees with the findings of the experimental research, content analyses have for a long time overestimated the amount of violence that people are 'exposed to' on television and at the cinema. The problem is partly the way media content is coded in large-scale surveys. If you want to study the content of TV over several years across a large number of channels, you won't have time to carry out any detailed analysis of the shows themselves. So, if there is a brief exchange of gunfire in an otherwise romantic or comedy show, a tick goes down in the column marked 'violence'. If a romantic couple have a fight in an otherwise highly moralistic film, violence – tick. By the end of it, a night's TV appears to be a bloodbath.

The same mistake has reappeared in claims about the violence in video games. Various authors have estimated the number of violent games to be anywhere between 49 and 79% of the market (Weber et al., 2006, 2009), which might be a cause for concern if it were true; but in a close analysis of the content of the most violent 'shooter' games, Weber et al. (2009) calculated that only 7% of playing time actually involves violent activity. So much for the rest of the games then.

Of course, the proportion of content to time tells us nothing about the *impact* of media. A viewer may only remember the single gunshot from an otherwise non-violent show. But the close analysis of media content makes some of the more lurid claims about violence seem rather ridiculous.

Field studies and natural experiments

Outside the laboratory, a number of researchers have tried to overcome some of the problems caused by artificial stimuli and settings by conducting what are known as **field experiments**. These have a long tradition in social psychology, which has often used children's summer camps as natural research settings. One interesting study of this type was conducted in Belgium by Leyens et al. (1975), where 'delinquent' boys in different cottages of a 'corrective institution' were shown either violent or non-violent films over the period of a week and their subsequent levels of aggression recorded. Physical aggression increased in the 'violence' cottages during that time and in the week following viewing, irrespective of the amount of aggression shown previously by the boys in those cottages.

One of the problems with the Leyens et al. (1975) study is that the authors measured instances of aggression displayed by individual boys and then added the observations together to produce a total for each cottage. However, being a group of delinquent boys, and a measure of physical interaction, it's highly unlikely that any one instance of violence would involve one child alone. This is a statistical problem known as the 'non-independence of data'. Suppose that one boy had been inspired by one violent scene and decided to re-enact this with his neighbour, inspiring the other 10 boys to pile in and have a mass brawl. This would be recorded as 12 instances of aggression in that one observational period. This looks like a large effect of violent media, but in fact, only one child was 'influenced' by the film.

Another interesting field experiment, this time using six residential (boarding) schools, was conducted by Feshbach and Singer (1971). It is particularly interesting because it is a rare test of the **catharsis hypothesis**, which argues that, contrary to most of the research on media violence, viewing violence actually decreases aggression by providing a vicarious outlet through which we can 'purge' our naturally aggressive impulses. The authors randomly assigned the children to 'violent' and 'non-violent' groups that differed only in the entertainment that was offered to them over a six-week period. In three of the six schools, the non-violent children displayed more aggression; however, it was also noted that this group were frustrated by not being allowed to watch the violent films.

The notion of catharsis has its roots in psychodynamic theory and does rather rely on the belief that we begin with a set of aggressive impulses to purge in the first place. However, it has rarely been tested, if at all, in the laboratory, and there is an argument that for some individuals, particularly those high in daydreaming and imagination, violent films may act as a mechanism for 'living out' aggression (Gunter, 1981). Other authors (e.g. Hill, 1997) have suggested that watching violence is something of a rite of passage for young men, and is used (along with horror films) to 'test boundaries' of what degree of shocking visual material is tolerable.

Another type of real-world study is the **natural experiment**, where the independent variable occurs without any intervention by the experimenter. A number of such studies have been conducted following the introduction of television into a society, such as St Helena, a remote South Atlantic island (Gunter et al., 2002). Here, viewing patterns were matched to teachers' ratings of antisocial behaviour, with few significant relationships emerging: pre-TV antisocial behaviour was the best predictor of all.

Other researchers have carried out statistical analyses of naturally occurring data, organizing them in order to infer cause and effect. A well-known example is the boxing and homicide studies of Phillips and colleagues (Phillips, 1983; Phillips and Hensley, 1984). In these studies, the authors collected data on US homicides and the results of major championship boxing matches that appeared on TV during the same period. They claimed a variety of effects from their data, broadly suggesting that an increase in homicides was related to the result of a prize fight in the preceding days. However, much criticism has been levelled at the findings, which, when broken down, seem to consist of an incoherent pattern of significant associations. For instance, the link was strongest on the third, sixth and ninth days following the fight, and for fights that took place outside the US. No theoretical explanation had been given to account for this odd pattern, leaving critics to suggest that the significant data were simply the result of spurious statistical 'noise' (Freedman, 2002).

Clearly, naturalistic studies are less likely to produce significant results than tightly controlled laboratory experiments, and for this reason, they are less likely to receive research funding. However, the higher ecological validity of such studies – their applicability to real life – means that they really should be the method of choice for anyone interested in the actual effects of media violence.

Paik and Comstock → **Types of violence**

One of the criticisms frequently levelled at laboratory studies of media violence is that the actual stimuli used in the studies vary too widely to draw meaningful inferences from the literature. Let's have a look at Paik and Comstock's (1994) meta-analysis of television violence and antisocial behaviour. Among the stimuli in the 217 studies covered, there are, in descending order of the size of their effect size (d):

- Cartoons/fantasy shows (1.21)
- 'Behavioural demonstrations' (e.g. the videos in the Bobo doll studies) (1.14)
- Pornography/erotica (0.94)
- Sports (0.87)
- Action/adventure/crime (0.69)
- News/public affairs (0.51)
- Westerns (0.39).

No satisfactory explanation was given for why cartoons should top this list, except for the fact that children were the participants in the studies and more likely to be affected by the 'violence' condition. Behavioural demonstrations we can leave alone, since they tell us nothing about actual media. Pornography and erotica are not of course violent by definition, but one assumes these materials were, which is consistent with Zillmann's (1971) research, suggesting that excitation transfer might be the most important factor in short-term aggression effects.

Sports is ambiguous, but probably refers to a number of studies that have used boxing as a stimulus, itself a debatable category of violence (rarely treated as problematic by researchers). The media that cause most concern – violent films – come some way down the list, producing an effect size not all that much greater than that of news and current affairs.

Surveys

Perhaps the most stinging criticism of laboratory-based media violence research is that it ignores the actual media experience of its participants, reducing it solely to a one-off 'exposure'. If, as suggested earlier, keen viewers of violence are desensitized to its effects, then these choice snippets of film should not really work as they seem to do. Therefore, much faith has been placed in studies that measure viewers' actual consumption of media violence and demonstrate associations between this and their actual levels of aggression.

For some, the 'missing link' in the violence research has been supplied by a longitudinal panel study by Huesmann et al. (2003), which tracked media use and aggressive behaviour across two decades. The researchers first measured TV preferences in over 500 American children at ages 6–10 (Huesmann and Eron, 1986), and then followed this up when the same group had reached their mid-twenties. They found that early preference for violent programmes was significantly correlated with aggression in later life.

Of course, one of the first things that psychology students learn about statistics is that you cannot infer causation from correlation, and many authors have urged caution in interpreting panel study findings for this reason (Grimes and Bergen, 2008). For one thing, perhaps the aggressive adults had always been aggressive, and this is what led them to prefer violent television in the first instance. Huesmann et al. (2003) checked this explanation, finding that childhood TV preferences, and notably childhood aggression, did not predict adult TV preferences. In other words, the damage, if we can call it that, is done through childhood exposure to media violence rather than adult exposure. This would seem to tally with Paik and Comstock's (1994) finding that cartoons are the form of media most strongly associated with antisocial behaviour.

In general, survey findings are less emphatic than those obtained in the laboratory – a consistent finding across all the meta-analytic studies. This can largely be explained by the fact that surveys allow researchers to examine more potential predictors of behaviour, so that the final correlation between media violence and aggression is watered down by the other factors. Experiments, designed to focus on the independent variable alone, inevitably produce stronger effects.

At the same time, critics of this research cite many of the same flaws that beset the experimental studies. While the survey data may at least refer to actual media, rather than cleverly stitched together highlights of violent films, they are equally diverse in what they measure in terms of aggression. As Grimes and Bergen (2008) argue, there are as many different definitions of aggressive behaviour as there are media violence researchers. Huesmann et al.'s (2003) measures of aggression include such minor transgressions as calling a person names and receiving a speeding fine.

More recently, research on media violence and aggression has diversified further, exploring different types of aggression. 'Indirect aggression', which consists of malicious gossip, hostile gestures and damage to property, is found frequently in TV popular with teenagers (Coyne and Archer, 2004). A related concept, 'relational aggression', where interpersonal relations are exploited for 'aggressive' ends, through gossip, slander and ostracism, has also been linked to television (Ostrov et al., 2006). However, this type of aggression was found to differentiate between boys and girls, with girls who watch more television engaging in more relational aggression, and boys in more physical aggression.

What is being communicated here? The variety of different types of media violence is matched by the variety of aggression categories and antisocial behaviours. This should really require a return to theory, as clearly some of the mechanisms elaborated by earlier media violence researchers, such as modelling and excitation transfer, cannot be held to account for all these different behaviours. Are the same psychological processes that cause someone to respond to violent media by beating up a passer-by really the same processes that cause someone to drive their car faster than the legal speed limit, or to yell a few choice insults at someone who has treated them badly?

Interviews

It is a shame that actually asking people about their responses to media violence should be the last method that is considered in this section, but I have tried to reflect the chronological order of the literature, and it is faintly absurd that it has taken so long for social scientists to adopt the qualitative approach to this heavily researched question. Nevertheless, there have been numerous interview-based studies in the past couple of decades, which have yielded data that act as a fascinating counterpoint to the traditional approaches.

One fairly consistent finding in the qualitative literature is that audiences are much more discriminating about different types of portrayal than has been assumed in most of the traditional research. David Morrison at Leeds University (1999) interviewed adults and children of various ages about their understanding of violence, and found clear distinctions between *playful* violence (e.g. cartoons), *depicted* violence (with graphic and bloody consequences) and *authentic*, or naturalistic violence. He argued that people base their violence judgements on whether or not the scene looks convincing, and whether or not the violence is actually justified. A wild punch thrown by a cornered victim, for instance, could just be regarded as instinctive self-defence.

Our decisions about violence are also influenced by the type of social environment we have grown up in, and the corresponding sets of values and norms we use to make sense of social interactions. Philip Schlesinger and colleagues at Glasgow University (Schlesinger et al., 1998) interviewed 88 men about their responses to a set of violent films, and found that men from rough backgrounds, in which fights were a frequent occurrence, were more excited by realistic portrayals of film violence than those from gentler homes. They were also less likely to apply the 'violence' label to scenes that they saw as justifiable punishment, such as either the husband or wife slapping a spouse suspected of infidelity.

The real-life parallels with violence have been studied more in the UK than the US, probably because so much of the US literature has been generated by different concerns over violence, that is, films that are actually set in America. Like Morrison's interviewees, Schlesinger's men drew a clear line between realistic and fantasy portrayals of violence, such as those encountered in Hollywood blockbusters. British audiences do seem to have a somewhat different relationship with media violence. As Gunter (1985) found in an earlier study, scenes involving knives were rated as more violent by British audiences than those involving guns, probably because, like Schlesinger et al.'s participants, they identified less closely with the gun–oriented violence of US television.

Another context that we need to apply to understand reactions to media violence is that of **narrative context**. One of the failings of traditional laboratory research is the reduction of 'media' to an artificially constructed set of random violent scenes that fail to fit into a broader narrative. Shaw (2004) interviewed groups of viewers about the 1994 Oliver Stone film *Natural Born Killers*, held responsible for 14 murders worldwide (Ruddock, 2001). Half the participants had seen the film, and were able to discuss selected scenes in relation to their meaning within the overall narrative, and narrative elements such as characters and sequence of events; the other half perceived them as more disturbing and violent because they were unable to select a meaningful frame for their interpretation (for more on framing effects of media, see Chapter 9).

Narrative context supplies us with an explanation for any given film scene and, in doing so, an explanation for why media violence occurs at all. While the vast majority of research on media violence is motivated by the belief that any violence on screen is undesirable, there are occasions when it is not only acceptable but desirable. For instance, one study (Schlesinger et al., 1992), investigated women's understanding of media violence after screening several films including Jonathan Kaplan's *The Accused* (1988), which famously concludes with a notoriously explicit rape scene. The women in this study, while disturbed by the scene, argued that it ought to be shown, because the entire plot revolves around the rape charge itself and the defendant's plea that the victim had experienced sexual pleasure.

Finally, one group of people curiously absent from the research on media violence are those who we are most concerned about – violent young offenders themselves, the people whose exposure to media violence has steered them towards a life of violent crime. Oddly, the only substantial research conducted with this group (Hagell and Newburn, 1994) has found that the criminals themselves actually watch less television than others. One might assume this was largely due to the fact they spent most of their time on the street committing crimes, but even when they did talk about television, they seemed to lack any sort of engagement with the medium.

Concluding thoughts on the media violence debate

The authors of a recent media violence meta-analysis (Savage and Yancey, 2008) sum up the state of affairs. They conclude that there is not one single study that tests the hypothesis using meaningful measures – a dependent variable of violent aggression or crime rates, and an accurate measure of actual exposure to violent media that uses a consistent and independent rating of violence. They argue that this does not mean that there is no relationship at all between media violence and aggression, but we are probably using the wrong methodologies to demonstrate it. Furthermore, even if we can demonstrate a theoretical and empirical media violence link to aggression in the laboratory, in real life, social background factors such as poverty, education and actual violence are so powerful by themselves that the media alone provide negligible top-up value. In trying to lay the blame for social breakdown on the media, we are probably worrying about the wrong things.

The special case of pornography

Why is pornography special? Pornography differs in one fundamental and important way from other taboo media. No film director, however provocative and unprincipled, has ever produced a violent film with the avowed intention that viewers subsequently imitate its content. Film directors and others in the world of cinema are forever quoted as denying the link between screen violence and actual violence, or downplaying it at the very least. Alfred Hitchcock and other horror directors might talk of their intention to scare the pants off audiences, but no one has ever said: 'I made this film so that psychologically healthy children leave the cinema itching for a punch-up.'

Pornography, however, is different. Pornography is made solely to produce specific effects on viewers and, on occasions, it has been advertised as an aid to sex itself. No (soft) porn producer has ever claimed that sexual arousal is an accidental by-product of their films, or that nobody would ever act out the scenes they witness. In fact, most porn producers are firm believers in the catharsis hypothesis, which states that, for men, at least, porn exists largely as stimuli to help lonely single individuals derive some sexual satisfaction. As far as soft porn is concerned, few would challenge this belief. Of course this may not be true of harder and specialized varieties of porn, which are another category of material entirely.

Inevitably, the concern over porn, particularly in the Internet era, is that it may be more easily accessed by children. Recent studies suggest that early exposure to Internet porn is associated with a greater incidence of casual sexual relationships and less progressive gender role attitudes by both sexes (Brown and L'Engle, 2009; Peter and Valkenburg, 2009), although there is no evidence here for causation. As with the media violence research, other social factors are likely to be overwhelmingly important.

Can media make us better people?

The final section of this chapter returns us to a frequently asked question of media influence. If violent content can have a negative effect on us, should altruistic and generally benevolent content likewise have a positive effect?

Research on prosocial media has lagged some way behind that on antisocial media, but it is possible to identify two broad categories of study: those that explore the beneficial effects of positive content within mainstream media, such as a prosocial soap storyline, and those that study the explicit effects of educational interventions or information media.

Probably the most fundamental difference between antisocial and prosocial behaviour in relation to media is that the former are almost always *incidental*, while the latter are mostly *intended*. The effects should, by definition, be much stronger, otherwise we would have to argue that completely different psychological processes are involved in the transmission of media effects.

One meta-analysis of prosocial media effects did indeed find that the effects of prosocial media were more enduring than those of antisocial (Hearold, 1986), although of course the sociocultural environment, school in particular, is more likely to enforce these than antisocial behaviour. A later meta-analysis (Mares and Woodard, 2005) suggested that the overall effect of prosocial media is not substantially greater than that of violent media, and then only in studies where participants' actual media use was calculated; in other words, the children preferred, or were encouraged by parents, to watch prosocial media in the first place. However, the authors argue that it is difficult to do any meaningful comparison of antisocial and prosocial media effects, because the amount of research in the two areas is so different. Compared to Paik and Comstock's (1994) analysis of 217 antisocial studies, they were able to include only 34.

Despite mixed findings, some authors have nevertheless attempted to develop a psychological model that accounts for both types of effect. The incidental effects of violence were originally accounted for by the General Aggression Model (GAM; Anderson and Bushman, 2002), where the stimulus (a violent film or video game) generates aggressive thoughts, feelings and behaviours in the short term, and desensitization, aggressive scripts and attitudes in the long term. The GAM was later expanded into a General Learning Model (GLM; Buckley and Anderson, 2006) in order to account for prosocial effects as well. The processes described by the GLM are similar to the GAM. Short-term processes have affect, cognition and arousal components, while long-term processes include attitudes, beliefs and scripts, and elements of personality, which also operate at short-term intervals. Ultimately, both the GAM and GLM are generalized descriptive models that simply reflect what appears to be happening in the experimental and survey literature. They do not incorporate different types of media, which would weaken their generalizability, and they do not specify different types of (real-world) behavioural outcome, so they have little use as explanatory devices.

What are prosocial behaviours and prosocial media?

Prosocial behaviour has been defined by Penner et al. (2005, p. 336) as 'a broad category of acts that are defined by some significant segment of society and/or one's social group as generally beneficial to other people'. While we tend of think of 'beneficial' behaviour as being associated with generally kind, altruistic individuals, as Gentile et al. (2009) point out, prosocial acts can be carried out by the filthiest villains. The Kray twins might have maimed and murdered rival gangsters throughout the East

UNIVERSITY OF WINCHESTER
LIBRARY

End of London in the 1960s, yet they performed many prosocial acts towards people in their own circle of friends and family (Pearson, 1972).

Perhaps the question is better answered by recourse to the elements of prosocial media: after all, if their effects are intended, we should begin by exploring what the desired outcomes are. Much prosocial media seems to have an educational aim, from programmes aimed at developing young children's vocabulary and number skills, to public health awareness campaigns that seek to encourage healthy behaviours.

There are also storylines and series that aim to have largely moral or even political effects, such as encouraging more women into education and the professions. Finally, there are prosocial media that tap into the behaviours defined by Penner et al. (2005), encouraging cooperation and altruistic behaviour, although here the prosocial definition is applied by researchers; as with media violence, these are largely incidental features of general drama series. In a rare micro-analytic study of media content, Greenberg (1980) found that antisocial and prosocial acts occurred with similar frequency in TV shows popular with children.

◁◉▷ Experimental research on prosocial media

Relatively few laboratory studies have been conducted with prosocial media. One of the earliest concerned the US show *The Waltons*, a 1970s family-based drama with strong moral overtones. Groups of 7- to 9-year-old children were shown clips from the show that featured either cooperative, non-cooperative, or neutral behaviours. Then a 'stooge', or associate of the experimenter, walked past the room and dropped a pile of books. Children who had watched the cooperative scenes were more likely to offer help to the stooge, and more quickly, than children in the other groups (Baran et al., 1979).

In a much later study using video games, Gentile et al. (2009) got college students to play violent, neutral, or prosocial games and then got them to interact in a puzzle completion task. Those who played the prosocial games were more likely to help other participants to complete puzzles, while those in the violent condition were more likely to select difficult puzzles for the others. Interpreted using the GLM, it could be argued that the students were learning behavioural patterns while playing the games and then operating these patterns in an actual social situation.

Not only might prosocial media provide models for people to imitate, they may also prime more positive cognitions. Greitemeyer (2009) played German students pop songs by the same artists with either prosocial or neutral lyrics. Afterwards, without prompting, they were given the option of contributing €2 to a charity box: in the prosocial condition, 24 of the 45 participants contributed, while in the neutral condition, only 14 of 45 did so. Had the participants been played songs about specific charitable acts, we might be able to infer a direct effect. However, neither of the prosocial songs in question so much as uses the verb 'to give'. One, in English, refers repeatedly to 'love', but without any clear philanthropic message (Bob Sinclair, 'Love Generation'), while the German one advocates togetherness, but largely for the ostensibly selfish reason of avoiding loneliness (2raumwohnung's *Kommt Zusammen*, or 'Come Together'). The author interprets the results using the GLM, and it is the kind of study perfectly suited to the descriptive powers of the GLM – no specific inputs or outputs, just a broad set of processes. One might just as well talk about a general 'vibe' being 'transmitted'.

Other experimental research has explored prosocial cognitions rather than behaviours: feelings of empathy in response to media characters, and the use of media in moral development. It is striking how much less time psychologists have devoted to exploring the potential positive benefits of media. As Mares and Woodard (2005, p. 316) conclude, television has 'real potential ... to help children feel and behave more pleasantly toward each other'. However, we still know little about the actual way in which it does this.

Educational television

Most of the longitudinal research on prosocial effects of media has been directed at the educational value of shows like *Sesame Street*, which was first broadcast in the US in the late 1960s in order to harness the popularity of television to educate 'hard-to-reach' preschool children, typically from poor and ethnic minority backgrounds. The show had an explicit theme of teaching vocabulary and number skills, but also had a more implicit role of promoting a multiethnic society, featuring mixed groups of children drawn from different ethnic groups. The stars of the show – the 'muppets' – represent animals, thereby avoiding any overt cultural bias.

The adaptability of the muppets has allowed *Sesame Street* to be exported around the globe; starting with Brazil and Germany in the early

1970s, over 120 countries now broadcast some version of the programme, often with fascinating local adaptations. In the 1990s, a joint Palestinian–Israeli production was developed, with the goal of promoting harmonious race relations, even if the original plan of having Arab and Jewish characters living on the same street never came to fruition. In 2002, a South African version was launched, featuring an HIV-positive character, and later in the decade, an Indian version, with professional female characters intended to act as positive role models for girls.

US media researchers have for many years collected data on educational achievements in relation to *Sesame Street* (Fisch et al., 1999). Broadly speaking, there have been positive findings, with frequent viewers of the show performing well at school, and displaying non-racist attitudes (Huston and Wright, 1998), although in the early days, it tended to be the middle-class children who benefited most from the show, counter to its producers' objectives (Ball and Bogatz, 1970). Indeed, in their meta-analysis of prosocial media effects, Mares and Woodard (2005) found that stronger effects of prosocial media generally were found in the most affluent socioeconomic groups.

One reason for this may be that middle-class parents are more likely to watch television with their children, thereby being on hand to explain and elaborate any ambiguous or puzzling content. This is known as **parental mediation**, and in a wide range of studies has been found to enhance the positive effects of media and reduce negative effects (Buijzen et al., 2008). Indeed, one of the original aims of *Sesame Street* was, through the creation of characters like Bert and Ernie, to appeal to watching adults in order to encourage them to accompany their children.

There is less research on *Sesame Street* in other countries, although the Palestinian–Israeli version has been studied for its impact on viewers, with some positive results. Although some of the children in both communities held unfavourable stereotypes about either Jewish or Arab adults, they did not bring these stereotypes to bear when discussing conflict between children (Cole et al., 2003).

Raising awareness of social issues through media

Not all prosocial television is as explicit as *Sesame Street*. Many countries have used soaps and other fictional series as vehicles for promoting topical issues by embedding storylines in established dramatic formats. Series on Indian radio (*Tinka Tinka Sukh*) and television (*Hum Log*) have been found to resonate with audiences by creating realistic characters and promoting educational issues, especially targeting female viewers (Sood, 2002).

Health is one of the most popular areas for raising awareness through media. Soap operas regularly run stories on cancer, HIV and other issues of current concern. Governments can become directly involved in the use of media to promote health behaviour, for example anti-smoking messages have been regularly transmitted for years through advertising in various contexts. It pays to be careful when designing mass media health campaigns, however. Two separate campaigns launched in Australia and the US both tried to shame women into cancer screening, either for cervical cancer ('pap testing') or breast cancer (mammography screening). They did this by presenting a list of popular excuses for not being tested ('I'm too old' and so on). However, when it came to evaluating the campaign, they found many non-attenders recycling these same excuses (Fernbach, 2002; McCaul et al., 1988).

Increasingly, television has been used in many countries to raise money for charitable concerns. In the UK, this began in the 1980s with large-scale events such as Live Aid, where although the focus was on an open-air concert, much of the fundraising was done through the television broadcast. Although during the 1990s, a degree of 'charity fatigue' seemed to have set in, the fundraising 'telethon' format has been successfully channelled into two annual BBC events, Red Nose Day for Comic Relief each spring, with a focus on UK and African charities, and Children In Need in the autumn. Both events have proved enormously popular, often the most watched programme of the week, and have raised millions of pounds for various causes. They have also become national events, involving schools in particular, in a way that demonstrates the power of television, even today, to influence nationwide behaviour. This is an unambiguous example of a prosocial media effect.

◉ Further reading

Barker, M. and Petley, J. (eds) (2001). *Ill effects: The media/violence debate* (2nd edn). London: Routledge.

Freedman, J.L. (2002). *Media violence and its effects on aggression: Assessing the scientific evidence*. Toronto, Canada: University of Toronto Press.

Chapter 4

Persuasion and advertising

◉ Introduction

Is advertising really a 'medium' at all? Maybe not, but wherever you search in the media landscape, you will find advertising, and – given the amount of money spent on it – its effects are presumed to be spectacular. In this chapter I review two approaches to the psychology of advertising. One, the social cognitive approach, focuses on advertising's power of persuasion on the fully aware, thinking consumer, who can recognize and act upon a clear message. The other, the perceptual (or even 'subliminal') approach, sees advertising's effects as largely *unconscious*, whereby the actual message is relatively unimportant. These two approaches have combined in a rather muddled debate on the effects of advertising to children, which has resulted in legal restrictions in certain countries.

◉ Advertising is everywhere

Take a look around, wherever you are. The chances are that you will see at least one advertisement. I'm writing this book in my study and without moving from my chair I can see three adverts: one, a glossy flier for a pizza delivery service, sticking out of my waste paper bin; two, a pair of fluffy bathroom slippers pinched from some hotel with the hotel's logo clearly visible; and three, a discarded plastic bag bearing the name of a supermarket chain. Three separate appeals for me to buy something – a cheap snack, a night of luxurious pampering, a sack of potatoes.

Advertising is the odd man out in this book. It is *not* a medium. The media in the above example are, respectively, paper, clothing, plastic. Advertising is a parasite that attaches to media; it needs media for its survival. But unlike most parasites, it is also crucially important for media themselves; in fact, without advertising, many media would not exist in the first place. Not things like paper and plastic, perhaps, but individual media products such as newspapers, magazines, television channels.

The whole history of newspapers goes back to advertising. The very first newspapers, appearing in the 17th century in Northern Europe, were barely recognizable from handbills, which were mostly collections of ads for local traders, fairs and markets. Newspapers just seemed like a good way of making these more attractive, and therefore more likely to be read. Today, one of the first questions a publisher will ask the editor of a new magazine is who their advertisers will be. The idea of setting up a newspaper or magazine *without* adverts is unthinkable.

The BBC in Britain is a rare example of a state-run radio and television service that is funded by the taxpayer in the form of an annual licence, which has for many years been the subject of some controversy, since it acts effectively as the right to *own a television set*. Today, with the BBC competing with hundreds of satellite channels, one might argue that, as a subscriber to an expensive satellite package, one has no interest in watching, and therefore propping up, the state service, but it wouldn't stop the bailiffs from carting your TV away. Despite the BBC's hallowed status as ad-free radio and TV, there is nevertheless a commercial wing of the corporation that markets its products aggressively: it doesn't just sell archive DVDs but increasingly swallows up other media. Recently, the UK government warned BBC Worldwide about its activities after it bought up the Lonely Planet series of travel guides (Holmwood, 2009). Furthermore, the BBC frequently slips in references to its own programming through 'news stories' about its presenters, even where the outcome is unflattering.

During 2008, BBC radio presenters Jonathan Ross and Russell Brand were the subject of a press scandal after they left insulting messages on the ansaphone of a much-loved actor whose daughter had had an affair with Brand. The presenters were subject to a chorus of disapproval about falling broadcasting standards, but the BBC were as active as anyone in promoting the story (and advocating swingeing punishments). At the time of writing, Ross and Brand are still broadcasting in their cutting-edge style, perhaps even with a few extra listeners. As they say, there's no such thing as bad publicity. (However, Ross's show on Radio 2 will end around July 2010 when his contract at the BBC ends.)

In this chapter, I will discuss various psychological theories that have been advanced to explain the effects of advertising, and ways of thinking about advertising that need to be adapted to the changing face of adverts and their audiences.

👁 Advertising as persuasion: the processing of a message

In the same way as media have been studied by psychologists largely as vehicles for delivering content (violence, sex, prosocial behaviour), so advertising has been studied as vehicles for delivering messages. The simplest model of advertising specifies a sender, a medium, a message, and a receiver. If we are interested in the persuasive appeal at a car ad in a local newspaper, this is probably a reasonable set of theoretical tools for us to work with. But, as I'll go on to explain, this basic model is pretty useless for much contemporary mass media advertising.

The psychology of advertising has a longer history than the psychology of attitudes and persuasion, although both these are now much more significant concepts in modern psychology. Walter Dill Scott wrote the first book on the subject in 1908, over a hundred years ago. The psychological processes he specified haven't changed much since: visual perception, attention, memory, and source credibility (today we're likely to be using brain imaging to look at the same things, but the ads themselves are unrecognizable).

The study of advertising actually helped to shape the discipline of social psychology. The whole field of **persuasion**, for instance, arose directly from theory developed to account for the effectiveness of advertising – and was then generalized to account for all types of persuasion, such as political influence. Since then, of course, it has been applied to all manner of social phenomena, in particular **attitude change**.

Persuasion and attitude change

One of the most influential figures in the early days was Carl Hovland at Yale University in the US, who became interested in the power of wartime propaganda when serving in the US army. After the war, he applied the principles of behaviourism to study the impact of a message in terms of its 'reinforcement' on the receiver. He identified five stages that a message needed to go through in order for it to produce a change in behaviour: exposure, attention, comprehension, acceptance, and retention (see Figure 4.1).

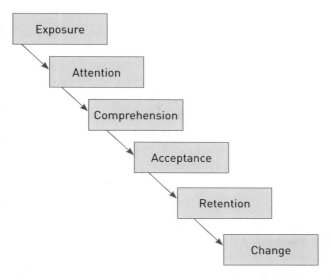

Figure 4.1 The Yale-Hovland model of message effectiveness

Applying this to advertising, clearly, the message needs to:

- reach the consumer in some way
- be stimulating enough for the consumer to pay attention to it
- be understood, although this is a point of some controversy
- be accepted – we need to believe it
- be retained – we need to remember the gist of the message, even if we forget the source itself.

Behaviour change is the desired outcome: we decide to ditch our old mobile phone and purchase the exciting new model instead.

The behaviourist part of this process, which admittedly looks fairly cognitive up to now, is that the message must *reinforce* the behaviour in some way that is of benefit to the consumer. For example, the new mobile might be much trendier than the consumer's old model, so this change is reinforced in terms of peer approval (your friends will be envious). Or it could be of financial benefit (the new model doesn't differ much from the old one, but the tariffs are much lower).

One of the important influences in this process is **source credibility**. Hovland and Weiss (1951) argued that the acceptance stage in the model was strongly affected by the status of the source, in other words, if a leading expert recommends a particular product, we should be more likely to accept the message of the ad than if it is someone who we don't trust, or whose judgement we don't respect.

Hovland and his team also identified a phenomenon known as the **sleeper effect** (Hovland et al., 1949), by which we may forget things such as source details after we've 'slept on' the message. Subsequent research has found that this effect only occurs if the message is powerful enough by itself to affect change, and would have been effective from a credible source in any case. In this case, it wouldn't matter who the source was, the message would get through in any case.

Cognitive dissonance

Another early social psychological theory that has been applied to advertising is **cognitive dissonance theory** (Festinger, 1957). The basic idea of cognitive dissonance is that individuals strive to maintain 'cognitive consistency' and are thrown into confusion when discrepancies occur between their beliefs and what they perceive as reality. For instance, if you have just bought a brand new car but have read an article in a motoring magazine about this particular make of car being accident-prone, it will generate a degree of discrepancy, or dissonance.

Festinger demonstrated this principle in an ingenious series of experiments where he asked undergraduate participants to describe a thoroughly tedious sorting task to other students waiting to take part (Festinger and Carlsmith, 1959). Along with an unpaid group, two groups of participants were paid $1 and $20 respectively to lie about the task and describe it as enjoyable. The participants were then asked how enjoyable they themselves had found the task. Those paid $20 (a considerable sum of money in the 1950s) rated the task as boring, as did the unpaid participants. Those paid only $1 rated the task as significantly more enjoyable than the others. Festinger interpreted this finding as an instance of cognitive dissonance. The unpaid participants did not receive any incentive to lie about the task; no dissonance here. The $20 participants received good money to lie; they experienced no dissonance either. The $1 participants were in more of a quandary; they had been paid to lie, but not very much. In the end, Festinger argued, they lied about the boring task in order to try and reduce the dissonance.

To return to our motoring example, reducing dissonance might mean that you change your mind about the make of car, maybe you even decide to sell it. Alternatively, you change your mind about the motoring magazine you have subscribed to for many years. How dare they write such rubbish about your new model. A third possibility is that you 'compartmentalize' the two ideas. Perhaps you decide to wait until you notice something wrong with your own car before you change your mind about either the make or the magazine.

Self-perception theory

An alternative explanation for Festinger's findings was offered by Daryl Bem (1967), who argued that the reason the participants in the $1 condition said they enjoyed the task was because, in retrospect, they decided they *had* actually enjoyed the task. In telling the lie, they actually convinced themselves. Bem argued that this was because we only come to understand our attitudes through observing our behaviour – just as we do with other people. With regard to advertising, if someone buys a flash sports car, we assume that this is the kind of image they wish to present to the outside world. If you buy a flash sports car, then you decide that you wish to present a worldly, sophisticated image to other people, even if that wasn't your original intention – you may have simply thought you were a connoisseur and were demonstrating your good taste.

'Self-perception theory', as Bem termed it, does have a somewhat counterintuitive feel about it. Rather like the James-Lange theory of emotions, where you only feel sad because you find yourself crying, it argues things from what appears to be the wrong way round. Surely it is attitudes that predict behaviour, not vice versa? It's unlikely that you would buy a sports car without having some idea what image you wished to portray to others. However, for rather less costly items, it may be that you don't have a very clear idea of why you purchase the products that you do.

Let's say John has always thought of himself as a bit of a 'metrosexual': he likes to flirt with sexual ambiguity, to keep people guessing. But one day his flatmate asks him why he always buys men's toiletries – shampoo, shower gel, deodorant – with a clearly masculine, even macho, image. On reflection, John considers that he may be a little bit more conservative and traditionally masculine than he has always liked to think. In most cases, John might well have a ready reply, and not allow his flatmate's comment to trouble his self-perception. But it could be that, over time, we do occasionally analyse our own behaviour in order to work out what attitudes we hold. After all, the average research participant may never have had to consider their attitude on a particular subject until a psychologist sits them down and hands them a scale to fill in.

Elaboration likelihood

Later theories of persuasion explored in more depth individual differences that might affect advertising effectiveness. One influential model is the **Elaboration Likelihood Model** (ELM; Petty and Cacioppo, 1981), whose central theme is the degree of product *involvement* the consumer engages in. If you're fed up with your old mobile phone, then you are likely to be more involved in an ad for a new make than someone who loves and cherishes their current model. This will increase the amount of *elaboration* they engage in with respect to the ad. Here, elaboration involves paying more attention to, and thinking more, about the ad, what its message is, what the virtues of the product are and so on.

Petty and Cacioppo (1986) specified two routes to persuasion, which they called the central and peripheral routes:

- *The central route* involves high elaboration, with much scrutiny of the message, and ultimately determines the degree and direction of attitude change. This is where you focus on all the functions and attributes of the new model – its price, special features, tariffs and so on.
- *The peripheral route* involves the 'environmental', or incidental, features of the message – things like source credibility, attractiveness, advertising slogans and so on.

Mostly, advertising works through a combination of the two routes, although their operation is strongly influenced by the characteristics and interests of the individual consumer. The key factors are 'motivation' and 'ability'. The consumer needs to be motivated to engage in message scrutiny, so it helps if the product has personal relevance, and that the consumer has high 'need for cognition' (a tendency to enjoy thinking in general). They also need to have sufficient cognitive resources (attention and so on) to scrutinize the message, and sufficient knowledge. If you don't know how a mobile phone works, you are unlikely to be persuaded by technical information.

In recent years, the ELM has been applied to advertising on the Internet, with mixed results (Karson and Korgaonkar, 2001). However, some support has been found for a combined effect of central and peripheral routes when considering websites as ads in themselves (SanJosé-Cabezudo et al., 2009). In this study, the researchers designed two travel agent sites, one serious and one amusing, and found that both approaches had equal effectiveness for a student sample.

Individual differences between consumers also affect the way they process different types of advertisement. Early on in the industry's history, two distinct forms of advertising became apparent, hard sell and soft sell. These correspond roughly to Petty and Cacioppo's two routes to persuasion:

- *Hard sell* ads are those that appeal directly to the product and its basic elements. So a 'hard' mobile phone ad would focus on the central route to persuasion – lots of technical and pricing information.
- A *soft sell* approach would appeal more to the peripheral route, so an advertiser might use music, imagery and narrative to seduce consumers in an indirect fashion.

But not all consumers will be swayed by the indirect, impressionistic approach. Snyder and de Bono (1985) found that the appeal of hard and soft sell was affected by the degree of self-monitoring that people engage in:

- *High self-monitors* – people who are very image-conscious, and likely to modify their behaviour to make a good impression on other people – rely on peripheral persuasive features and are therefore more susceptible to the soft sell approach.
- *Low self-monitors* – much more dogmatic and pragmatic – know what they like and are more attuned to the central persuasive elements of the hard sell approach.

Another element in persuasion is the appeal to imagined future selves. The concept of **possible selves** (Markus and Nurius, 1986) is long-established in social psychology as an important influence on behaviour, and has a clear link to advertising, where we are invited to imagine how our lives might be enhanced by purchasing a particular product, often in conjunction with the endorsement of idealized others (e.g. celebrities).

Advertising generally appeals to *positive* imagined selves (ideal selves), which is why glamorous figures are routinely used in commercials. It has been argued that the use of unattainable celebrities might affect repeat sales of products due to cognitive dissonance – the failure of the use of lipstick advertised by Claudia Schiffer to transform the consumer into a Schiffer lookalike ought to increase dissatisfaction with the lipstick. However, the findings from research in this field offer mixed support for this argument (Marshall et al., 2008).

Not all imagined future selves in advertising need to be positive. A famously successful campaign featuring a *negative* possible self is the First World War recruitment poster in which a very glum father sits in an armchair with his daughter on his knee while his son plays toys soldiers on the floor. The wording at the top of the poster, which we can attribute to the daughter, reads: 'Daddy, what did YOU do in the Great War?' This poster was designed to shame conscientious objectors and encourage others to enlist in the army before it became compulsory. Daddy's answer, presumably, was not intended to be a proud statement of pacifism.

Criticism of this research

There is no doubt that cognitive social psychological theories of persuasion and decision-making (we can call this the information processing (IP) approach) have had enormous influence in consumer research, and on the advertising industry itself. Routinely, consumers are asked questions in market research studies geared to measuring the conscious processing of an ad – memory, attention and so on – as much as the emotional or affective meanings of the product (or the ad itself).

However, Heath and Feldwick (2007) have argued that the IP process is fundamentally flawed when it comes to measuring the effectiveness of advertising. They argue that the industry has been using 'the wrong model' for over 50 years. The IP model was developed to account for the kind of unsophisticated advertising that appealed to the central route to persuasion during the 1950s and earlier, whereas modern-day advertising is highly impressionistic and appeals much more to consumers' emotions – the peripheral route, which according to the IP model, and the ELM in particular, is supposedly less effective for persuasion. Intuitively, this argument makes a lot of sense. The authors present numerous examples of some of the most successful advertising campaigns of the past 30 years or so – from the Andrex puppy (a cute dog that runs off with the toilet roll) to the Guinness surfers (waiting patiently for the ultimate wave) that have relied exclusively on 'peripheral' appeals, with scarcely any 'central' product information apart from the brand name.

There are logical reasons for why an advertiser might use the peripheral route. After all, how would you use the central route to advertise a toilet roll – 'it wipes your bottom without chafing as much as the rival brand'? With some products it is now illegal to advertise using central route information for health reasons, such as cigarettes and beer. Indeed, some of the most peripheral appeals of all time were those of the Benson & Hedges' Silk Cut billboard and magazine campaigns of the 1990s, where the product was reduced to a series of symbols – scissors, purple silk, a cut or slash somewhere in the poster.

The other problem with the IP approach to advertising effectiveness is that it relies on the consumer being able to identify a coherent, unambiguous message from the ad. As Heath and Feldwick (2007) put it, the Andrex puppy commercials did more than just communicate the information that its brand of toilet roll is 'soft, strong and very long', and the Guinness surfers ad, which has been voted the best television commercial in a variety of polls, does more than remind the consumer that the drink takes a long time to pour.

A model of advertising effectiveness that relies solely on consumers being able to comprehend, and recall, a simple message, would identify the Andrex puppy and Guinness surfer ads as confusing and irrelevant, and unlikely to persuade or change attitudes about the products. The fact that these campaigns – and many other highly impressionistic ads – have proved so successful at establishing their brands and products in the market suggests that there are many other psychological factors at work, including many of which consumers are not necessarily aware.

Thinking about advertising effectiveness

How do we know when an advert has been successful? What counts as success? One of the problems that besets the psychology of advertising (and marketing) is that it is extremely difficult to disentangle the various components of a marketing campaign in order to analyse the effectiveness of any one.

Let's suppose you have been asked to organize a campaign to advertise a new biscuit that was launched two years ago on the market and has since suffered a dip in sales. You wouldn't just run a series of radio ads. You'd probably commission some TV ads too. And maybe some print ads. And an in-store marketing campaign. And some links to other products (maybe get supermarket chains to advertise your biscuits as part of their promotional package). You might also organize some press – try to get a story in the papers about the biscuits. And some product placement – make sure there's a packet visible on a kitchen table in *EastEnders*.

A few months later, someone asks you how successful the radio ads were. They would be buried beneath all these other influences. You can only say that the whole campaign was a success (or not), unless there was something special about the radio ads, for example they were only broadcast in Lincolnshire, and then you could see if sales in Lincolnshire were significantly higher than elsewhere.

This is why the methods used by psychologists and other social scientists to measure advertising effectiveness sometimes seem so artificial. Trying to get real-life results that relate to specific ads is really a very difficult task.

Advertising: the perceptual approach

If the IP approach to advertising – studying message reception, retention and elaboration – is wide of the target, what other theories might psychologists employ to explain how advertising 'works'? If Heath and Feldwick (2007) really are right, and emotional processing is more important than cognitive (information) processing, the influence of advertising may be unconscious. We know, for example, that the third person effect is particularly strong with regard to advertising (Hoorens and Nuttin, 1993). If advertising were a simple matter of hard thought, then surely we would acknowledge its influence on us: 'I pay attention to the ads and use them to make my own decision about what things to buy.' I think very few of us would agree with this statement. We are suckered by ads despite ourselves.

During the 1950s, at a time when American society was beside itself with fear of the threat of communism, concerns about 'brainwashing' were raised following a controversial study of **subliminal perception**. Advertising expert James Vicary claimed, in an unpublished report, to have increased sales of coca-cola and popcorn at a particular cinema over a six-week period through exposing viewers to the messages 'Drink coca-cola' and 'Eat popcorn'. These messages, he said, were flashed briefly (1/3000th of a second, too fast for conscious awareness) and repeatedly onto the screen during the projection of a feature film. Challenged subsequently to replicate his findings, Vicary tried and failed. The cinema itself was found incapable of holding the number of customers Vicary claimed constituted his sample. Further attempts to replicate the methodology by Vicary and other researchers were unsuccessful. Several years later, he admitted the whole experiment had never taken place.

Nevertheless, the concept was reported widely and – like Andrew Wakefield's infamous MMR–autism link many years later (see Chapter 9) – the idea that 'subliminal advertising' posed a devastating threat to Western civilization wormed its way into the public consciousness in a much more effective way than any brief sales message. The British, Australian and US governments all announced bans on subliminal advertising, and for years to come, presumably unaware of the fact that Vicary had himself declared the study a hoax, various bodies all warned of the dangers of such propaganda.

Over the years, the notion of subliminal learning has opened the door to all kinds of quackery, such as audiotapes that claim that, if you play the tape while you are asleep, you will unconsciously process material that can make you learn a new language, or conquer various psychological issues such as giving up smoking or boosting self-esteem. In a controlled experiment of such claims, Greenwald et al. (1991) found little evidence for subliminal learning other than a slight placebo effect, that is, those listeners who believed they were listening to self-esteem messages did actually perceive a slight increase in their self-esteem.

Notwithstanding the Vicary data, could subliminal perception influence consumer behaviour in any way? Studies of **iconic memory** have demonstrated that we certainly process this kind of briefly presented material (Sperling, 1960). In a typical study, participants are presented with a 3 × 3 grid of nine digits for 50 milliseconds, too short a time for us to recall all the digits in the right place. However, if we are subsequently asked to recall at random any single line of three numbers, we can do it. The information has been processed, but it is only consciously available for a few seconds.

It does seem that truly subliminal presentations, that is, those that are literally below the attention threshold of the observer, are unlikely to have much long-term effect. There is, however, evidence that unperceived material can be retained for longer periods. Eagle et al. (1966)

presented a series of slides to participants, most of which contained animals, and asked them later to say which animals they had seen. They then asked them to write a story about a farmyard. In the experimental condition, one of the slides contained a tree trunk with the outline of a duck embedded within it. The participants in this condition did not include ducks in their lists of animals, but they were more likely to mention them in their farmyard stories.

More recently, a team of French researchers found some similar results using three-second pop-up ads on a specially constructed website (Courbet et al., 2008). Eight days after being exposed to the ads (for a fictitious brand of bottled mineral water), participants denied having ever seen the brand name, but rated the brand significantly more positively than a control group who had not been exposed to the ad. Moreover, this effect was still observed at a three-month follow-up. Also, participants who had seen the brand name and a picture of the product were able to link the two better than controls and a group who had been exposed to the name alone.

Do these results mean that manufacturers could sell more products using these techniques, or do they just demonstrate our hidden memory abilities? Certainly they show how 'brand awareness' might develop, so that certain names become familiar – and perhaps more trusted. This has been called the **mere exposure effect** (Zajonc, 1968). According to this, any exposure to a particular stimulus (e.g. a brand name) is sufficient by itself to effect a change in attitude or effect – there is no need for any elaboration, or cognitive deliberation, or even recall of the stimulus.

For this reason, advertisers are prepared to spend a good deal of money on **product placement**, whereby advertisers pay film and television companies in order to expose their products on screen. Although companies have placed their products in films from the early days of Hollywood, perhaps the most famous example is in Steven Spielberg's *E.T. The Extra-Terrestrial* (1982), where the character Elliott tries to lure the alien into his house by scattering Reese's Pieces (peanut butter-flavoured sweets) in his path. In the month following the film's release, sales of the product increased by 65% (*Time*, 1982).

There is relatively little academic research on the effectiveness of product placement, although a study by Matthes et al. (2007) on TV placement found that the degree of involvement with the show was a critical factor. However, neither the show nor the product used in this study is really likely to have engaged the participants. Two groups of university students were shown the same documentary about farming in which an advertising hoarding for an agricultural company was visible in the background. One group was asked to pay attention in preparation for a subsequent test, while the others simply watched the video. No relationship was found between participants' recall of the brand name and their evaluation of the brand, which the authors interpreted as a mere exposure effect of sorts.

A subsequent study using a more engaging programme (*Seinfeld*), with more appealing products (shampoo and M&M chocolates) found that greater liking for the show predicted poorer evaluation of the advertised product, regardless of recall (Cowley and Barron, 2008). In addition, the products were actually used by characters in the show, like Reese's Pieces in *E.T.*, rather than just randomly appearing somewhere in the background. Therefore, a crucial factor in product placement could be the extent to which the advertised product enters into the narrative of the film or show.

A highly lucrative option for modern-day advertisers is the use of product placements in computer games. The enormous popularity of games, and the captive nature of their players, allows multiple opportunities for brand exposure, such that firms like Coca-Cola have announced a shift away from TV towards games (Mackay et al., 2009). Again, the function of the product is important: car racing games afford opportunities for motoring manufacturers to advertise models that players are intimately involved with during the game. In a study comparing racing games featuring two different car models, Mackay et al. (2009) found that, unless players already had a favourable impression of the car model, attitudes toward the brand increased significantly as a result of the product placement.

◉ Celebrity endorsement

In the US and UK, up to a quarter of all advertising uses celebrities in some way to endorse the product (Amos et al., 2008; Fowles, 1996). A celebrity may simply be pictured alongside a product; sometimes they are referred to as 'the face of' a particular brand or product; sometimes they play a substantial role in the campaign and may be forever connected to the product. Former England football star-turned-TV presenter Gary Lineker has advertised Walkers crisps since the mid-1990s, appearing in a new set of commercials every few years. It is hard to dissociate him from this particular product.

Celebrity endorsement works, it is claimed, through a process of **meaning transfer** (McCracken, 1986), whereby the image or persona of the celebrity transfers to the product they endorse. Gary Lineker's unthreatening amicability has always been referred to as 'clean-cut': as a player, he did not receive a single yellow or red card in his entire career.[1] As a TV presenter, he has maintained this image (despite a divorce), and Walkers have played on the metaphorical connection of 'clean-cut' potato crisps by associating with him; there is also a geographical link, since both Lineker and Walkers come from Leicester in the English Midlands.

A meta-analysis of 32 studies of celebrity endorsement effects found that there were three factors that best predicted its success: trustworthiness, expertise and attractiveness (Amos et al., 2008). Advertisers need to be careful that consumers trust the celebrity they've chosen to represent a particular product. Use the wrong face at the wrong time and the campaign might backfire. This happened in 2009 when the frozen food supermarket chain Iceland dropped the former Atomic Kitten singer Kerry Katona as its celebrity following alleged drug abuse.

It also helps if the celebrity has some degree of expertise in relation to the product. Clearly this depends on the product: Gary Lineker does not require a doctorate in food science to successfully endorse a packet of crisps. In practice, it is not necessarily expertise as such that appeals to the audience but some kind of rationale for associating the celebrity with the product – so Lineker would be a better endorser of a new brand of football boot than a pop star. This is more commonly referred to as 'celebrity/product fit'.

In an earlier study, Alperstein (1991) found that people's attitudes towards celebrities were often impaired as a result of their involvement in commercial activities, particularly if they were believed to be promoting the product purely for financial gain. One interviewee, for example, was disappointed to see the Hollywood legend Orson Welles advertising wine. On the other hand, where products were integrated into celebrities' day-to-day personae, the match was more successful. One woman, who had related strongly to US TV presenter Joan Lunden through the course of her pregnancy, admitted buying a particular brand of baby food on her recommendation.

These are examples of media influence resulting from parasocial interaction with media figures such as TV presenters and celebrities in general, a topic explored in more depth in Chapter 6.

👁 Advertising and children: the great debate

The final section of this chapter is devoted to a long-running debate in advertising and psychology: the advertisement of various products aimed at children. As with (fictional) media violence, there has been considerable concern about children's ability to understand the implications of advertising, and, regardless of whether they understand it or not, concern about the knock-on effect of 'pester power', whereby adults are indirectly targeted by advertisers. Most of all, there has been widespread condemnation of the practice of advertising unhealthy food products to children.

Theoretical perspectives

Although it is rarely characterized as such (although see Livingstone, 2009), the debate has arisen largely from the two distinct approaches to the psychology of advertising: one, the IP approach, arguing that it is the processing of messages that is important; the other, the perceptual approach, arguing that advertising will influence consumers regardless of their ability to understand a message and base a decision on it. Applied to child development, the former approach would suggest that children can only become vulnerable to advertising once their thinking has become sufficiently sophisticated to comprehend the messages. The perceptual approach, on the other hand, suggests that children of all ages are inherently vulnerable to advertising's seductive powers.

Nevertheless, much of the research in this area has ignored both approaches, arguing that children are actually *more* vulnerable to advertising when they cannot understand the message, and that there is a developmental stage at which they become more sophisticated thinkers and are able to understand the implications of advertising and (presumably) capable of resisting its allure. Much of this research has taken its cue from Piaget's theory of cognitive development, with researchers such as John (1999) and Valkenburg and Cantor (2001) describing stage models of consumer development. This has led to much speculation about the 'magic age' at which children can be said to fully understand advertising (and, by implication, become 'fair game' for advertisers).

During the early years, Valkenburg and Cantor (2001) argue that children begin requesting advertised products as early as 18 months. They are therefore most vulnerable in the preschool period, when their understanding of television is said to be 'literal', in that they can be misled by advertising into thinking that products have magical powers and other exciting effects. Only by the ages of 9–12 have children developed the critical skills to enable them to understand the function and purpose of advertising. Meanwhile, their negotiation skills are also developing at the same rate, enabling them to become more effective 'pesterers' of their parents.

For some years, the age of 12 has been touted as the cut-off point in advertising to children. Livingstone (2009) suggests there are three reasons behind citing this as the 'magic age':

1 It is believed that children having only begun to attain 'advertising literacy' at this age, that is, they have learned to 'read' ads for what they are (Young, 1990).
2 Until around 12, they are said to lack the cognitive defences to avoid being influenced by advertising (Bjurström, 1994).
3 It is, therefore, considered unethical to advertise to children who are both illiterate and vulnerable.

Legislating advertising to children

On the basis of Bjurström's findings, both Sweden and Norway passed laws in the early 1990s to prevent advertisers from promoting their products on television to children under 12. More recently, a ban on advertising food with high fat and sugar content during children's television has been applied in both the UK and the Netherlands (Buijzen, 2009).

Of course, television counts for a proportion of contemporary advertising to children, and the research supporting the above restrictions has largely been based on television (Livingstone, 2009). There are many reasons why television advertising bans might be somewhat ineffectual by themselves. The first is that digital media are not governed by national legislation, and in the Swedish case, the ban could only be enforced on state television, while increasing numbers of ads – from the UK in particular – reached child audiences through satellite TV (Caraher et al., 2006).

The second is that, as with so many media, advertising effectively pays for the programmes, and it has been argued that through financial restrictions on advertising, these kinds of bans harm the very media they are instigated to protect (Ambler, 2008). That said, does quality children's television really require the financial support of the food industry to flourish?

An additional criticism concerns the 'magic age' itself. Researchers have traditionally relied on purely verbal data in order to investigate children's understanding, and appreciation, of advertising. However, some developmental psychologists have begun to use alternative methods of eliciting this information from children, either by offering them a cartoon that represents the meaning of the ad (Owen et al., 2008), or by using pictorial cues such as smiley faces to represent the degree of liking (Nash et al., 2009). Using such materials, children as young as 7 are able to display the same level of advertising literacy as 10-year-olds, and alcohol advertising, designed for adults, was appreciated by 7-year-olds.

In terms of practical applications, these findings send conflicting messages. On the one hand, the earlier-than-expected attainment of advertising literacy could be interpreted to suggest that television channels under advertising legislation could be allowed to drop the age at which children are able to view, for example, food ads. On the other hand, the surprisingly young children's appreciation of alcohol ads implies that all children are equally vulnerable to advertising effects and perhaps legislation should be broader. Nash et al. (2009) argue that children should not be attracted to unsuitable products, but the real problem may be the longer term implications of associating fun, entertaining imagery with alcohol.

Modern advertising and marketing strategies

Nairn and Fine (2008) argue that, with sophisticated modern-day advertising, children are more vulnerable to **implicit persuasion** – of the sort discussed earlier in relation to product placement and mere exposure effects. The authors are particularly concerned about the growth of 'stealth marketing', where advertising is embedded in other media, including not only familiar techniques such as celebrity endorsement and product placement in popular children's media such as social networking sites, but also more sinister phenomena such as 'brand pushers' – children who are commissioned by companies to plug products by word of mouth.

This phenomenon began in the early 2000s, when multinational giant Procter & Gamble (P&G) developed a network of 250,000 teenagers who became known as 'connectors', to plug P&G brands among their friends. The project was so successful that the company created an even bigger network of mothers to promote products like washing-up liquid and dog food. The company claims that none of its pushers are actually paid, but they are sworn to secrecy (Martin and Smith, 2008).

Many authors have criticized the cognitive stage approach more generally, arguing that the stage approach suffers from the same flaws as the IP approach to advertising in general – its reliance on consumers being able to identify an unambiguous message, and to consciously reflect on the ad and the brand in order to arrive at purchasing decisions. A review of 50 studies of the effects of food advertising on children found little difference across age groups ranging from 2 to 16 years: indeed, the weakest effects were found in studies involving the youngest children (Livingstone and Helsper, 2006). It seems, therefore, that the relationship between advertising literacy and vulnerability to advertising is more complex than Piagetian theory might predict. It could be argued, of course, that if adults were invulnerable to advertising, the industry would have collapsed years ago.

A recent study on the immediate impact of food advertising neatly illustrates this paradox. Harris et al. (2009) screened cartoons to children and a comedy show to adults, half with food ads embedded in a commercial break. In both experimental and control conditions, snack food was made available to participants, but the experimental participants in both age groups consumed up to 45% more food than the controls. The authors concluded that the ads triggered 'hedonic hunger' – unconscious cravings for food – since the extra food consumed did not necessarily correspond to the actual food products advertised.

This finding suggests that, for all the blame laid at the food industry, some responsibility should also be borne by parents, by not making the snack food available in the first place. So controls on food advertising need also to be balanced by sensible parenting. As with media violence, some degree of parental mediation is advisable here, where parents help to explain the goals of advertising and persuasion to their children (Buijzen, 2007; Buijzen and Valkenburg, 2005). This has been found to be more effective where there are some restrictions on children's media use (Buijzen, 2009).

Perhaps it is the debate on children and advertising that should guide future thinking about persuasion. Clearly, the IP model cannot be right if preschool children are effectively able to make 'purchasing decisions' about Christmas toys, unless we have to concede that all advertising effectively carries the same message ('buy this product'). The perceptual approach implies that issues such as emotion and meaning-making are central to understanding how advertising works, and where better to observe this than in the developing child?

Note

1   FIFA, the world governing body of association football, adopted the yellow and red card system of punishment in the 1970 World Cup. A yellow card is issued for relatively minor transgressions, such as a wild challenge or disrespectful behaviour, while a red card is for more serious offences and results in the player being dismissed from the field.

Further reading

Fowles, J. (1996). *Advertising and popular culture*. Thousand Oaks, CA: Sage.

Sutherland, M. and Sylvester, A.K. (2009). *Advertising and the mind of the consumer: What works, what doesn't, and why*. Sydney: Allen & Unwin.

Chapter 5

Body image, eating disorders and the media

👁 Introduction

A third – and highly controversial – area of media influence concerns the alleged effects of certain body types on the eating and health behaviours of media consumers. Specifically, the constant viewing of thin models and celebrities, and muscular male figures, causes females and males respectively to become dissatisfied with their own bodies, and to indulge in unhealthy behaviours to try and emulate the thin, or muscular, 'ideal'. In this chapter I discuss the research (mostly experimental and correlational) that has tested the impact of mere exposure, or repeated use of 'thin' media and men's magazines, on body dissatisfaction, eating behaviour and drive for muscularity. I also consider the fascinating pro-ana phenomenon, a community of websites that seems to promote, and arguably glamorize, the condition of anorexia.

👁 Body shape and the media

Hairdressers, beauticians and cosmetic surgeons are all familiar with the scene: a client walks in with a glossy magazine, points to a glamorous model or celebrity and says: 'Make me look like him/her!' For years we have used beautiful people in the media as models for our own personal style, copying a particular hairstyle, wearing an item of clothing popularized by a star, or even, more recently, requesting a new nose to match the one sported by a Hollywood actress. To what lengths are we likely to go in order to emulate our favourite celebrity? Some people spend thousands of pounds each year to keep up with the designer lifestyle of the rich and famous, while others will undergo excruciating pain to change their appearance to resemble an idol. Generally, we see these things as rather eccentric, a bit sad even, but ultimately the decision of the individual as to how they spend their time and money.

However, what psychologists have become more concerned about in recent decades is a more general influence of media on the body image, and subsequent dietary behaviour, of adolescent girls and increasingly boys. The proliferation of certain, privileged, body shapes – painfully thin females and painfully muscular males – is thought to be a major factor in extreme dieting in girls and excessive, sometimes dangerous, levels of exercise and steroid use in boys. In some cases, it is alleged, the fascination with thin celebrities can trigger the onset of an eating disorder, as individuals struggle with keeping their weight down to size 10 levels and embark on a straightforward starvation route to attain the 'perfect', skeletal image. In media terms, this is most commonly associated with the reading of glossy celebrity magazines and watching drama series filled with model-standard actors and actresses. An additional media influence, in recent years, is the emergence of 'pro-ana' websites, where the obsession with attaining a pure, anorexic figure is fuelled by advice and discussions about the best ways to manage an eating disorder and to conceal it from friends and family.

⊙ Body shape and dissatisfaction over the decades

Towards a 'thin ideal' for women

Is our current preoccupation with thinness (in women) and muscle size (in men) really peculiar to our historical period? It would be surprising, since recent figures suggest that up to a half of all women in the US and UK are overweight by clinical standards (Dittmar et al., 2009). Nevertheless, content analyses of magazines, beauty contests and even children's toys tell a different story. Two studies of the winners of Miss America beauty pageants and the centrefold models of *Playboy* magazine between 1959 and 1988 found that, counter to a general trend towards larger body shapes in the American female population in the same period, these models became increasingly thinner (Garner et al., 1980; Wiseman et al., 1990).

Changing standards of female beauty out of step with the real world have even been found to influence the shape of children's toys. By the mid-1990s, Barbie dolls had attained a body shape that was physiologically impossible. In one study, researchers estimated that the average woman would have to gain 24 inches in height, five inches in the chest, and lose six inches around the waist to match her (Brownell and Napolitano, 1995). However, her makers Mattel later introduced a new model with a wider waist to counteract claims that the doll was encouraging unhealthy eating.

It has been argued that these conflicting trends (increasingly thin models, increasing weight in the general population) have contributed to an increase in the amount of **body dissatisfaction** experienced by media users (Halliwell and Dittmar, 2006). It leads to discrepancies between the actual self and ideal self, whereby people see themselves as so far from having the 'perfect figure' that they either use unhealthy methods to attain it, or simply sink into low self-esteem and despondency (Cafri et al., 2005). Indeed, incidence of body dissatisfaction has become so high that as many as 50% of girls and undergraduate women in the US report being dissatisfied with their bodies (Bearman et al., 2006). It also appears that these attitudes are now developing early in childhood, with girls as young as six desiring a thinner ideal figure (Dohnt and Tiggemann, 2006).

It is in the mid-to-late adolescent period, however, that body image disturbances are likely to have the most damaging effects, since during that period, it is customary for girls to experience increases in the distribution of fat around the hips and thighs, thereby taking their bodies even further away from the **thin ideal** promoted by the media (Dittmar et al., 2000). Ironically, this is the period during which teenage girls are most likely to adopt extreme diets, pushing them towards dangerous levels of malnutrition. Not surprisingly, the media have attracted much of the blame for this, particularly magazines aimed at teenage girls, whose encouragement of low-fat diets and heavy advertising for dietary products has been seen as a major contributor to body dissatisfaction and unhealthy eating behaviours (Grabe et al., 2008).

Changes in the ideal male figure

Meanwhile, in the male population, there are similar historical trends relating to body shape and cultural ideals as for women. The current cultural ideal for men is the 'mesomorphic' body shape – the classic 'inverted V', with broad, muscular shoulders and chest tapering down to a thin waist and hips (Pope et al., 2000). Content analysis of media has found an increasing predominance of the mesomorphic shape over recent decades. Along with the trend towards thinness found in female models, so images of men in publications from *Playgirl* to *GQ* and even *Rolling Stone* have increased in muscularity (Law and Labre, 2002; Leit et al., 2002).

Consistent with changing trends for girls' toys, boys' toys have also reflected changing media ideals, with action figures such as GI Joe and his UK cousin Action Man increasing in musculature over successive decades, to such an extreme degree that even body builders would require steroids to emulate them (Pope et al., 1999).

As with media aimed at young women, charges have been levelled at men's magazines in particular for encouraging a more body-conscious culture, particularly magazines supposedly oriented towards men's health, which routinely offer 'miracle' and 'crash' diets and body-building programmes as a way of attaining the muscular ideal and, implicitly if not explicitly, attracting women. These magazines have been joined in recent years by the emergence of 'lad magazines' (Taylor, 2006), which first appeared in the UK in the 1990s (*Loaded, FHM, Esquire*), and later in the US (*Maxim* and *Stuff*). Lad mags appealed to the young male who has grown up in a world where sexist attitudes have been curtailed to some extent by antidiscrimination laws but where they have been able to prevail (partly) disguised as ironic, or 'postmodern' humour. Stevenson et al. (2000, p. 371) claimed that they had 'changed the face of men's magazine publishing' when they first appeared. Increasingly, titles like *Zoo* and *Nuts* have begun to resemble old-fashioned pornographic magazines, despite editorial claims that they remain essentially ironic (Mooney, 2008). Nevertheless, lad mags (and related TV channels such as Spike TV in the US) have reinforced some of the sociocultural norms observed in mainstream popular culture in relation to idealized body shape for men and women, and the magazines in particular devote much advertising space, despite apparent editorial counterclaims, to grooming and appearance products (Stevenson et al., 2000). In other words, men have become objectified in much the same way as women, while being encouraged to develop implausible physiques.

While some might applaud the apparent levelling effect, whereby men have become subject to the same social pressures as women, these changes have nevertheless been accompanied by growing body dissatisfaction among males, with adolescent boys and young men suffering from low self-esteem around appearance and adopting excessive exercise regimes to try and build muscle (Cafri et al., 2002). More disturbingly, changing media trends have coincided with an increase in the use of anabolic–androgenic steroids in men (Pope et al., 2000). Even in younger males, rates of steroid use have been found to mirror the incidence of eating disorders in females (Schooler and Ward, 2006).

Are these changing cultural ideals the direct result of media, or do media and body dissatisfaction both simply reflect other changes that have taken place in Western society over recent years? Is there anything we can do to increase people's body satisfaction irrespective of media content? These are questions I will attempt to tackle in the remainder of the chapter.

The effects of 'thin media' on body shape

As with media violence and advertising, much of the research linking body image and media consists of experiments that seek to isolate the effect of media on body dissatisfaction. And as with the media effects tradition in general, there has been criticism that the research focuses only on one-off exposure to thin stimuli, while most authors support a cultivation explanation of long-term preoccupation with thin celebrities and models resulting in unhealthy eating practices (Gerbner et al., 2002).

Nevertheless, the short-term laboratory effects of mere exposure have been quite impressive. In most instances, participants have been presented with a sequence of images featuring thin models taken either from fashion magazines, television advertisements, or more general 'appearance-focused' media (Grabe et al., 2008). Typically, participants complete the same measure of body satisfaction before and after the images are viewed, so the researchers can measure the difference between the pre-exposure and post-exposure scores, a research design known as **A-B-A**, or **pre-test/post-test intervention** study.

Many different measures of body dissatisfaction have been designed over the past two decades. One popular instrument is the Visual Analogue Scale (Heinberg and Thompson, 1995), where respondents are presented with a series of body shape outlines and asked to indicate which outline best describes their current self and their ideal self. In experiments using this measure, greater discrepancies between current and ideal self have been found after the viewing phase than before (Birkeland et al., 2005; Tiggemann and Slater, 2003). Outlines exist for both male and female bodies, making them a useful device for research with both sexes.

Many other measures of body dissatisfaction have been used in the literature, which makes comparison between studies somewhat difficult, but in general the A–B–A design has been used for most of the experimental research, and a meta-analysis of 80 such experiments by Grabe et al. (2008) found that there was a small-to-moderate (although statistically significant) effect size of image exposure. Other studies in the meta-analysis used measures of eating attitudes, 'drive for thinness' and scales to measure 'internalization' of media or cultural ideals, all of which have shown some degree of change following exposure to thin images.

One problem with this literature is that, while demonstrating the effectiveness of mere exposure as a stimulus, there is little attempt by researchers to explain what is actually going on in participants' minds during actual exposure, and how this mechanism results in increased body dissatisfaction. Do participants *routinely* continually compare themselves to celebrities (regardless of the presence of a researcher with a questionnaire), and if so, does this eventually result in long-term self-esteem problems? Or, is it simply an 'artefact' of the experimental setting, whereby participants are forced to confront issues that they might otherwise happily shrug off?

In addition to experiments measuring the short-term effects of image exposure, Grabe et al. (2008) also included 60 correlational studies where, rather than manipulating participants' exposure to thin models, they assessed their actual media use. Here, there was no attempt to collect 'before' and 'after' discrepancies in response to some artificially presented stimulus, but solely 'after' data, assuming that body dissatisfaction in the long term is a response to media consumption. The researchers found that the correlational research produced similar results, in that high consumption of thin media was significantly associated with high levels of body dissatisfaction, internalization of media values and disturbed eating.

The **internalization** measure (Heinberg et al., 1995) is particularly interesting, because it directly assesses the extent to which the values promoted by media are integrated into the individual's belief structure about the world. For example, respondents are asked to what extent they agree with the statement that 'looks are essential if you want to get on in today's society'. High agreement with this statement indicates internalization of this particular value, which is seemingly consistent with the thin ideal. Of course, since these are correlational measures, one can always argue that people are attracted to media that reflect their pre-existing values or beliefs about the world, so those who have always believed that looks are important will orient towards appearance-focused media.

One criticism of studies of media effects on body image is that they have tended to overgeneralize media use, particularly in the earlier (pre-2000) studies. Stice et al. (1994), for example, found that the use of media featuring a high proportion of ideal body images was related to eating disturbance. However, this included a diverse range of sources that incorporated both game shows and arts magazines. Increasingly, researchers have paid more attention to the nature of the media content their participants consume.

Individual differences

One of the most common criticisms of mere exposure theories of media effects, as we saw with violence and advertising, is that exposure may have different effects on different people. However, relatively few studies have explored individual differences in responses to thin media. An exception is the study by Tiggemann et al. (2009), who instructed their experimental participants (all female undergraduates) to think in different ways about the images they were presented with. The participants were asked to examine magazine advertisements featuring a picture of a thin female model. A third of the participants (social comparison condition) were instructed to compare themselves to the women in the images, another third (fantasy condition) were asked to fantasize about what it would be like to be the women, while the remaining third (control condition) were given no instructions. Participants in the social comparison condition reported significantly higher body dissatisfaction than those in the other two groups, which did not differ to a significant degree. Those in the fantasy condition reported more positive mood after viewing the images than those in the other conditions.

These findings suggest that cognitive processing of thin media images is more complicated than mere exposure suggests. It also indicates that personality factors are a potential explanatory factor for thin media effects, in that people may be predisposed to view attractive models in different ways. Highly anxious individuals may interpret the pictures as a threat to their self-esteem, while more stable individuals may be more inclined to use them as tools for daydreaming and imagination.

This study may also answer the question that has always intrigued researchers in this field: why, if viewing thin media increases body dissatisfaction, are people still drawn to thin images, and keep buying magazines that promote them? Might it be the case that *most* magazine readers are fantasists, for whom reading fashion and celebrity magazines acts as a harmless and pleasurable diversion from everyday life, while only a minority find the images disturbing for their self-esteem? All these are issues that have barely been addressed by the existing research.

Eating disturbance and media

Some controversy surrounds the use of eating attitude scales in this kind of research. The link between eating disorders and the media is made frequently, often casually, without any really firm evidence, and so it is useful to have some data that might support the argument. However, many of these scales are designed for clinical use, to indicate a cut-off point at which an individual is said to meet the criteria for an eating disorder. Most people score very low on the scale, making it a difficult measure to include in analyses like the one by Grabe et al. (2008).

Despite this, Stice et al. (1994) used the Eating Attitudes Test in their study, a measure used primarily by clinicians to identify individuals who are potentially at risk for eating disorders, and found significant associations between these scores, media consumption and body image dissatisfaction. Likewise, in an experimental study, Hawkins et al. (2004) managed to induce significant increases in anorexia and bulimia symptomatology simply through experimental viewing of images.

Men, boys and the muscular ideal

The research on thin media and female body dissatisfaction has been mirrored in recent years by an increase in similar studies of males in response to the muscular body ideal promoted in the media. The methods used, and the pattern of findings, reflect those used in research on females and thin media: body dissatisfaction typically increases in experiments where male participants (boys and adult men) are exposed to muscular and athletic male images (Hargreaves and Tiggemann, 2009), and correlational studies have also pointed to a significant relationship between various types of media use and body dissatisfaction (Schooler and Ward, 2006).

Male body image research, perhaps because of its somewhat later development, has focused more closely than that on female body image on actual media use and precise messages or images encountered in those media. For example, consumption of men's magazines, and particularly lad magazines, has been associated with higher 'body surveillance', and the internalization of sociocultural attitudes towards appearance (Aubrey, 2006). Other research has claimed that exposure to ideal male images in the media can result in a condition called **muscle dysmorphia**, where the individual believes that his muscles are less developed than they really are (Leit et al., 2002).

Most research on male body dissatisfaction has been measured in terms of **Drive For Muscularity** (DFM; McCreary and Sasse, 2000), a psychometric scale that assesses the preoccupation with building muscle, where respondents are asked to what extent they agree with statements such as 'I wish that I were more muscular'. Various studies have related high DFM with media use, from the reading of fitness magazines (Morry and Staska, 2001) and broadly male-oriented magazines (Hatoum and Belle, 2004), to watching a variety of television genres (Tiggemann, 2005). These studies have also found that DFM is enhanced by the internalization of sociocultural attitudes towards appearance, in other words, the desire to enhance musculature arises from the internalization of media ideals.

A study by Giles and Close (2008) examined these processes in relation to lad mag use and dating in heterosexual men. While it found that the relationship between lad mag use and DFM was significant for the sample as a whole, it was significantly higher among single, non-dating men than among those participants who were in steady relationships. The study also found that, if you divide the DFM into its subscales 'attitudes' and 'behaviour', the effect for 'attitudes' practically disappears.

It was argued that, while dating men might still internalize media values and increase body dissatisfaction through reading lad magazines, they were less likely to deal with it by heading to the gym to pump iron. Single men, on the other hand, showed a stronger link between lad mag use and DFM behaviour, which includes items about visiting gyms and even steroid use. They may, however, simply have more time in which to visit the gym.

Why the thin ideal? In whose interests?

A question rarely asked in all this research is why there should be a trend towards thinner female images in the media, especially given the female population's gradual trend towards weight gain. Who wants to look at super-skinny women? Certainly not (heterosexual) men, who are more attracted to less thin women than is often imagined (Bergstrom et al., 2004).

One argument is that clothes designers have always believed that clothes hang better on women with flat chests and imperceptible hips, and show off the garments to better effect on catwalks and in photo shoots. This has created an 'iconography' that prioritizes superslim models, that is, we associate fashion styles with that type of body shape to the point where the garments simply look 'wrong' on anyone slightly overweight.

Improving satisfaction?

If viewing a series of images of thin models makes us dissatisfied with our own bodies, is it also possible to achieve the reverse effect by using images of large, heavy models? Dittmar and Howard (2004) did actually test this hypothesis, although their images were described as 'average', that is, slightly overweight, and found, indeed, that there was less body-focused anxiety after viewing the images than before, suggesting that the greater use of average-sized models in the media might lessen the degree of dissatisfaction in the overall population. Interestingly, the authors also found that, when the average-sized models were perceived as attractive, they were just as effective at advertising products (specifically, perfume) as thin models. This finding once again begs the question: why has a preference evolved for thin models and celebrities in the media? Would we really be less interested in, and attracted to, media if it were populated by average-looking people?

Other studies that have focused on reversing body dissatisfaction have, like those bent on countering the effects of media violence and advertising, sought to educate young people in particular about the effects of media in order to increase their levels of media literacy and thereby make them less vulnerable. Grabe et al. (2008) do report the findings of a number of these studies, but there are mixed results, with some authors reporting lower dissatisfaction following 'media literacy discussion' and others finding no significant changes. The ability of a short discussion to change lifelong attitudes is limited; only a longer term educational programme is likely to have any effect in this area.

Why don't media consumers become obese instead?

If media (in general) promote a thin ideal, and mere exposure to thin images brings about dissatisfaction with one's body, why is it that more and more people in Western society become obese? Either the media effects are trifling in comparison with the factors that promote obesity, or they are highly selective (see the earlier section on Individual differences).

Another explanation is that obesity may, ironically, arise out of failed attempts to diet. A five-year **longitudinal study** (where the same group of participants was followed up five years later) by Neumark-Sztainer et al. (2006) found that dieting at time one was a significant predictor of obesity at time two. In fact, the younger dieters were twice as much at risk from becoming obese five years later as the other children, and those who practised unhealthy weight restriction (skipping meals and so on) were three times as much at risk. If media use plays a role in encouraging these dieting behaviours, it could be argued that it is an indirect factor behind obesity. But much more research is needed to explore this possibility.

Eating disorders online

A related area of research has explored the growing number of websites dedicated to eating disorders, particularly a notorious community of what has become known as **pro-ana websites**. These are not sites set up by health professionals or 'recovered' anorexic individuals, but by people who themselves have an eating disorder and generally have no wish to 'recover' or undergo anything more than a basic stabilizing treatment.

Pro-ana websites have attracted enormous controversy throughout the world since they started appearing in the early 2000s, from scare stories in the press to considerable outcry on behalf of health professionals and parenting organizations, and eventually the intervention of governments. The general nature of the complaints is that the websites – in an echo of the claims made about media violence – are a threatening and potentially dangerous influence to 'impressionable' and vulnerable young people.

The specific charge is that pro-ana sites promote, glamorize or glorify the condition of anorexia, and dissuade their members from seeking medical or psychological treatment.

What is all the fuss about exactly? At first glance, pro-ana sites do seem rather alarming. A typical site home page carries plenty of disclaimers (very often the term 'pro-ana' is taboo, not surprisingly, since if it can be picked out by a search engine, it could spell disaster), but usually has some statement demonstrating the owner's attitude towards eating disorders. Links to other material on the site may include a discussion forum (or several), a chat room, member profiles, blogs, diaries, and usually plenty of artwork, poetry and lyrics relating to eating disorders.

The discussion forum, or message board, is probably the feature of pro-ana sites that has attracted the most attention over the years, since it is here that community members post messages, share tips for weight loss that may carry enormous health risks, and exchange advice for concealing their eating disorders from family and friends, teachers and medical professionals. This aspect has also been most heavily researched by psychologists (e.g. Chesley et al., 2003; Dias, 2003).

The pro-ana community and social identity

One of the most striking features of pro-ana discussion forums from a social psychological perspective is the way that group identities are formed and maintained by the community members. In my own research on this topic, I examined the identities produced during online discussions and came up with the list in Table 5.1 (see Giles, 2006).

The ingroups listed in Table 5.1 are clearly hierarchical in nature, with 'ana' occupying the pole position. Typically 'ana' is constructed as the ultimate goal of anyone using the websites, who has attained a condition of complete purity through the loss of 'disgusting' body fat. While anyone with an ED is welcome in the community, there is clear sympathy with 'mias', whose condition (bulimia) is widely regarded as 'failed anorexia' (because the individual eventually succumbs to eating binges). Some pro-ana sites have separate discussion forums for 'mias' that act almost as a kind of 'second XI' to the 'anas' forum. EDNOS, the diagnostic label used when individuals fail to meet all the criteria for either anorexia or bulimia, is regarded as yet further failure, although clinically it is easily the most common diagnosis (Button et al., 2005).

UNIVERSITY OF WINCHESTER
LIBRARY

Ingroups		Outgroups	
EDs	Anyone with an eating disorder	Normals	Anyone without an eating disorder
Ana/anas	Anorexia/individuals with anorexia	Haters	People who post hostile messages on pro-ana discussion forums
Mia/mias	Bulimia/individuals with bulimia	Wannabes	People who aspire to an 'ana' identity but fail to meet the criteria
EDNOS	Individuals diagnosed as having an eating disorder not otherwise specified	Dieters	People with weight loss aims that fail miserably to meet the criteria for an ED
Cutters, burners	EDs who also self-harm	Parents, friends, teachers	Significant figures, often sympathetic, but who typically fail to understand EDs
		Psychologists, GPs, doctors	Professionals bent on recovery or treatment of EDs

Table 5.1 Ingroups and outgroups in the pro-ana website community

The outgroups are revealing because they create further ranks to the hierarchy, in that 'wannabes' and 'dieters' are groups of so little consequence they are unwelcome in the pro-ana community, either because they don't shape up (literally), or because they are seen as having other objectives (dieting for relatively minor weight loss). Significant others, such as boyfriends, parents and siblings, are discussed as outgroups whether they are sympathetic or not; likewise health professionals. All these groups have a vested interest in the individual receiving 'treatment' and 'recovering', while the goal of pro-ana sites is to maintain and manage an eating disorder while functioning as a relatively normal member of society.

Some authors have talked about the pro-ana phenomenon as if it were a philosophical standpoint, or even an ideological position (Fox et al., 2005). However, one of its most noticeable characteristics is that there is no shared belief system among pro-ana sites about the nature, cause or origins of anorexia, and the result is a rather contradictory set of opinions on eating disorders. Despite this, the community defends itself aggressively, not only from the obviously hostile interlopers ('haters') who post inflammatory messages on the forums if they can, but on 'wannabes' who are often screened out through harsh initiation routines.

One of my students explored this issue by posing as an ana and gaining entry to a number of different chat rooms on pro-ana sites (Brotsky and Giles, 2007). She posted an identical profile on each of the sites and then entered into discussion with other members using the same opening messages and maintaining, as far as possible, a consistent persona. In several of the sites, she was greeted warmly by the existing members, invited to disclose her ana credentials, and treated as a genuine 'newbie' (slang for new community member). In the other sites, however, she was put through a fierce series of challenges by community members who simply did not believe her credentials or thought that she was naive in her use of the term 'ana'. She found the vitriol hurled at her persona in these chat rooms quite upsetting at times (having had a genuine eating disorder history), and it demonstrated both the high level of defensiveness that the community has sometimes adopted to counter attempts to rein in its activities and the degree of 'cliquishness' in some of the closed (password-protected) sections of the community.[1]

Liberating or suicidal? Standpoints on the pro-ana phenomenon

As more and more researchers have investigated the pro-ana community, so a range of different viewpoints have emerged. The dominant standpoint from the health and medical fields is that pro-ana websites are dangerous, potentially lethal, and have got to go. The Royal College of Psychiatrists (2009) called on the UK government to raise the status of such sites to 'harmful', alongside pornographic and other undesirable Web content.

Inevitably, it is these groups who have been most seriously listened to by those in authority around the world, and there have been one or two attempts by governments to legislate against pro-ana sites. French MP Valerie Boyer tabled a bill to fine or even imprison the creators of sites that 'provoke' or 'encourage' unhealthy eating practices. The bill was initially approved in April 2008 at the Assembleé nationale (the French parliament's 'lower house') but not by the Senate the following year, who has the final say on what becomes law. Similar proposals have also been stifled in Spain and the Netherlands.

Meanwhile, social scientists from fields such as women's studies and sociology have taken a more liberal perspective, and in some cases a feminist argument has been made almost in favour of the sites, or, at the very least, defending their existence from what they see as patriarchal surveillance by the male-dominated medical profession (Harris, 2001). Psychologists, on the whole, tend to be curious rather than judgemental, seeing the sites as fascinating natural settings for social interaction.

One final point. Care must be taken not to regard pro-ana websites as an easy way of obtaining data that tell us about the 'true' or hidden nature of anorexia, or any other eating disorder. It is tempting though, as at no time in history has so much self-disclosure by the members of marginalized groups been put on record as with the advent of the Internet. And it has highlighted a few interesting issues that eating disorder experts have long been familiar with, such as the desire to conceal the condition from significant others, and the aspirations to purity that motivate the desire to become weightless, even to disappear.

However, what an ana posts on a message forum can in no way be analysed as the 'innermost feelings' of an individual with an eating disorder. As media psychologists, we should be sensitive to the mediated nature of any data we sample. Pro-ana is not an 'underground movement' that suddenly became famous because of technological advances. It never existed until a discernible cluster of websites became recognized by users and observers. It is phenomenon peculiar to the Internet, and it should only be studied with reference to the medium.

Note

1 It must be added that this last study might well have struggled to gain ethical approval in many university psychology departments, where Internet-based research is still subject to a number of restrictions (British Psychological Society, 2007). Following British Psychological Society and American Psychological Association ethical guidelines, deception is only permissible if the research question is deemed significantly important, and where the study will fail without it. We believed that both conditions applied in the context of this particular study and, fortunately, the British Psychological Society agreed.

Further reading

Dittmar, H. (2008). *Consumer society, identity, and well-being: The search for the 'good life' and the 'body perfect'*. New York: Psychology Press.

Section summary

In these next three chapters, I am going to introduce the concept of the media audience. So far, most of the research covered in the book has dealt with the individual as a rather lonely figure, a victim even, of random stimuli to which she is exposed – violence, advertising, images of thin celebrities. These stimuli trigger some kind of private event, be it a change in bodily arousal, cognitions, or neural activity, and the lonely individual then 'responds' in a way that leads the researcher to claim that he has isolated an effect that is specific to that particular medium, or, more typically, to that particular type of media content.

But as we know, media are often social events. We watch television in groups, couples, even whole crowds at a bar; we play video games with one another; we discuss what we've found on the Internet with our friends. And we are not alone in our media use either; every time there is an ad on TV, it will be watched by thousands or millions of others. For this reason, media researchers tend to talk more about 'the audience', or even 'audiences'.

However, we're psychologists, and while the audience is an important social psychological construct, we need to consider individuals as part of audiences. But not necessarily just as passive recipients of stimuli. Individual audience members have some degree of choice over what media they consume, even if they are subject to unconscious processing of adverts and other media imagery. We have preferences for certain media and certain content; from an early age, we are highly selective about what we watch, listen to and log on to. For these reasons, the term 'media user' may be the best description of our individual audience member.

This imaginary individual is very different from the passive figure envisaged by the media effects researchers. She chooses what programmes to watch, what websites to visit, what advertising to pay attention to. She gets involved in the media herself, appearing on TV shows, or contributes even just by voting people off the latest *X Factor* competition. She may be a self-confessed fan, organizing her life around her favourite media figure. She may even have broken through the 'fourth wall' and met that media figure in real life. In this section of the book we will move through all these levels of media use, from the 'feeling of knowing' that we get simply through encountering figures in the media, through to the participation of audience members in media productions and the activities of fans.

Chapter 6

Parasocial interaction

👁 Introduction

The concept of **parasocial interaction** is introduced in the first part of this chapter: the psychological processes through which media users treat media figures as if they were real people, even if they are fictional creations. The concept of **parasocial relationships** is then discussed, which are longer lasting psychological constructs through which we come to feel as if we 'know' media figures as members of a virtual social network. The remainder of the chapter deals with issues pertinent to parasocial phenomena – relationships with different types of media figure, the similarities between parasocial and social behaviour, and the conceptual limits of parasocial interaction.

👁 Encounters with familiar strangers

If you've ever had the fortune (or misfortune, even) of bumping into a celebrity in real life, the chances are that it was a very strange experience. Typical celebrity sightings start off with a vague sense of recognition: you're sure you know that person, but for a moment you can't quite place them. Is it someone from school? A neighbour? Someone who you knew once and then lost touch with? Then suddenly the penny drops, and it all becomes clear. It's somebody you've never actually met before, but you seem to know them so well – their face seems as familiar as that of a family member. But they have no idea who you are. No idea at all.

For years, psychologists lacked a concept for this 'feeling of knowing' that evolves through repeated encounters with celebrities and other media figures. Since the 1950s, communication scientists have talked of the 'parasocial interaction' that takes place whenever a media user encounters a figure – real or otherwise, human or non-human – in the media. The term was coined by a psychiatrist called Wohl and a sociologist called Donald Horton in a paper in the journal *Psychiatry* (Horton and Wohl, 1956). They had become fascinated with the responses of radio listeners to certain fictional figures, most notably a young woman who was known as 'The Lonesome Gal'. This was a show broadcast on US radio late at night, in which a young woman with a seductive voice addressed the listener as her lover, inviting 'him' to lie down on the couch with her and have 'his' hair stroked.

Evidently large numbers of lonesome boys were captivated by this broadcast, because thousands of letters subsequently arrived at the radio studio proposing marriage. In those naive times, did the men honestly believe that the Lonesome Gal was for real? Horton and Wohl argued that the manner of her delivery had led impressionable listeners to form imaginary relationships with her, which developed with each broadcast until she became such a regular presence in their lives that they became obsessed with meeting her.

Of course, most modern-day media users are much more sophisticated. And yet, we can all relate to similar experiences when we have become preoccupied with someone whose photograph we have gazed upon, whose voice has captivated us, and who we may have fantasized about one day meeting – a film star, pop star or sports idol. Perhaps it's someone we just like a lot, because we share their views or admire their talents, or we are simply charmed by their personality. Perhaps it's someone we absolutely hate. Whatever the case, it seems as though the medium itself is no barrier to the basic human instinct to form relationships: in this case 'parasocial' relationships.

Little interest was shown in parasocial activity of any kind until the late 1970s, when US communication expert Mark Levy (1979) conducted a focus group study on TV viewers' relations with local newsreaders, or newscasters (in America, a 'local' newscaster may be broadcasting to an area the size of the British Isles). He found that, for many of these viewers, newscasters were perceived almost like friends, they kept viewers company, they missed them when they were on vacation, and they even addressed verbal comments out loud to them.

Levy and later researchers subsequently adapted these viewers' remarks as items for a psychometric scale, known as the Parasocial

Interaction Scale (Rubin et al., 1985). This instrument has been used in communication research ever since, to measure the strength of parasocial interaction with favourite celebrities, radio presenters, comedians, and even soap characters and cartoon characters. Researchers have found that many of the psychological features of parasocial relationships are exactly the same as those of social relationships, such as 'uncertainty reduction', or trustworthiness (Perse and Rubin, 1989), and that parasocial attachment styles reflect our general attachment styles (Greenwood et al., 2008).

◉ Parasocial interaction and parasocial relationships

At this point, it is worth making a distinction between parasocial interaction (PSI) and parasocial relationships (PSRs). Parasocial interaction refers to the activity that takes place during the act of media use itself. Hartmann et al. (2008) have identified three psychological processes that constitute PSI: cognitive, affective and behavioural:

- *Cognitive* processes are thoughts we have regarding the media figure – Do I like them? Do I agree with their views?
- *Affective* processes are emotional responses to the figure – laughing, or becoming angry.
- *Behavioural* processes are actual behaviours that we perform when, for example, we watch a TV show, such as directing verbal comments at the media figure, or making gestures.

PSI processes are clearly related to PSRs, but once a relationship is established, it develops independently of episodes of PSI. After the TV is turned off, we don't stop thinking about media figures. We talk to our friends about them; this interaction itself has a powerful effect on our PSRs. If, for example, our friends disagree with our opinion about a new character in a soap or reality show, we might eventually modify or change entirely our original opinion to fit in. And think of the effect that bad news might have on a PSR. When former UK glam rocker Gary Glitter was arrested in the late 1990s for downloading child pornography, he lost thousands of fans in one fell swoop. Their PSRs changed from those of admiration to those of disgust.

Figure 6.1 contains a hypothesized sequence of events that take place as an initial parasocial encounter gradually develops into a PSR. It consists of a network of ellipses (stretched circles), which refer to episodes of PSI, and boxes containing elements of a PSR.

The large ellipse at the top refers to a given viewing episode, say, an episode of a soap, during which we make use of our knowledge about the figure (he's called Tom and he's married to Joanne, works in a bank and so on) and our judgements about the figure (he's charming and good looking, but he's having an affair with his secretary, so he's essentially untrustworthy). The ellipse below ('Other encounters') refers to occasions when we come across Tom once the TV set is turned off. Maybe we read about the character and look at pictures of him on the soap's website, or read about upcoming episodes in the newspaper or in TV listings magazines.

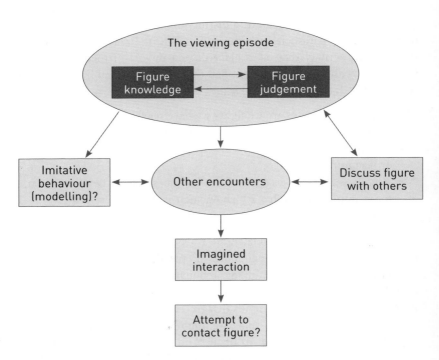

Figure 6.1 Stages in the development of a parasocial relationship
Source: Adapted from Giles, 2002a

The boxes in the diagram relate to possible outcomes of the PSI from a PSR perspective. The left-hand box 'Imitative behaviour' allows for the behavioural expression of influence from the figure. If you identify with Tom – perhaps you are a young man in a similar situation – you might use Tom's behaviour to guide your own. Perhaps you have also considered having an affair at work, but by giving you Joanne's perspective as well, the soap makes you reflect on the impact that an affair might have on your marriage. Or, alternatively, you might think: if Tom can get away with it, so could I.

The right-hand box 'Discuss figure with others' allows us to be influenced by our fellow media users. What do your friends think of Tom's behaviour? As discussed in Chapter 2, much media psychological research treats the media user as a solitary individual, abstracted from all social contexts. But we often watch TV, and use other media, with friends and family. Their comments will have a profound impact on the way we perceive the figures we encounter.

Finally, there are two further options for the PSR. We can daydream about meeting Tom, particularly if we find him attractive. We might be so strongly attracted to him that we feel compelled to seek out the actor that plays him, or even, in some cases, to try to contact the actor 'in character'. Because there is a real person involved (the actor), actual contact is a possibility. We may simply settle for the prospect of running into him in a nightclub somewhere, someday.

Similarities between social and parasocial relationships

Perse and Rubin (1989) argued that there are three ways in which parasocial relationships resemble real relationships:

1 They are entered into voluntarily – we choose our real and our parasocial friends.
2 Both types of relationship fulfil a need for companionship.
3 They arise from social attractiveness.

While the first of these claims is undeniable (except that we might feel that often our real friends choose us), the second two points are debatable. The idea that parasocial relationships fulfil companionship needs is not really supported by much of the research. In the early days, it was imagined that TV viewers might form stronger parasocial relationships if they were lonely or isolated; however, Rubin et al. (1985) found low correlations between loneliness and strength of parasocial interaction with favourite newscasters. It seems, then, that we are quite able to handle multiple parasocial relationships regardless of our actual social networks.

Perse and Rubin's (1989) third point is also in doubt. Most of the research, using the Parasocial Interaction Scale, asks respondents to select a single 'favourite' figure, whether a celebrity, newsreader or fictional character. But what about less favourite figures, and indeed figures that are thoroughly disliked? Do we not also form relationships with these figures? The continued focus in parasocial research on 'favourite' media figures has restricted our knowledge about these relationships.

Disliked media figures

One study that looked at negative PSRs is that of Hartmann et al. (2008), who asked fans of Formula 1 motor racing a series of questions about their 'favourite' and 'most disliked' Formula 1 drivers in order to discover which drivers they had established positive and negative PSRs with. They found that the nature of the existing PSRs reflected the level of suspense that fans experienced when watching a race. Suspense was high when they were rooting for their favourite driver to win, but less so when hoping that their most disliked driver would lose.

Other studies have found similar outcomes for fictional characters. Raney's (2004) work on fiction in particular has found that much of the enjoyment we derive from reading novels lies in our expectations that our favourite characters (typically the hero or protagonist) will enjoy positive outcomes, and that disliked characters (villains) will meet a sorry end. 'Affiliations' develop during reading, rather like PSRs, and these are constantly shaped by each new piece of information, for example revelations about a character's background.

Little other research has been conducted on disliked media figures. However, a recent study (Giles, 2008) asked sixth formers and university students to nominate their favourite and least favourite celebrities and fictional characters. Not surprisingly, their PSRs with favourite figures were much stronger and more positive, and in many cases their least favourite figures were very strongly disliked. Interestingly, the most disliked celebrities tended to be young females, and they were disliked by female participants just as much as by male ones.

◉ Media figure type

So far in this chapter I have talked about PSI with real and fictional figures interchangeably. This is a common feature of parasocial research: very little attempt has ever been made to distinguish between our PSRs with real people, such as newsreaders, and PSRs with fictional, even non-human, figures. In a previous study (Giles, 2002a), I developed a three-level 'model' of parasocial relationships, in which I distinguished three types of **media figure**:

1 First-order figures (MF1) are human figures whose real existence is unambiguous, such as celebrities and other people in the news and entertainment media
2 Second-order figures (MF2) are fictional characters who nonetheless possess a visible human form, typically a character in a film or TV series
3 Third-order figures (MF3) are fictional figures who do not possess a visible human form, such as a cartoon character or a fantasy character.

My distinction between each of these three types is related to the potential relationship resulting from an encounter between a media user and a media figure. Even if I only encounter an MF1 through television use, it is possible, either through deliberate pursuit or by accident, for me to have a subsequent social encounter with that figure. A passionate fan of a television presenter could, in theory, end up having an intimate social relationship with that television presenter (this does sometimes happen).

With an MF3, such an eventual outcome is impossible, because the figure does not 'exist' as such. MF2s occupy the middle ground because, while it is impossible to have a social relationship with the character themselves, it is nonetheless possible to have a social relationship with the human form that the character inhabits, in other words, the actor who portrays the character. Indeed, when actors are encountered by media users 'in the flesh', they are sometimes responded to as if they are still in character (Tal-Or and Papirman, 2007). Soap stars often complain that they get abuse in public because of the way their character has behaved in the previous night's episode.

In a recent study, I compared these three types of media figure according to various characteristics of PSRs (Giles, 2008). I found that, on some dimensions, such as similarity, there was no difference between types: the participants perceived themselves as similar to their favourite celebrities as to their favourite fictional human and non-human characters. Only on some fairly obvious dimensions was there a difference: wanting to meet that figure, wishing to emulate that figure and so on.

It seems, therefore, that there are some common processes at work in the formulation of PSRs with media figures regardless of their actual reality status. This goes back to the parallels made between parasocial and actual social relationships. One argument that has been advanced for the similarity between social and parasocial relationships is that, as in so many cases, human psychology has not been able to keep pace with technological change. In other words, our brains have not evolved quickly enough for us to be permanently conscious of the mediated nature of parasocial relationships (Kanazawa, 2002). This is what Reeves and Nass (1996) have termed 'the media equation', citing numerous instances where, for example, computers are treated as if they were people (especially when they don't do what we want them to).

Sometimes, PSRs can seem simply bizarre. During the 1960s, the American actor Robert Young received over a quarter of a million letters during the five years he played the leading role in medical drama *Marcus Welby M.D.*, most of which were asking for medical advice. In the pre-Internet era, when we relied on a doctor's appointment for any healthcare information, this might have seemed like a reasonable gamble for a desperate viewer who had already formed a strong parasocial relationship with a fantasy doctor with a nice bedside manner. During the 1970s, the UK soap opera *Coronation Street* ran a storyline in which a popular character, Hilda Ogden, lost her raincoat. The following day several mysterious packages arrived at Granada studios. Inside each was a replacement garment sent in by a worried viewer.

Parasocial bereavement

One way in which we can observe PSRs in action is in people's reactions when celebrities die. Michael Jackson's death in 2009 triggered a variety of responses, from those who mourned a great musician to those who could only relate to a controversial figure who had been involved in several dubious incidents concerning his relations with children. Many arguments and debates raged in the media as to which was the 'real' Michael Jackson, although ultimately it all depended on how the later controversies had shaped the PSR that people had developed with him during his most successful years as an entertainer.

Similar confusion occurred around the death of Princess Diana in 1997. 'I would say that I am a fairly hard-nosed cynic, but tears came despite that', wrote one contributor to a BBC website dedicated to Diana tributes. Another wrote: 'As a happy, well adjusted woman, I was stunned by the emotions I felt ... I couldn't stop crying and I didn't know why.' In both cases, it appears that there is something essentially irrational – or at least something that seems irrational to us – about developing such strong attachments to people we have never met.

Eyal and Cohen (2006) coined the term 'parasocial breakup' to refer to the death or disappearance of a fictional character. They studied fans' responses to the final episode of the TV sitcom *Friends*, and found that the enforced termination of the parasocial relationship created a sense of regret and even loneliness. These responses are not as strong as those to celebrity deaths, suggesting that this is one area where we can clearly distinguish between PSRs with real people and PSRs with fictional characters.

Other types of media figure

The Giles (2002a) **typology** of media figures is, inevitably, oversimplified. There are several categories of figure that fail to match any of the types. MF1s – real people – assumes that PSRs exist only with figures that are actually alive. However, many people have very strong attachments to figures that are no longer alive, such as Elvis Presley, Marilyn Monroe and, possibly, Princess Diana.

In some ways, PSRs with dead figures are more like those with MF2s or even MF3s: since the relationship cannot possibly be reciprocated, it can only ever exist at a level of pure fantasy. There is no opportunity to meet Elvis, unless one is absolutely convinced that he is, somewhere, still living (for older figures even this remote possibility must be ruled out). In their study of Elvis impersonators, Fraser and Brown (2002) describe a number of people whose lives are intricately linked to the star, although in most cases their relationships date from a period when he was still alive.

One other way in which dead media figures differ from live ones is in terms of the trajectory of the relationship. We can follow the day-to-day events in a celebrity's life as they occur in real time, which means we can have a closer affinity with them. Of course, this doesn't mean to say that the PSRs with living figures are more intense, stronger, or more meaningful than those with fictional or dead figures. They just allow for different possibilities in the way the relationship is incorporated into our everyday existence.

The MF2 category (fictional human) is also problematic since it is limited to visual media. It relies on the assumption that a fictional character is portrayed by an actor, and so we can make contact with the character indirectly (by meeting the actor). But what about (human) characters in books? Here, we may have a strong affiliation – or dislike – with a character whose visual image is entirely constructed out of the author's verbal description and our own unique interpretation (Culpeper, 2001).

Where the book is televised or adapted as a film, our visual image undergoes a strong challenge. The actor cast in our character's part will inevitably be different to our preconceived 'vision' (Martin, 2005). A parallel situation occurs when we encounter fictional characters in the guise of several different actors. James Bond and Doctor Who have both been represented by numerous actors, and fans continually debate which actor is the 'true' Bond, or the best Doctor. We each have our own personal favourites, typically the first actor we saw in the part. For me, those are, respectively, Sean Connery and Jon Pertwee. Other Bonds, and Doctors, just don't really cut the mustard.

What's *not* parasocial interaction?

I will end this chapter with a brief discussion of alternative concepts that arguably cover the same ground as parasocial phenomena. The literature is divided on this topic, largely because the use of the Parasocial Interaction Scale over the past two decades has restricted the way in which researchers have conceptualized parasocial relationships.

The tendency to equate the concept with the measure – with its items about addressing remarks to the screen and so on – has led a lot of communication experts to assume that this is the only context to which the whole idea can be applied. This is a shame, because other similar concepts are simply inadequate for capturing all the relationships between media users and media figures.

There is also a tendency for authors to casually refer to parasocial phenomena in ways that misrepresent the basic concept. This is particularly common when referring to human–computer interaction, or computer-mediated communication. So, while considering other terms, like 'celebrity worship', that ought really to fall under the broad concept of PSRs, it is equally important to be clear what is *not* a PSR.

Several authors have tried to separate PSI from **identification**, a concept with a long history in psychology. We can trace it back to Freudian theory, where it was used particularly to refer to children's relationships with their parents, and to film theory, where authors employed psychoanalytic theory to account for viewers' involvement with the protagonists, or central characters, in films.

Feilitzen and Linne (1975) distinguished between 'similarity identification', where viewers identify with media figures because they share similar characteristics (age, gender, ethnicity and so on), and 'wishful identification', where we put ourselves in the shoes of the media figure – typically the hero in a film – and fantasize that we are that person. Or that we could, in time, become (like) that person. Of course, it is possible for both types of identification to exist simultaneously, where we idolize a successful figure who resembles us in some way. This is a powerful form of media influence, particularly for members of minority social groups – think of a young African-American boy idolizing Barack Obama.

How is identification different from PSI? Cohen (1999) devised a typology of relationship with media figure that distinguishes PSI from the two types of identification and 'affinity', arguing that we can *like* media figures without parasocially interacting with them. However, he didn't account for our relationship with figures who we *don't* like, or consider the development of PSRs over time. It is perhaps fair to argue that all four processes – PSI, similarity identification, wishful identification and affinity – are part of the PSR-building process.

Another concept that has emerged to account for audience relationships with media figures is **celebrity involvement** (Brown et al., 2003). This concept is limited in that it deals solely with living people (or MF1s, following our typology), but it is measured using a scale that is not unlike the Parasocial Interaction Scale (typical items include 'X is a hero to me', 'I feel I can easily relate to X'). Also the authors argue that celebrity involvement arises from a combination of PSI and identification. It is possible, therefore, to regard celebrity involvement as simply one form of a PSR.

Likewise, the concept of **celebrity worship** (to be discussed in more detail in Chapter 7) could be regarded as a specialized form of PSR, in that it involves celebrities, and that the PSR is fundamentally positive. Beware of statements such as 'parasocial interaction is a form of celebrity worship', which you will read in papers on the subject. It is nonsensical to think of the association this way round.

The arrival of Internet technology has created a whole new 'grey area' for parasocial theory. Email, online dating, social networking and other forms of computer-mediated communication allow us to interact with other people all over the world without ever meeting them 'in the flesh', or even knowing what they really look like (as I will discuss in Chapter 12, this is a particular problem with online dating). Some authors have used the parasocial concept – wrongly, in my opinion – to describe these interactions.

First, PSI was invented to account for one-way interaction with figures only encountered through traditional one-way media such as radio and television. The Internet requires a new concept to account for interactions between remote users who cannot actually see one another. The term 'virtual relationships' would seem to cover these perfectly well, no need for any 'parasocial' business at all.

Second, parasocial relationships, by their very definition, cannot be reciprocated (returned). Once reciprocation occurs, the relationship ceases to be parasocial, it becomes a straightforward social relationship. Even if a fan of the Queen ever got to meet her, they could be said to have a social relationship, albeit one that is heavily circumscribed (limited) by social conventions, hierarchies and so on. A British person sending an email to a person in Australia, and receiving a reply, has established a social, although virtual, relationship. There is nothing parasocial about it after that.

Just because the Internet enables us to establish relationships across the globe without meeting people, it doesn't mean that parasocial theory has been made redundant, or that we can't interact parasocially with media figures via the Internet. Even on social networking sites, interaction can still be one way: on my *MySpace* page, I am 'friends' with all my favourite bands. I am even friends with William Shakespeare.

When things become really interesting is with fan websites that enable users to – apparently – engage their idol in online chat, or, at least, some kind of online dialogue. Here, fans can be under the impression that they have established an actual social relationship with their heroes, even if the site is managed by another fan, who might be impersonating the star themselves. You can never be sure, just as you can never be sure when you write a fan letter to your hero that the signed letter you receive in return hasn't been just typed out by the fan club secretary.

A final category of media figure, and one that really should belong in the MF3 compartment, is the game character, or avatar. These have developed along quite complex lines in recent years, so we need to consider not only figures like Lara Croft, whose character is simply a scripted part of a game, but also user-generated figures in role-playing games like *Second Life*. Researchers have referred to these relationships as 'character attachments' (see Chapter 11).

Authors have, of course, been interacting parasocially with their characters since time immemorial, except nobody ever thought to research the phenomenon as such. What makes user-generated game characters different is that they have a powerful representative function. Authors' characters – except in explicitly autobiographical fiction – are supposed to develop a life of their own independent of their creator. Game avatars are intended to *represent* the player. These may well be a special kind of PSR, and, as they are becoming increasingly common among Internet game players, probably deserve a category to themselves. In any case, they will be considered at some length in the final section of the book New Media.

◉ Further reading

Giles, D.C. (2002). Parasocial interaction: A review of the literature and a model for future research. *Media Psychology*, 4, 279–302.

Chapter 7

Celebrity and fandom

Introduction

In this chapter, I consider three discrete, though related, literatures: the psychology of fame and celebrity, where the nature of celebrity itself is the centre of attention; the research on fans themselves and their various activities; and the concept of 'celebrity worship', which provides the link between ordinary fandom and pathological obsession, with celebrity stalking at its most extreme pole. Certainly, fame is highly desirable now as ever, with more and more opportunities for people to enter the world of celebrity, but, without any marked talent, it has also become more short-lived. Nevertheless, the problems of privacy and unwanted attention sour the fame experience. Fan activities resemble religious rituals in many ways; most of the time these are harmless and serve a primarily social function, but researchers are divided over how concerned we should be about more private, obsessional devotion, and how closely this is linked to stalking or abusive behaviour towards celebrities.

Fame and celebrity

Fame has been with us for centuries – millennia even. In the outstanding work on the topic, Braudy (1997) identifies Alexander the Great as the first famous individual, as he moved around the Mediterranean adding various countries to his empire, and word spread from one community to another about his deeds and his achievements. To be famous in the 4th century BC, you really did have to achieve. Communication media were thin on the ground (clay tablets and parchment at best) and it was only by word of mouth, over many years, that tales of Alexander's exploits would have reached the most privileged citizens. Most of them wouldn't have got to hear about him until he had been long dead.

Today, becoming famous is a rather different matter. A new name can be broadcast across the world's media in a matter of hours, and the ubiquity of media outlets among the world's population means that the vast majority of people worldwide will soon become familiar with it. Such immediate fame would require quite a noteworthy deed. Around Christmas 2009, for example, the world had just got to know the name Umar Farouk Abdulmutallab, a Nigerian man who tried to ignite a bomb on a plane to Detroit and raised airport security everywhere a further notch. Everyone recognized Abdulmutallab's name for a few days, but he is unlikely to outlast Alexander.

Perhaps the most striking difference between ancient fame and 21st-century fame is that the latter can be obtained without an individual having to do very much – they simply appear on television and entertain the audience by dint of their personality. The remarkable fame of 'reality TV' contestants and other instant celebrities has fascinated audiences and commentators for several years. Its most noticeable feature is the speed with which it disappears, leading many people to recall 1960s' pop artist Andy Warhol's famous maxim: 'In the future, everyone will be famous for 15 minutes.' Well, maybe not everyone, and maybe not for 15 minutes, but fame's time frame has certainly shrunk since Warhol's day.

One of the most common debates around fame and celebrity concerns the business of definition. Braudy (1997) and many others see **fame** itself as something that is earned through merit: it is legitimate to talk about a famous author, painter or musician, but not a famous criminal or reality TV contestant. Fame needs to be earned over many years of hard work and well-won plaudits. It could equally be argued that, while through most of history fame is associated with worthy deeds, cultural and technological change has forced us to redefine it because people can, and do, now become famous quickly, through achieving less. Building a reputation is no longer a difficult task requiring years of hard work and brilliance. Fame is the social process through which individuals become famous, regardless of what they've actually done (Giles, 2000).

Meanwhile, a similar level of debate surrounds the definition of **celebrity**. Gamson (1994) and others have argued that celebrity is a uniquely 20th- (or 21st-) century phenomenon that has arisen because of the expansion of the media. The number of media outlets that exist, the sheer size of the audience for each outlet, and the speed with which information can be communicated through them has created a culture that is completely unlike, and probably incomparable to, any other in history. The reasons for today's fame, and the nature of that fame, are fundamentally different and need a new concept to capture them.

Some researchers have attempted to distinguish between celebrities and other, worthier individuals, whether such individuals deserve such descriptions as 'heroes' (North et al., 2005), 'luminaries' (Cheung and Yue, 2004), or 'greats' (Simonton, 1994). North et al. (2005, p. 42) asked their participants to select heroes and celebrities on the basis that celebrities do 'not create any objects or ideas of permanence or lasting importance'. Needless to say, most of the 'heroes' chosen by participants in their study were historical figures; Princess Diana managed to slip through the celebrity net somehow, which is interesting, given that most researchers regard her as the ultimate celebrity (see, for instance, Cashmore, 2006).

In my own work, I have defined fame as a process and celebrity as a state (Giles, 2000). Neither fame nor celebrity has anything intrinsically to do with the nature of people's activities, why someone is famous, how long for, and in which media. Fame can be contained within an institution (some children are known by everyone at a school, others only by their classmates and class teacher), or it can be worldwide. Some people are literally famous overnight simply for fulfilling a role: the president of the United States, irrespective of their personality, will be world famous, as will most important political figures. Minor politicians could become famous, but they would need to do something exceptional.

However, it is important to bear in mind Gamson's argument that celebrity as a phenomenon could not really have happened without the contemporary media. Even at a local level, the media can create a form of celebrity – on the school website perhaps. Maybe the Internet, and its social networking capacities for making us all famous (albeit in a much smaller community) for 15 minutes, will eventually force us to redefine the terms.

👁 What is it like to be famous?

The experience of fame is roughly the reverse side of the coin described in Chapter 6: to be the individual who is the object of a parasocial relationship, who is known by millions of media users but has only ever met a tiny portion of their audience. Meanwhile, stars have parasocial relationships too, and one of the attractions of fame is that it opens up real relationships with other celebrities who have hitherto only been admired from afar. Most celebrities have been fans at some time in their lives.

A measure of success might be the importance of the people you get to meet. Even a relatively modest civil award such as an OBE (Order of the British Empire) will be pinned on by the Queen. If you have been widely exposed through the media, the Queen may even know about you – effectively she has a parasocial relationship with you – as the TV entertainer Rolf Harris found out when receiving his OBE: 'She knew the whole history of my career! It was bloody amazing!' (cited in Giles, 2000, p. 93).

One of the difficult things that famous individuals have to cope with, however, is the lack of control they have over new relationships. While it may be hugely rewarding to meet your own heroes, and come to the attention of highly attractive admirers, these are but a tiny sub-sample of the thousands of people who are clamouring for contact with you. It is nice to strike up a conversation with an attractive actor or model; it is rather less convenient to be harangued in public by people who you would normally cross the street to avoid. At modest levels of fame, before you require the assistance of bodyguards and chauffeurs, this lack of control is perhaps at its most disagreeable. The singer Robbie Williams, early in his career, spoke of getting abuse on the train three or four times a week. Even a radio presenter, without extensive TV coverage, may be forced to share his personal space with curious strangers, as journalist Stuart Cosgrove found out:

> I took a train from Edinburgh to Glasgow … and eight people talked to me about the show. Even the man selling tea and sandwiches sat down and chatted for about 20 minutes. You don't get any space.
> (cited in Giles, 2000, pp. 94–5)

The loss of privacy is perhaps the most obviously unwelcome trapping of fame. Not only fans, but the media themselves are tracking your every move, so there is an acute sense of living, as it is often put, 'in a goldfish bowl', constantly under observation. Movement becomes restricted, as you are often chaperoned for your own protection, either because the sheer number of fans trying to reach you would be overwhelming (such as the arrival at a concert or screening), or because there may be individuals who wish you harm (see the section on stalking later in the chapter). Even inside the security cordon, you are subject to the attention of paparazzi snapping away, catching you off guard.

Academic research on the experience of fame is thin on the ground, not surprisingly, since the famous are not an easy population from which to recruit. A rare exception is the work of Donna Rockwell, an American psychotherapist who used her professional contacts as a former CNN journalist to interview a small sample of celebrities (Rockwell and Giles, 2009). Taking a **phenomenological** approach, through which the researcher attempts to delve into the 'lifeworld' of the interviewee, Rockwell found that the experience of fame was characterized by a process that incorporates four phases over time:

- *Love/hate:* Initial phase where some elements of the fame experience are deeply gratifying, such as being recognized, while others are extremely discomforting, like never having a moment to yourself.
- *Addiction:* After a while, celebrities find that they become preoccupied with doing all they can to remain famous. Rockwell's participants spoke of being 'on a high' in this period.
- *Acceptance:* This is the period during which celebrities finally come to terms with the ups and downs of fame and become more philosophical about the celebrity experience.
- *Adaptation:* Having accepted fame, the celebrity then makes changes to their life to cope with it. These are not necessarily positive changes: some celebrities choose at this stage to lead a reclusive existence, simply avoiding social contact where possible.

In another study on celebrity, Mrowicki and Giles (2005) looked at the paths to fame in a sample of young people striving for musical careers. For these individuals, fame was seen as a destination, involving a journey that took them through the highs and lows of success and failure. It seems that budding celebrities are not really prepared for the less appealing aspects of fame. Very few of them had any idea how to deal with things like media intrusion and loss of privacy. Clearly, the allure of its positive aspects rather blinds fame-seekers in the early days.

Ultimately, the variety of different fame experiences simply reflects the different reasons for becoming famous. For a sports star, it is easy to see how media can be regarded as an unwelcome intrusion, since, from the performer's point of view, it is solely through football, tennis, or whatever that you have earned your fame. For a reality TV contestant, the link between fame and the media is undeniable; one could not exist without the other. Ironically, the media role accounts for sporting fame just as much as reality TV fame, televising their finest moments, broadcasting them to millions. Those who accept their debt to the media probably cope better with fame than those who see the media as simply providing a window through which others can admire their brilliance.

👁 Why do so many people want to be famous?

In October 2009, the US media became transfixed by an unfolding story in Colorado. A giant helium balloon had broken free of its moorings and was drifting across fields with, according to his parents, a six-year-old boy inside. TV cameras and network news teams broadcast live footage as it finally came to earth near Denver Airport, disrupting flights. But the balloon was empty: as it turned out, Falcon Heene had been in his bedroom throughout the drama. Two months later, Falcon's parents were jailed, accused of orchestrating the stunt in order to publicize a reality TV show that his father Richard was in the process of creating. It seems that the pair had an unquenchable thirst for fame, having already appeared on various reality shows such as *Wife Swap*, and that this episode was simply a career move. Richard Heene was also prevented for profiting from the incident for four years, but whether this includes launching the reality show is not clear.

The long line of people queuing for auditions to *Big Brother* or *The X Factor* is testimony to the enduring desire for fame that seems to persist from one generation to the next. What drives them? Given the potential pitfalls of fame, why are so many people – mostly young people – prepared to do almost anything to see their name in lights? And what makes the rest of us settle, quite happily it seems, for relative obscurity?

A recent study by Maltby (2010) identifies six different dimensions of **Interest in Fame**, as opposed to 'wishing' or 'desiring' fame. These are:

- *Intensity:* 'I would do anything to become famous'
- *Vulnerability:* 'Being famous would bring some meaning to my life'
- *Celebrity lifestyle:* 'I want to see my picture in magazines'
- *Drive:* 'I work hard every day to be famous'
- *Perceived suitability:* 'I have got what it takes to be famous'
- *Altruistic:* 'I want to be famous so I can make a contribution to society.'

Some of these dimensions were found to be associated with personality traits and other psychological and social variables. For instance:

- intensity and perceived suitability were associated with the perceived encouragement of family and friends
- the vulnerability dimension is associated with high neuroticism, low self-esteem and insecure attachments
- altruistic is associated with agreeableness – efforts to get on with other people
- drive is associated with conscientiousness.

Like the fame experience itself, the desire for fame reflects the nature of the fame that is available in any given culture. Poets and authors were once content to be 'discovered' after their death, since in all probability it was not until a writer was dead that their fame had spread widely enough to make a significant impact. Today, instant fame is possible and is therefore the variety with the most appeal to the potential audience, auditioning for any reality show going. At the same time, the modern work ethic is reflected in Maltby's 'drive' dimension of fame interest.

◉ Evolutionary explanations for fame and celebrity

Might there be an evolutionary explanation for our interest in fame and celebrity? One surprising suggestion is that we are fascinated with the intricate details of celebrity behaviour for their educational potential. Not in terms of conventional education, that is, but the kind of useful day-to-day social learning about potential hazards in the social environment – 'fitness-relevant survival information' (de Backer et al., 2007). Gossip about celebrities then operates as a way of alerting us to potential hazards – what might happen if we cheat on our partner, what kinds of outfits are likely to earn us admiration or provoke derision, and so on. Researchers have found that interest in celebrity gossip is inversely correlated with age, suggesting that these issues are important to younger people, whereas older people don't need this kind of reassurance.

But what about becoming famous ourselves? One of the most frequently cited reasons for becoming famous and successful is that it widens the pool of available sexual partners for the individual. At the very least it affords them a higher status, thus making them more attractive to potential partners. One other argument is that fame is a way of achieving symbolic immortality, a cultural equivalent of replicating one's genes: in this case the entire self is passed on, through thousands of photographic reproductions, video and audio recordings, and legendary accounts (Giles, 2000).

Whatever the various theories behind the enduring popularity of fame, when I put the question to a psychology class I taught at Coventry University some years ago, they could only come up with one explanation: money. In their eyes, no other incentive seemed necessary. Perhaps this tells us more about contemporary celebrity – the flouting of designer labels and flash cars – than about fame through the ages. Or maybe it tells us more about the pecuniary ambitions of psychology students!

◉ Fans and fandom

Of course, media coverage alone is not enough: fame is sustained by the presence, actual and virtual, of an army of adoring fans, who exist to remind the celebrity of their social importance. Famous individuals have always had their admirers, from 18th-century writers to early Hollywood stars, drawing crowds wherever they went. Some fans, it seems, will go to extraordinary lengths simply to catch a glimpse of their heroes in the flesh, camping outside their homes just to see them drive off, while others collect trivial belongings that have passed through celebrity ownership.

If there is something vaguely religious-sounding about fan behaviour, it may not be entirely coincidental. The term 'fan' derives from the Latin word *fanaticus*, meaning 'belonging to the temple', and numerous authors have identified fan activities that map neatly onto those of religious rituals: the collection of relics, creative artistic work based around the object of devotion, and the acceptance of whatever treatment their idols choose to mete out. In the early 1980s, Australian singer Nick Cave, then with The Birthday Party, would occasionally kick out at the heads of fans in the front row of the audience, who wore their bruises with pride afterwards.

In the early days of Hollywood, fans contacted stars on a regular basis to demand objects with which they had made physical contact – soap they had washed with, a handkerchief bearing lipstick traces, a used piece of chewing gum or even merely a blade of grass from the star's lawn (Tudor, 1974). These sacred items perform the same role, perhaps, as the relics collected by religious devotees since the veneration of saints and martyrs in the 4th century AD. Random bits of bone, hair and nails are still claimed as the remains of various saints, on view in reliquaries in churches throughout the world. Fans are not content simply to receive objects from stars: equally important is the communication in the opposite direction. Park Dietz, a psychiatrist who has been involved in several high-profile trials, published a list of the 'enclosures' that had been sent to Hollywood celebrities (Dietz et al., 1991). Some of the items were largely innocuous, such as personal business cards and press clippings; some were offensive, including a blood-filled syringe and even the severed head of a coyote; others were simply bizarre, such as a half-eaten candy bar, a disposable razor and a toy submarine.

The exchange of personalized objects opens up another possibility for fandom. Like religious devotion, it is not simply a case of lesser mortals fawning over greater ones; clearly, fans hope some of the star's charismatic powers will travel back in their direction. Centuries ago, Petrarch (1304–74) and Rousseau (1712–78) were hounded by admirers who travelled hundreds of miles simply to see them in the flesh, some of them bearing their own poems, hoping that the experience would rub off on their own literary ambitions. While the purpose of sending a toy submarine to a celebrity is slightly less obvious, it may simply be enough to think that the star is going to handle an object that the fan has handled, establishing some remote connection.

There are many fans who have no burning desire to meet their idols, in fact, sometimes the experience of encountering one's heroes can be deeply disillusioning. Some prefer to worship from afar, building shrines to their favourite performers. One Boy George fan I met claimed to have amassed 11,714 images of the star in the form of pictures, posters, and badges (note the specificity of the figure). She spent large sums of money on clothes that would enable her to resemble him, and travelled across the UK to fan club meetings and concerts where she joined forces with fellow devotees. She had actually spoken to Boy George on one occasion, so making contact with the star was no longer an incentive (Giles, 2000).

Other fans express their devotion through creative activities. Henry Jenkins (1992) has documented in detail the work produced by fans of TV series such as *Star Trek*, ranging from reworked scripts of specific episodes to spliced-together footage of Kirk and Spock to generate a gay love story. Jenkins describes such activities as 'textual poaching', and we can now see a good deal of this kind of creativity on fan websites.

Many media scholars are dismissive of the links between fandom and religiosity (Hills, 2002), arguing that fans draw on the discourses of religion, often in a playful way, to avoid having to justify their enthusiasms, but also that there is great diversity in the fan community. Hills is ultimately concerned that religious parallels are used to undermine fan activity by making unflattering comparisons between media phenomena and matters of life and death – and it is true that parallels between fandom and religious devotion are often made (by the media themselves, even) in conjunction with general complaints about the 'worthlessness' of modern society.

In actual fact, there are many different types of fan, and different reasons for being a fan. Following years of research on fan communities, Stever (2009) has developed a classification system of fandom comprising three elements:

1   Eight different *levels of intensity* ranging from a broad interest in stars and media through to pathological attachment, where, for example, a fan might commit suicide on hearing of their idol's death.
2   Nine different *motivations* for fandom, ranging from 'task attraction' (liking a musician for their artistic qualities) to various types of attachments.
3   Whether fans are *isolated* or *interactive* in their activities.

Celebrity worship

In recent years, some psychologists have attempted to capture the essence of fandom by creating a Celebrity Worship Scale (McCutcheon et al., 2002). This is a psychometric scale not unlike that used to measure para-social interaction, in which fans are asked to agree or disagree with a series of statements about their favourite celebrity.

Over numerous studies, researchers agree that there are two fundamentally different aspects of celebrity worship that roughly map on to Stever's (2009) distinction between interactive and isolated activity:

1   an *entertainment-social* factor, akin to being a member of a fan club
2   an *intense-personal* factor, like building a personal shrine to a celebrity.

The entertainment-social factor is measured by items such as 'My friends and I like to discuss what my favourite celebrity has done', while the intense-personal one is tapped by items like 'I am obsessed by details of my favourite celebrity's life' (Maltby et al., 2002). While there is clear overlap between these factors (after all, a great many people might be obsessed by celebrity details, if only to share them), it is the psychological function of each aspect that is of most interest to researchers. While the entertainment-social factor seems innocuous enough ('Learning the life story of my favourite celebrity is a lot of fun'), it was the scale constructors' intention to problematize celebrity worship, although they conceived it as a unitary concept (a **single factor construct**), with high scores *in general* indicating pathology (McCutcheon et al., 2002).

Later researchers felt that it was important to dissociate the social (fan club-style) elements of celebrity worship from the potentially pathological ones. It seems that the authors had already decided that extreme fandom contains elements of obsessive-compulsive disorder, since several of the statements are worded so as to reflect the clinical literature. 'I have frequent thoughts about my favourite celebrity, even when I don't want to' and 'I often feel compelled to learn the personal habits of my favourite celebrity' both seem to indicate a compulsive element to celebrity worship to go with the explicit obsessional component.

While there is clearly a pathological element associated with high intense-personal scores, several studies have identified a third dimension – 'borderline-pathological' celebrity worship, for example 'If I were lucky enough to meet my favourite celebrity, and they asked me to do something illegal as a favour, I would probably do it'. High scores on this subscale would clearly raise concerns about individuals' behaviour. A further four subscales have been suggested (Maltby and Giles, 2008) that identify aspects of celebrity worship – attempts to establish contact, collecting and other painstaking activities in relation to a favourite celebrity, sexual desires, and stalking tendencies, including the item 'I wish my favourite celebrity was dead'.

In a variety of studies in the UK and the US, different aspects of celebrity worship have been found to relate to other psychological phenomena. As anticipated, the intense-personal subscale is most closely associated with psychological disturbance – higher levels of depression, anxiety, stress and even physical illness (Maltby et al., 2004). The borderline-pathological dimension is associated with fantasy proneness – vivid fantasies and memories, even hallucinatory or paranormal experiences (Maltby et al., 2006). In another study, Maltby et al. (2003) related celebrity worship to personality traits, and found considerable overlap between its dimensions and the three factors of Eysenck's personality model. Scores on the entertainment-social dimension tend to correlate with high extraversion, scores on intense-personal correlate with neuroticism, and borderline-pathological with psychoticism.

How does celebrity worship develop in childhood? There is less research on this age group; indeed, the reliance of most celebrity worship studies on undergraduate samples, rather than, say, fans themselves, has been criticized by some authors (Stever, 2009). However, one study found that the emergence of attachments to celebrities coincided with a decrease in attachments to parents during adolescence, greater independence, and high attachments to peers, suggesting that celebrities may act as a set of parasocial friends for teenagers (Giles and Maltby, 2004).

One word of caution: do not confuse the concept of celebrity worship with that of parasocial interaction (PSI; see Chapter 6). Celebrity worship is a highly selective form of PSI. First, not all PSI requires 'worship', or even liking (parasocial relationships can be based on hatred). Second, celebrities only constitute one type of media figure with whom we can form parasocial relationships. But the two concepts are frequently muddled, and PSI has even been described, bizarrely, as a form of celebrity worship.

Given media scholars' dislike of the fandom/religion comparison, how valid is the term 'worship' for fan activities? Maltby et al. (2002) compared scores on the Celebrity Worship Scale with those on a measure of 'religiosity' (how religious an individual is) in an undergraduate sample, and found a broadly **negative relationship** between the two overall scores. Whether this means that the two are entirely separate activities, or that celebrity worship has replaced religion in terms of serving psychological needs requires further research.

◉ Pathological fandom

Extreme celebrity worship can result in overidentification with stars, which can be measured by the Celebrity Worship Scale, with items such as 'The successes of my favourite celebrity are my successes also'. In rare cases, it can result in such a strong desire to make an impact on the celebrity that individuals are prepared to go to ludicrous lengths to demonstrate their adulation, from **stalking** them obsessively to actually attacking them.

Perhaps the most well-known instance of a celebrity obsession that got out of hand was that of John Hinckley Jr, a psychologically disturbed young man whose earlier obsession with becoming famous through music soon developed into a specific obsession with the actress Jodie Foster.

Foster was, at this time, still studying at college, which made her an easy target for stalkers. Hinckley would break into her dormitory at night and slip love letters under her door. In one letter, he admitted that he was content simply to be the subject of conversation between Foster and her friends, 'however full of ridicule it may be' (Franzini and Grossberg, 1995).

Soon, however, being talked about was not enough. As Hinckley's psychological state worsened, he began to plot ever more dramatic ways of securing her attention, such as hijacking planes and committing suicide in front of her. Eventually he turned for inspiration to one of Foster's early films, *Taxi Driver* (1976), in which the central character plots to assassinate a presidential candidate. Why not just shoot the president himself and have done with it, thought Hinckley. After stalking Jimmy Carter towards the end of his time as president in the late 1970s, and being arrested on a firearms charge, Hinckley had a spell of psychiatric treatment for depression. By that time, Ronald Reagan had replaced Carter in the White House, and was leaving the Hilton Hotel in Washington DC in April 1981 when Hinckley fired six bullets at him. All six missed, injuring other members of his entourage, but one ricocheted off his waiting limousine and struck Reagan in the chest, puncturing his lung. Hinckley was arrested there and then – given his motives, it would have made little sense to run away – and was later found not guilty by reason of insanity and confined indefinitely in a psychiatric institution.

Jodie Foster was lucky, as several other celebrities have been killed by their fans. In December 1980, former Beatle John Lennon was returning from a recording session to his New York apartment with his wife Yoko Ono when he was shot five times, once fatally in the heart, by Mark Chapman. Lennon had signed an autograph for Chapman several hours earlier in the same spot, but clearly making contact with his idol was not enough. Nor did it seem to be the motive for murder: although a fan of Lennon's music, Chapman was repeatedly angered by his anti-religious statements and deliberately moved to New York in order to kill him (Jones, 1992). Unlike Hinckley, Chapman overruled the initial decision of not guilty by reason of insanity and pleaded guilty to murder.

Could we have been able to identify Hinckley and Chapman as potential celebrity assassins by their scores on the Celebrity Worship Scale? Chapman maybe, although he would have scored highly on the religiosity scale in the Maltby et al. (2002) study as well. Hinckley would certainly have been labelled a risk to Jodie Foster, but who would have drafted in extra security for Reagan on the basis of obsessive sexual love directed at an actress? The one thing that Hinckley and Chapman share with many other individuals who attack public figures is a delusion of grandeur, and a desire for some kind of fame or infamy (Meloy et al., 2008). Perhaps, ultimately, the answer may come not from studying fans and celebrity worshippers, but from those who are preoccupied with becoming famous.

Further reading

Braudy, L. (1997). *The frenzy of renown: Fame and its history* (2nd edn). New York: Vintage Books.

Giles, D.C. (2000). *Illusions of immortality: A psychology of fame and celebrity*. Basingstoke: Macmillan – now Palgrave Macmillan.

Meloy, J.R., Sheridan, L. and Hoffmann, J. (2008). *Stalking, threatening, and attacking public figures: A psychological and behavioural analysis*. New York: Oxford University Press.

Chapter 8

Audience participation media

◉ Introduction

The media have always relied upon audiences to contribute to their output, whether in the form of readers' letters or as TV quiz contestants. In recent years, so much television in particular has drawn its participants from the viewing public that we have devised terms like 'reality TV' to describe shows whose stars are ordinary viewers transformed into celebrities. In this chapter I present some psychological explanations for the popularity of reality TV and other genres that rely on the public for their success, and discuss what it means for the viewer to identify so strongly with the person who could be their next-door neighbour snatching the limelight away from the remote, untouchable figures of traditional celebrity.

◉ The psychological appeal of audience participation media

Ever since radio and television have been beamed into our living rooms, the viewing public has had a powerful presence in the programmes. The term 'audience participation media' covers any show that relies on the participation of the general public, from tightly edited and scripted 'lifestyle' television (property shows, for example) to reality shows such as *Big Brother* where viewers can watch 24-hour live footage of unscripted, naturally occurring social interaction.

The appeal of **audience participation media** is of interest to psychologists because it relates closely to some of the concepts discussed in the previous two chapters, particularly parasocial interaction and identification. It can be argued that audiences identify more strongly with public participants because they recognize them as peers, as distinct from people who work in the media (e.g. TV presenters), and traditional celebrities, who earned their fame through other activities such as acting or music.

What has become increasingly interesting in recent decades is the way in which public participants have been turned into celebrities through their appearances on such programmes. In the UK, the most striking example of all is that of Jade Goody, who shot to fame during her first participation in the 2002 *Big Brother* series, and who died from cervical cancer seven years later in the full glare of the media headlights. But Goody is something of an exception. Most people who make their name through audience participation media tend to exit the stage shortly afterwards, other than those who take up careers in the media as presenters.

This apparently new form of fame has raised a lot of questions about the social function of celebrity and its audience appeal. Most reality TV stars are not endowed with talent, good looks or charisma, as in Goody's case, their audience appeal lies in their very ordinariness. Goody's funeral in 2009 attracted thousands of people, many of whom described her as 'the girl next door' and 'our Essex princess' (BBC, 2009). This sets Goody completely at odds with traditional celebrities such as Hollywood stars, whose remoteness and exoticism contributed to their allure.

The psychological implications of this type of celebrity, and the popularity of audience participation media, will be discussed later in the chapter. But first, it is necessary to trace the evolution of such shows across the history of radio and television.

'Ave a go Flo! Public participation on radio and TV

Wartime radio

In the early days of BBC radio in Britain, it was quickly realized that a cheap and popular form of broadcasting involved a presenter visiting 'ordinary people' performing mundane, everyday activities, and getting them to speak into the microphone. For example, the Manchester BBC studio broadcast shows in which a personality presenter, Harry Hopeful, interviewed people in various parts of the north of England about their daily activities. During the Second World War, this format became more popular as it was seen as a way to boost public morale by featuring groups of factory workers and other people engaged in the war effort.

Quiz shows

After the war, quiz shows became the dominant form of audience participation media, especially in the US, where at one point in the 1950s, five of the top ten rated network TV shows were quizzes (Goedkoop, 1985). These shows had high stakes for the participants, as substantial monetary prizes were on offer. The quiz show format suffered a temporary setback following a famous scandal involving the show *Twenty-One*, where it transpired that several contestants had been supplied with answers in order to keep them on the show so that they would become familiar faces to viewers, thus generating further publicity for the show. Here we can see the prototype for today's 'reality TV' star.

Later on, the basic quiz show format became extended to incorporate all kinds of competitions involving public contestants. While many of these continued to reward winners with money prizes, such as *The Price Is Right*, others appealed to contestants' (and audiences') romantic side, notably *The Dating Game*, first broadcast on US TV in the 1960s, and ITV's *Blind Date* (1985). Fuelled by huge viewing figures, some of the *Blind Date* contestants became minor celebrities for a brief period, such as Paul Nolan, a window cleaner from Dorset, who entertained the audience with his impressions of TV presenter Bruce Forsyth, and later, after being chosen by that week's female contestant, turned out to be rather less single than the show's prerequisites demanded.

Talk shows

A popular audience participation format in the 1980s and 90s was the **talk show**, which had its roots in 1950s' US television, where the likes of Steve Allen invited the studio audience to interact with his guests, actually moving around the audience himself with the microphone. This type of interaction evolved into a format in its own right with *The Phil Donahue Show* in the 1960s, and later Oprah Winfrey, whose highly popular 1980s' talk show was probably the most influential of them all, and certainly the longest running, set to end in 2011 after 25 'seasons'.

Although the format of *The Oprah Winfrey Show* was to become increasingly diverse, incorporating a book club and celebrity interviews, it initially focused on a separate theme each week, usually a topical social issue such as drug use or AIDS. The same format was briefly popular in the UK in the early 1990s, with former MP Robert Kilroy-Silk presenting a show (*Kilroy*) every weekday morning on the BBC. ITV launched a simultaneous rival show. Themes were typically social issues of varying degrees of seriousness.

The nature of the TV talk show began to change radically during the late 1990s, however, as audiences became younger, brasher and increasingly bored with discussing healthcare and unemployment benefit, preferring more personalized topics. This was in part due to the success of younger, less authoritative hosts such as Ricki Lake in the US and Trisha Goddard in the UK, but also due to the cult success of *The Jerry Springer Show*. Here, presaging the likes of *Big Brother*, the stars of the talk show were not specially invited 'experts' or celebrities as in *Kilroy*, but members of the public with a story – usually a scandalous one – to tell. The drama would unfold in the show as jealous partners, rivals, exes and relatives emerged from behind the curtain to challenge the protagonist, often with explosive consequences and, on occasions, actual violence, although there have been many claims that the brawls were largely staged for the cameras.

Springer and similar shows came under a good deal of criticism from within and outside the media, with social commentators concerned about falling moral standards, 'trash' TV and the ethical responsibilities of the TV channels. Were these people released from the show in order to go home and kill one another? It seems that is precisely what happened in 2002, when guest Ralf Panitz was jailed for the murder of his ex-wife Nancy just hours after the broadcast of the show. Springer was successfully sued by the couple's sons (BBC, 2002).

Almost as great a concern was the suspicion that individuals (and entire families) were appearing on the show simply for publicity, and doubts were raised as to the authenticity of the storylines and the emotions on display. These issues are vitally important for the psychological appeal of audience participation media, as I will go on to discuss later.

Lifestyle shows

In the 1990s, the full potential of audience participation was realized, both in terms of audience appeal and cheap programming. Two types of

lifestyle show became particularly popular during this period, containing elements that were to become critical to the success of reality shows in the following decade – the makeover show and the challenge. In the **makeover show**, members of the public have themselves, their love lives or their properties transformed through the help of experts. This format began in earnest with the BBC's *Changing Rooms* (1996), but had quickly mushroomed into an identifiable genre by the end of the decade (Moseley, 2000).

Makeover shows are a large subset of a broader genre of lifestyle programme in which audiences – and their representatives on the show – are invited to update, transform or improve some aspect of their lifestyle, typically during the course of a single episode. An army of experts is on hand to challenge the current state of affairs, for example a scruffy or dated hairstyle, and assist the participants throughout the show. In the BBC's *Ground Force* (1997), it was participants' gardens that received the makeover, while in its *What Not To Wear* (1999), self-styled fashion 'experts' Trinny and Susannah mocked participants' existing wardrobes before advising them on new purchases.

One of the key cultural features of makeover television is – as Moseley (2000) and other authors have commented – that they serve as a way of creating certain 'hierarchies of taste' and privileging some fashions and lifestyles over others, sometimes for commercial ends. In one episode of a short-lived gardening makeover show, BBC's *Gardening Neighbours* (1998), Taylor (2005) describes how one couple were ridiculed by the so-called 'design experts' for making the focus of their back garden a bed of Bizzy Lizzies, even though the owners were clearly fond of this colourful centrepiece. The makeover, meanwhile, consisted of the 'crisp formality of ... box hedges and standard bay trees' (p. 118), privileging trendy contemporary concepts over supposedly sentimental and old-fashioned styles of garden design, but ultimately sacrificing any visual focus.

At times – particularly with fashion-related shows – such innovations provide close commercial tie-ins with sponsors and other benefiting industries. The ultimately disastrous 1990s and 2000s boom in UK property values was supported by numerous property shows in which home-owners were instructed on the various style elements that could be transformed in order to increase property prices even more, sometimes, apparently, by tens of thousands of pounds. So viewers were simultaneously taught contemporary tastes and market values (Giles, 2002b).

The second popular format, related to the first, although not exactly a lifestyle show, involves members of the general public taking part in an authentic, that is, naturally occurring, *challenge* of some kind, only the challenge takes place over the course of a series, with the public participants emerging as the real stars of the show rather than the experts. The BBC's *Driving School* (1997) is a typical example. This series featured genuine learner drivers at a specific establishment encountering weekly challenges in their ambitions to learn to drive. By focusing on the participants rather than the experts, 'challenge' series allow personalities to emerge over the course of time, such as Maureen Reece, a spectacularly slow learner who took eight attempts to pass her driving test, and then only in a car fitted with an automatic gearbox. For a while, Maureen was a household name in the UK, even scoring a minor hit single and fronting a safe driving campaign. As with Jade Goody, and other, later reality celebrities, Maureen's essential appeal was her ordinariness, but also her perseverance to master a skill that seemed initially to be beyond her.

⊙ 'Reality TV'

It is hard to say when the first true **reality TV** show first appeared, although the basic idea of setting up cameras and recording free, naturally occurring interaction between members of the public was seen in a number of one-off series during the 1970s and 80s. These became known as 'fly-on-the-wall' documentaries, or 'docusoaps', creating the impression that the viewer had gained privileged insight into the everyday interaction of an authentic community, but that also there was a narrative unfolding in the course of that interaction.

Perhaps the first true 'reality' show was the BBC's *The Family* (1974), which followed the day-to-day activities of a working-class family from Reading in the south of England, whose members, like Paul Nolan, attracted much press attention at the time, especially since one of the daughters became married during the course of the series. During the 1990s, the docusoap format became more occupation based, with various series charting the day-to-day activities of the workplace or people engaged in a particular profession. The BBC's *Airport* (1996) focused on the activities of staff at London Heathrow Airport, making a star (again, briefly) out of the Aeroflot ground services manager Jeremy Spake.

However, the first shows that were recognizably 'reality' were probably the Dutch show *Nummer 28* and the US variant *The Real World*, broadcast by MTV in the early 1990s, in which public participants auditioned to become flatmates in an authentic apartment. Although lacking the continuous footage later featured on *Big Brother*, the weekly summaries and 'confessional' monologues straight to camera were picked up by most later reality series, and the concept of a show based around the continuous interaction of public participants heralded the reality explosion later in the decade.

In the early 2000s, reality shows mushroomed on television networks across the globe. *Big Brother* led the way, first in the Netherlands in the late 1990s, then in the UK in 2000 and in numerous other countries during the same period, which reproduced the *Real World* formula, albeit with 24-hour live footage and various other contrivances to force the participants into an unfolding narrative. Most characteristic perhaps was the involvement of the viewing audience, who were able to vote for their least favourite contestant in order to oust them from the house, and then assemble to 'greet' them as they emerged. This element of 'viewer power' added to the impression of reality created by the show – a form of audience democracy, whereby it was the viewers rather than a team of media folk – scriptwriters, producers, celebrities – that dictated the unfolding narrative.

In the UK, *Big Brother* was followed by the BBC's *Castaway* (2000) and ITV's *Survivor* (2001), where public, and unacquainted, participants were thrown together in hostile environments and set a series of arduous challenges. Again, these were simply variants of internationally successful programmes, soon to be usurped by the success of a celebrity version (*I'm a Celebrity – Get Me Out of Here!*), the same fate ultimately befalling *Big Brother*. Indeed, as early as 2001, Channel 4 launched *Celebrity Big Brother*. Strangely, the appeal of seeing public participants in these shows began to fade shortly after.

At the start of the millennium, nobody would have imagined that, by 2010, the most popular TV series – in many countries – would be old-fashioned singing and dancing talent contests, but that is the large circle that reality TV has helped to complete. In 2001 in the UK, reproducing a successful Australian format from the previous year, ITV launched *Popstars*, a series in which young performers competed to form a singing group (Hear'Say), who were to go on briefly to have enormous commercial success.

Later in the same year, *Popstars* was followed by *Pop Idol*, a similar contest to find a solo performer, whose winner Will Young has gone on to sell over 8 million albums. In the US, the format was adapted as *American Idol*, going on to top the viewing ratings for several years, and many other countries had similar success with local versions. In the UK, the same format has been preserved throughout the decade, with minor variations. By 2010, *The X Factor* continued to make the headlines and produce celebrity performers, even from the cast of also-rans. In 2009, the biggest musical success story in the UK was that of Susan Boyle, an unlikely 48-year-old singer from West Lothian in Scotland with what the *Washington Times* described as a 'homely' appearance (McManus, 2009). Like Jade Goody and Maureen Reece, Boyle scores heavily in the ordinariness stakes, albeit with slightly more evident talent.

While the TV talent show concept itself is a long-established format (UK TV had *Opportunity Knocks* and *New Faces* in the 1970s), the 'reality' version introduced successful elements from other shows. From makeover TV came the unbridled mockery and ritual elimination of unsuccessful applicants in the early phases, an opportunity for preserving taste hierarchies, such as formal vocal mannerisms, popular musical styles and so on. From *Big Brother* came the power of the audience vote, which has often countered sharply with the views of the shows' experts.

However, the most striking feature of the modern talent contest has been the savage criticism meted out by the same experts, helping in the process to make celebrities out of certain panellists, most notably Simon Cowell, whose barbed critiques made him as much of a star as the eventual *Pop Idol* winners – especially since he would be back next series to continue. The same feature has continued on another highly popular UK series, the BBC's *Strictly Come Dancing*, where celebrity contestants are frequently subjected to withering verbal assaults for being only slightly less polished than their opponents.

How real is reality TV?

Early definitions of reality TV were hopelessly confused. Some claimed that it referred to any programme with natural, unscripted and unedited footage; others even that it referred to fictional re-enactments of 'real' events, although these are now usually termed **docudramas**. The essence of reality TV seemed to be simply that it wasn't fictional. Difficulty over identifying precisely what constitutes reality TV has led some media scholars to claim that the term is too general to be useful (Holmes and Jermyn, 2004). Nevertheless, it has become well established in the contemporary lexicon, and there are certainly features of modern-day programming that are instantly recognizable by audiences as reality TV, even if the shows themselves have precious little to do with reality per se. Whether we like the term or not, it seems we're stuck with it.

Su Holmes (2005, p. 148) has referred to pop talent contests such as *Pop Idol* as 'ultimate examples of reality TV', in that they subvert the workings of the music and entertainment industries by stripping away hype, marketing and internal contrivance and allowing the raw talent itself (and the audience) to be the centre of the selection process. In one sense, they have enabled television to triumph over the music industry itself. In 2009, the UK music sales charts were so dominated by current and former TV talent contestants that a *Facebook* campaign was launched to ensure that a 'genuine' act occupy the Christmas No. 1 slot, as the previous five years had seen that accolade falling to each year's winner of *The X Factor*. A 1992 track from US rock act Rage Against the Machine was dusted off and brought out of retirement and, thanks to the online campaign, received 50,000 more sales than 2009 *X Factor* winner Joe McElderry's debut single.

What makes Rage Against the Machine genuine and Joe McElderry fake? Following Holmes's argument, it should be McElderry that we acknowledge as the real deal, having fought through several rounds of competition and voted for by a huge viewing public, while, for all we know, Rage Against the Machine may have been entirely fabricated in the mysterious world of their multinational record company 17 years or so earlier. The difference is that TV played no obvious part in the formation of Rage Against the Machine. Nobody voted for them. They just emerged, as far as we can tell, from the creative urges of their constituent members, built up a following through live work and some modest recordings, before Sony came in, signing up an already fully fledged act with their own look and sound, untouched by TV-approved experts, professional trainers and advisers. When it comes to music, authenticity – at least for many fans – comes from *not* being involved with the media.

The essence of reality TV is surely the belief that the audience is watching real events unfold in real time, featuring real people. Much of the time this is simply not the case, even in classic reality shows like *Big Brother*. While there was a 24-hour live feed available for those with the time and interest to follow it, the vast majority of viewers relied on the tightly edited mid-evening highlights package, complete with selected chunks of 'action', straight-to-camera 'confessionals' from the diary room, commentary from in-house psychologists and former contestants and the reactions of a studio audience. Whatever viewers might have seen on the live channel, this was where reality TV happened. And then some: the subsequent media commentary, particularly in the UK tabloid press, online interaction in *Big Brother* Internet fan forums, and even Channel 4's follow-up show *Big Brother's Little Brother*, which extended the analysis conducted during the main show. To quote Su Holmes again (2008, p. 20), 'participants have to come out of the house to find out what they mean (or who they are)'. She cites some telling dialogue from the show where contestants speculate about how the media will portray them: 'I'll be seen as the posh one' (p. 21).

Ultimately, then, reality TV is never the 'window on the world' that it sets itself up to be. Even live sport, which surely is a better candidate for the title of 'ultimate reality TV show' than *Pop Idol* or *The X Factor*, is profoundly shaped by commentary, summary and postmortem debate. Research that has manipulated the commentary to televised sport has found that viewers' perceptions can be significantly affected by the commentators' delivery and bias (Sullivan, 1991). Ultimately, Holmes's (2005) argument implies that reality TV is reality *shaped by* TV. It's really happening, and we're watching it as it happens. How 'authentic' it is remains another matter entirely.

Authenticity and emotional display in audience participation media

Despite concerns over reality TV's claims to be 'real', the question of authenticity is central to understanding the psychological appeal of the programmes. Fundamentally, the important thing about all audience participation media is that we believe the participants are being true to themselves. This is precisely what differentiates audience participation shows from fictional drama, and provides the key to defining 'reality' TV. Never mind that the whole thing is a set-up, that the situations are contrived, and it's a terrible way of producing a half-decent pop group, the important thing is that, in the course of the programme, we see genuinely ordinary public participants displaying sincere emotions.

Emotional display in audience participation media is skilfully manipulated by producers and editors, designing and organizing programmes so that they build up to some kind of **revelation** that will produce a spontaneous outburst of emotion in participants (Moseley, 2000). We can see multiple instances of such revelations in different types of show:

- *Announcements of winners, losers, qualifiers and so on in relation to a contest:* Suspense is created by deliberately delaying the actual revelation, thereby increasing the intensity of the emotional response both in the audience and, more importantly, the significant individuals involved. This is a long-standing tradition in contests such as *Miss World*, perhaps the first televised contest specifically built around extravagant displays of emotion by public participants.

- *Unmasking of transformed persons or their homes/gardens:* Typical of the *Changing Rooms/Ground Force*-type makeover show, this is usually the climax of the show where the owners of the home or garden are led, blindfolded, to a location for optimum visual impact. The blindfold is removed and the camera zooms in on their faces. In personal makeover shows, a mirror is suddenly produced for similar effect.

- *Delivery of expert judgement or critique:* The moment of revelation on shows such as *The X Factor* and *Strictly Come Dancing*, almost more important than the performance itself, is when each member of the panel of experts delivers their verdict. Irrespective of the panellists' standing, the visual focus is the face of the contestant.

- *Unmasking of mystery persona:* Typical of 'candid video' shows such as *Candid Camera* and *Beadle's About*, where members of the public are lured into unfortunate situations before the salesman, inspector or whoever is revealed as a TV presenter. Also seen on shows such as *Blind Date*, where contestants are expected to select a potential date solely on the basis of vocal interaction.

- *Disclosure of correct answer:* Seen mainly in quiz shows. As with prizewinners, or public votes in reality shows, the modern tendency is to delay the revelation for an almost painful interval, although in shows employing multiple-choice items (e.g. *Who Wants to be a Millionaire*), much of the audience pleasure lies in trying to 'read' the answer from the presenter's facial gestures and tone of voice.

The main function of emotional display at these moments of revelation is to convince the watching audience that the participants, and the things that happen to them, are genuine, and not actors responding to staged events. This is such an important feature of audience participation media that disclosures of fakery (such as the US quiz show 'rigging' scandal in the 1950s) are met with great hostility by the general public.

Why is it so important that we believe in the authenticity of participant emotion? One possibility is that it enables us to recognize the participants as fellow members of the public; in other words, they are not part of the script. Defining what constitutes 'the general public' is an extremely difficult task. German philosopher Jürgen Habermas (1989) defined the 'public sphere' as an area where people can discuss political matters in an influential way without actually being politicians, rulers, lawyers and so on. Applying this concept to the media, you could argue that the general public are defined simply by *not being* celebrities, presenters or anything to do with the media.

In most TV programmes, it is easy to identify members of the public simply through the roles they are assigned in the production (Giles, 2002b). For example, a member of the public would never introduce the show; even if we have never seen the presenter before, we assume that they are a media employee of some sort. The most emphatic role assignment though is the on-screen description of each person who speaks: if you are billed by name alone, it is assumed you are sufficiently well known not to require a role, and are therefore a celebrity or other media personality. If you are billed as 'Joan Potts, housewife' or 'John Potts, local resident', then you are clearly assigned a public role until the show is over and other media have the opportunity of turning you into something more glamorous.

In short programmes, and particularly in edited shows, the appearance of public participants is not always long enough to fully convince a sceptical viewing audience that the individual is genuine (and not an actor). One of the most successful features of *Big Brother* and other reality shows is that the continuous coverage of live footage makes it harder for participants to sustain any kind of artificial front, and the expectation is that their 'real selves' will be exposed sooner or later (Holmes, 2008). It is, perhaps, for this reason that we saw a gradual shift in audience appeal from ordinary contestants to celebrity contestants on reality shows in the 2000s. Once the reality format was established, it became more fun seeing celebrities' real selves unmasked rather than those of public participants.

Participant experiences

While the audience at home is revelling in the tantalizing revelations and emotional twists and turns of the participants, what about the participants themselves? The welfare of individuals appearing on shows such as

Big Brother has been hotly debated by psychologists and the television industry, with long-running discussions in publications like *The Psychologist*. TV bosses are frequently accused of exploiting public participants, who, after all, don't command a fee, and of encouraging **voyeurism**.

The most important ethical issue concerns the psychological welfare of participants who – unexpectedly – find that they cannot cope with the social pressure of the show and yet are bound by the competition rules to continue. This kind of scenario has uncomfortable echoes of controversial psychological studies such as Milgram's 1974 obedience studies (see Chapter 11) and the Stanford prison 'experiment' (Haney et al., 1973). These examples prompted a tightening of ethical standards in social scientific research during the 1980s, with a scale of reform that has yet to be fully embraced by the media.

In *Big Brother 7* (2006), contestant Shahbaz Chauhdry walked out of the house after just five days after threatening to kill himself. It later transpired that four of the other housemates in the same series had previous or existing mental health issues, leading the founder of mental health charity SANE Marjorie Wallace to claim that the show was 'worse than bear baiting' (Wallace, 2006). Three years later, Sree Dasari, an evicted contestant, was hospitalized after cutting his wrist while watching a subsequent episode of the show.

The counterargument by media producers is that participants are free agents who are fully aware of the psychological risks of participation, and that they themselves are exploiting the medium for the good of their own self-publicity. Furthermore, should unexpected psychological distress occur, it is argued, there are counsellors on hand to look after contestants' welfare before, during and after the show (Addley, 2009). Despite this, there have been frequent statements from the British Psychological Society and the Mental Health Foundation about concerns over the actual ethical standards being observed by TV companies in producing reality shows that often seem to be exploiting vulnerable individuals in the name of entertainment.

◉ Further reading

Holmes, S. and Jermyn, D. (eds) (2004). *Understanding reality television.* London: Routledge.

The Mediated Social World

UNIVERSITY OF WINCHESTER
LIBRARY

Section summary

The two chapters in this section are devoted to issues of media influence in the social world of which we are often only dimly aware. Chapter 9 concerns the opinion-shaping influence of news media and focuses largely on the way in which media are said to 'frame' the material they present to their audience. There is also some consideration here of how a researcher might study this within the context of psychological methods. Chapter 10 explores the effect of growing up in a media-saturated environment and the sense-making processes of the developing brain. This is, or should be, one of the most important topics in media psychology, but it is also one of the most difficult to study, since we are forever trying to work out exactly how children understand the world around them, and we often make the error of assuming that adults themselves are fully aware of media and its many influences.

Chapter 9

Framing and the psychology of news influence

Introduction

This chapter introduces readers to the concept of 'framing', which has long been a popular concept in social sciences generally, but in psychology it has tended to be restricted to research on 'message framing', in which the source of the messages is deliberately vague, and the content overly artificial. Instead I outline a methodological approach known as Media Framing Analysis, which examines several features of news stories in order to identify a set of 'frames' that are used to present a specific topic in newspapers, magazines, news websites and TV news bulletins.

Where do we get our opinions on current affairs from? Partly these are 'handed down' to us from influential figures in our social network – relatives, teachers, peers – but where do they get their opinions from? For many years, 'peer influence' has been a rather misleading concept in social psychology, based on the assumption that knowledge circulates solely within social groups, sometimes ignoring cultural influences entirely. And the most important of these today is undoubtedly the media.

This chapter explores the phenomenon of **media framing**, the process by which a topic is presented from a particular angle (or variety of angles), inviting audiences to draw particular conclusions, and to make particular allusions to other topics. The same phenomenon might be called 'spin' when applied to politics, or marketing when applied to consumer goods. It is essentially a matter of how topics are dressed up when presented in newspapers, television bulletins and news websites.

Media framing has only recently become of interest to psychologists, largely through its application to health psychology (see, for example, Giles et al., 1999; Shaw and Giles, 2009). However, framing itself has generated an enormous amount of research in the social sciences in recent years.

Message framing

The concept of **message framing** has been popular in social and health psychology for some time (see Ferguson and Gallagher, 2007, as a typical example). Message framing derives from the work of Tversky and Kahneman (1981), who were largely interested in judgement, risk and decision-making. For them, the key properties of a message (e.g. an advertisement) concern the costs or benefits of responding to that message as perceived by the receiver.

According to Tversky and Kahneman, messages can either be *loss-framed* or *gain-framed*. For example, an advert for vitamin supplements could dwell on the dreadful illnesses that you might be prone to should you not use the product (a loss frame), or it could concentrate more on the health benefits – feeling good, added vitality and so on (a gain frame). Whether or not we choose to buy the product will depend on the type of message frame in conjunction with other psychological variables (personality, self-efficacy and so on), as well as the type of product.

While the basic concepts of message framing are relevant to media psychology, there are several shortcomings of the literature that make it less useful than it might seem. To begin with, it is trapped within the same 'wrong model' of advertising that was picked apart in Chapter 4, assuming that adverts consist of easily interpreted messages and that all frames can be categorized according to a simple binary (gain/loss, or whatever). As explained previously, modern advertising is far too complex for such simplistic theories to be useful.

Like many social psychological theories, message framing suffers from its apparent virtues. It is essentially a **paradigm** that has become popular because it lends itself to experimentation. In the classic message framing study, participants are presented with the same message, typically a paragraph in the researchers' questionnaire, with a few words changed to manipulate the framing variable, for example to make it a gain or loss frame. Where do we encounter such messages in the real world? Social psychologists deliberately ignore these details in order to construct basic-level theory. It is the job of applied psychology to make them relevant.

◉ Media framing

At the same time that social psychology developed the concept of message framing, researchers in other social sciences, particularly communication, journalism and political science, were more interested in real-life framing: the actual business of presenting topics in the media. Over the decades, framing has acquired an enormous literature, so vast that some commentators have argued that the term itself is no longer useful because it encompasses too diverse a range of approaches and methods.

Probably the best definition of framing comes from one of the leading experts, Robert Entman, who says that frames 'introduce or raise the salience or apparent importance of certain ideas, activating schemas that encourage target audiences to think, feel, and decide in a particular way' (Entman, 2007, p. 165). Other authors have characterized frames as 'interpretive packages' (Gamson and Modigliani, 1989), or as convenient short cuts for understanding (Scheufele, 1999).

Either way, the basic idea is that the frame is constituted by the combination of various elements of media. For example, the basic elements of a newspaper story consist of a headline, one or more photographs (with captions), and the basic text of the article, sometimes split into subsections with subheadings. Figure 9.1 contains an adaptation of a typical news story from a UK tabloid newspaper, illustrating some of these elements.

We can see that much interpretative work is done by the basic elements. The headlines and captions serve to introduce the two leading characters in the drama, a 'mum' called Michelle and a 'maniac' or 'lunatic' who has assaulted her by hurling a brick at the windscreen of her car. As it turns out, no one has yet been charged with this terrible crime, and in fact even the sex of the culprit has to be inferred by the police ('we must catch *him*'). The important point about framing is that, while the basic elements are free-standing, the arrangement of them is not an accident. The paper has deliberately chosen to frame this as a crime story rather than, say, a medical drama, as we can see by the byline

MUM MAIMED BY BRICKS MANIAC
Hit at the wheel
By JOHN FARLEY, Crime Reporter

A Mum of four will have to have extensive facial surgery after a mindless thug hurled a brick through the windscreen of her car.

Michelle Armitage, 41, was nearly killed when the missile fractured her skull.

She may yet lose the sight of an eye, say consultants, who were last night planning how to rebuild her shattered face.

Her Ford Fiesta – with her two youngest children on board – left the road and crashed into a garden fence.

The youngsters escaped serious injury and helped save their mum's life, police said.

Her son, 12, ran to get help from a nearby house in Bedworth, Warwickshire, where the attack took place. And her daughter, 11, stayed with her until medics arrived.

Michelle, who also has a daughter, 15, and a son, 16, was stable in intensive care last night.

Her former husband Alan said: 'Thank God she's still here with us. It was a close shave.'

'I'm so proud of the kids. They must have had a terrible shock, seeing her with those injuries.'

Cops warned that this is the fourth time that the lunatic has struck this month. On the same stretch of road three other vehicles have had their windscreens smashed.

Police said: 'We must catch him before he kills someone.'

Figure 9.1 Newspaper story: mum maimed by bricks maniac
Sources: Based on an article from *The Sun* (29/11/03): see Giles and Shaw (2009) for original

given to the 'crime reporter', although the first three paragraphs of the text are devoted to the surgical and anatomical details of the situation.

Of course, the story in Figure 9.1 is presented out of context: the original contained a picture of a car with a smashed windscreen at the top, and a small picture of the victim underneath the headline. Furthermore, on the day this story ran, it would have appeared in a specific section of the newspaper, alongside other (possibly related) stories, adverts, cartoons and references to other material in that day's edition. The placement of related stories and adverts is deliberate. You would not usually find an advert for a film appearing in the sports pages. Very often the simple placement of a story does the same framing work as the byline in Figure 9.1.

So far, I have concentrated solely on print media – newspapers – as opposed to broadcast media such as radio and television. Here, framing is accomplished by slightly different elements (sound effects or live video footage), and headlines themselves play a much lesser role. But story placement is equally important: where a story occurs in a bulletin plays an important part in framing, for example later items in a news programme generally have a lighter touch, or may form part of a specific section like sports or arts.

👁 Cognitive aspects of framing

We will return to the bricks maniac shortly, but in the meantime you might well be wondering what is *psychologically* important about whether a story is framed as a crime drama or a medical drama. To appreciate the relevance of perspective, we need to go back to some research from cognitive psychology in the 1970s, when several studies explored the effect that perspective-taking had on readers' comprehension of stories.

In their most well-known study, Anderson and Pichert (1978) presented participants with a description of the contents of a house and its residents, which included 72 details such as a leaking roof, a new bicycle, the fact that the house was empty at certain times, and that there was a rare coin collection stashed away. Participants were asked either to read the text from the perspective of a potential home buyer or a burglar, and were then asked to recall as many details of the property as they could. 'Prospective buyers' recalled significantly more items relating to property ownership, such as the leaking roof, while 'burglars' recalled significantly more of the valuable items, such as the new bike and the rare coins.

By implication, then, we could say that *Sun* readers' understanding of Michelle's nightmare experience will lead them to come away from the story with an ardent desire to catch and punish the bricks yobbo rather than a concern for Michelle's forthcoming surgery. If, however, the story had been framed as a medical drama, the inferences about the attacker might be substituted by more information about her operation, maybe even an interview with one of the surgeons involved, previous outcomes of such procedures and so on.

Staying with 1970s' cognitive psychology, we can see a good example of how framing works by reference to a series of studies conducted by Bransford and Johnson (1973), who demonstrated the importance of an interpretative frame for making sense of information. They read out a set of sentences containing around 14 'idea units' but without any textual inferences to link them together. They then asked participants to recall as many of the ideas as they could. Half of the participants were given a picture to look at during the listening phase, which depicted a man with a guitar serenading a woman from the bottom of a tower block. These participants, on average, recalled 8 of the 14 ideas, while those who had nothing to go on but the text were only able to recall 3.6.

While no newspaper item is ever quite as bizarre as the text in this study, the visual impact of a photo can have a profound impact on the way readers approach the accompanying text. At the height of the 1984 miners' strike in Britain, right-wing tabloid *The Sun* set up a front cover with a picture of left-wing miners' leader Arthur Scargill saluting his striking colleagues beneath the headline 'Mine Fuhrer'. The intention, witty pun apart, was to draw a parallel between Scargill and Adolf Hitler and further discredit him among the paper's working-class readership. They never got to find out if it worked: the paper's printers, in a gesture of solidarity with a fellow trade union, refused to cooperate, so the cover had to be withdrawn at the last moment.

◉ Framing and behaviour: the example of MMR

One of the most powerful 'media effects' in recent history is the MMR controversy that gripped the UK media during the late 1990s and early 2000s. In the early part of this period, the UK government announced that the National Health Service was to start offering a vaccination for children that combined three previously separate 'jabs' – inoculating children against measles, mumps and rubella (German measles).

Just as surgeries had begun to administer the new MMR vaccination, an article was published in *The Lancet*, a prestigious medical journal, that reported a possible link between the combined vaccination and an unusually high incidence of both autism and bowel disease. It was a small sample, and a one-off finding, but Andrew Wakefield, the author of the piece, had already contacted the media and soon newspapers were reporting the research amid a flurry of sensationalist headlines about the dangers of MMR. As time went by, more and more studies were published that failed to replicate Wakefield's original research. Needless to say, none of these attracted anything like the same headlines, usually appearing as minor news items tucked away in the inside pages. However, the damage had been done: worried parents throughout Britain were choosing not to have their children submitted to the potential risk, however small, of the MMR jab. The seeds of doubt had been well and truly planted.

Over the following years, uptake of MMR fell from a peak of 92% in 1995–96 down to 80% in 2003–04, a figure that is considered dangerously low and a potential risk for a measles outbreak. In a survey conducted for the UK Economic and Social Research Council, Hargreaves et al. (2002) found that less than half of a broad sample would choose MMR above other vaccination options if offered, and 20% believed there was a link between MMR and autism. Since 2005, the incidence of measles in the UK has increased alarmingly; 2,349 cases were reported in 2007–08, almost as many as in the previous 11 years combined. MMR uptake has improved slightly, but it has not quite recovered to the pre-Wakefield era (Thompson, 2009). Sure enough, the same newspapers that had stirred up anti-MMR sentiments following Wakefield's initial research subsequently backtracked, claiming that 'the media' were to blame for sensationalizing the 'now-discredited' *Lancet* article. They assumed that their readers had forgotten they *were* those media.

Much is made of the need for the media to present a 'balanced' argument, particularly towards scientific findings, but, as a study by Clarke (2008) points out, the balance in this case was entirely unwarranted by the sheer weight of evidence *not* supporting a link between MMR and autism. In the Hargreaves et al. (2002) study, over half the respondents agreed with the statement that there was 'equal evidence of both sides of the debate', but there was no debate. The media had 'framed' the MMR controversy as a debate.

⊙ Media framing analysis

One of the reasons that framing has been criticized is that it lacks a coherent methodology – a formal set of procedures for carrying out an analysis. Rachel Shaw from Aston University and myself have attempted to resolve this problem by putting together an analytic process that we have called **Media Framing Analysis** (MFA) (Giles and Shaw, 2009). Although it is more flexible than most research methods, it consists of a series of stages that researchers need to take into account when carrying out a framing study:

1 Identifying the story
2 Identifying character
3 Analysing narrative form
4 Analysing language use
5 Making generalizations
6 Final analysis.

I will address each of the stages in turn, but the first thing you will need to consider is what kind of scale you want to address. Are you examining frames across a big dataset, for example several years' worth of press coverage? Or are you going in depth on a narrow topic? The former approach might give you hundreds of articles to analyse, possibly requiring some statistics, while the latter might be more suited to a more discursive, qualitative study. Either way, you will need to decide where you're going to get your data from, and how you're going to search for the relevant material.

Identifying the story

What makes a story a story? Where does it come from? As a first step in a framing analysis, this one would seem too obvious to be worth taking, but as psychologists we must be careful not to simply assume that topics arrive at the news desk as fully formed entities. Topics such as road rage, happy slapping and asylum seekers are first and foremost media phenomena; they come to life through repeated use by social commentators and journalists. It is highly likely that the researcher will already have a clear topic in mind when they embark on a framing study, but, even so, you will need to discover what exactly generates the articles you have selected for analysis.

The analyst's first step in MFA, then, is to identify the source of each news item, and the way we do this is by identifying the **news peg**. This is the peg on which the story hangs: it could be a press release, the publication of a report or book, or a statement made by a government minister. Ultimately, it is the reason the news story was written in the first place.

Over the course of several news stories on the same topic, common news pegs might emerge. In our work on voluntary childlessness (why certain people choose not to have children), we identified a variety of news pegs that generated articles in our survey of two decades' worth of UK press coverage. Table 9.1 provides the full list.

1	Announcements by 'childfree' organizations, such as the British Organisation of Non-Parents and Kidding Aside (The British Childfree Association) (n = 10)
2	Announcement by the Bishop of Rochester about childless couples (n = 7)
3	Changes in tax law for couples with children ('pro-parent policy') (n = 5)
4	Publication of the book *Baby Hunger* (Hewitt, 2002) (n = 8)
5	Other publications of books, and TV appearances by authors of books, about being childfree or childless (n = 20)
6	Publication of various academic or market research studies on childlessness (n = 67)
7	Other (n = 11)

Table 9.1 News pegs identified in articles about voluntary childlessness
Source: Giles et al., 2009

One other important consideration at this point is to sort your articles or news items (don't forget, you can do this type of research with TV news as well as print or online news) into meaningful categories. Too many framing studies in social science ignore the contextual origins of their data, but there are huge differences between brief, supposedly impartial, news reports (e.g. on the front page of a newspaper) and longer, in-depth features or commentary articles such as columns, which are often highly subjective and have a celebrity name and picture at the top.

If you've used an online database to search for your articles, much of the contextual information will be removed, so you will need to check from the information given whether you need to consider the item separately from others – many articles retrieved through databases are readers' letters, which are not really suitable for a framing analysis.

Identifying character

News stories, like any stories, are populated with a cast of characters. Right from the start of your study you can begin building a cast list (or 'dramatis personae') of all the people mentioned in each article. Soon you will find some interesting patterns – the same individuals will reappear, cited by different sources, mentioned by different authors. For instance, in our research on older mothers, we found frequent mention of 'Britain's oldest mum', a woman from Sussex who was repeatedly referred to by journalists even though she had nothing directly to do with the 'news pegs' triggering the stories. Journalists seemed to be queuing at her door for quotes relating to the research discussed in the articles.

There are usually more characters in a news story than meet the eye. In the bricks maniac story (Figure 9.1), it is possible to identify the following cast list:

- Bricks maniac/lunatic/thug
- Michelle Armitage
- Medical consultants
- Cops/police
- Michelle's daughters (aged 11 and 15)
- Michelle's sons (12 and 16)
- Medics
- Alan (Michelle's ex-husband).

The characters in any set of news items will tell us a lot about the way the articles are framed. While it is not surprising to find various legal and medical personnel in the article, much emphasis is placed on the various members of Michelle's family. A man named Alan, referred to as Michelle's former husband, is quoted, although not involved with the incident directly. A second son and second daughter are also mentioned, even though they appear to be uninvolved. These fringe characters do little apart from help to reinforce Michelle's role as a mum (and ex-wife), with numerous dependants who are particularly concerned for her welfare. So while the overall frame is that of a crime drama, there is a secondary frame – that of family drama – that arguably might not have been used if the victim of the crime had been, say, a single unmarried man.

The important task for the analyst, when examining characters, is to try and work out which characters the audience is invited to identify with. As discussed in Chapter 6, the function of identification serves to bind audiences into parasocial relationships with the characters (assuming they don't already exist, as in the case of celebrity news stories). Clearly, the reader of this story is most likely to identify with Michelle, or possibly her ex-husband, depending perhaps on their own gender.

Analysing narrative form

Much of the framing work, particularly in a longer feature item in a newspaper, magazine or on television, may relate to the way in which the overall narrative of the item is structured. Given that we are dealing with stories here, the style of the storytelling is important. We can refer here to Vladimir Propp's (1928/1958) classic analysis of folk tales, in which he argued that all stories can be broken down into a relatively small set of basic stories pitting heroes against adversaries, overcoming challenges, rescuing damsels in distress, dealing with enemies in disguise and so on.

For an illustration, let's look at some of the early coverage of the MMR controversy in the longer feature article presenting Andrew Wakefield's side of the story:

> His story begins in Canada in the late 1980s, where he had been working as a transplant surgeon. He became dissatisfied with chopping out pieces of diseased bowel and wanted to know what triggered the disease process in the first place. One freezing night, drinking a pint of Guinness in a bar, he had an inspiration. What if inflammatory bowel disease was not a bowel disease at all, caused by bacteria in the gut, but a vascular diseased caused by damage to the blood supply to the gut wall? He returned to England 'in something of a crisis' and set to work at the Royal Free Hospital, north London, to test his hypothesis. (**The Independent, 3 March 1998**)

In this article from *The Independent*, Wakefield perfectly fits Propp's figure of the hero in a far-off land, returning home to do battle with his enemies, who turn out to be both the medical establishment (sceptical about his theories), and the UK government, trying to fob off MMR on their citizens. Here, Wakefield is the lone pioneer, struggling with the conventional limitations of his job as a surgeon, driven by the challenge (or even 'crisis') of solving a thorny medical conundrum.

In addition to the narrative form this extract takes, we can also detect certain literary conventions. The **turning point** is a classic narrative device that grows out of the type of hero-based plot typical of Propp's theory. Wakefield's turning point comes in the form of a **eureka moment** in the unpromising surroundings of a Canadian bar. Notice the author's rhetoric; the freezing night, the pint of Guinness, all mundane details that frame the setting as banal and commonplace as possible, thereby deliberately reinforcing the brilliance of the hero's flash of inspiration. Setting his eureka moment in an intellectual debate with other scientists simply wouldn't have the same impact.

Analysing language use

This stage might seem obvious, but there are many ways of doing it, and ultimately how you analyse language will depend on the question you want your framing analysis to answer. With small datasets, you might prefer to draw on techniques like discourse analysis (Parker, 1992) or membership category analysis (Baker, 2004). This is fundamentally a question of identifying key parts of language like nouns and adjectives and trying to work out what rhetorical functions they achieve.

In our study on voluntary childlessness (Giles et al., 2009), we selected a subset of articles that had all been written in the first person describing the author's reasons for choosing not to have children. Our analysis involved looking for descriptions that revealed the 'angle' or frame, for example one author's claim that 'motherhood is not a job I ever wanted' suggests that the frame here is one of career choice. Elsewhere, multiple mentions of nappies and smells reinforced the idea of mothering as dirty work, implying a physical revulsion to the idea of bringing up children.

With larger datasets, and maybe with larger questions, you might need to employ some form of quantitative content analysis and even inferential statistical tests. In the most widely cited framing study of them all, Entman (1991) compared the US news coverage of two similar airline disasters that took place during the 1980s. In one case, an Iranian airline had been shot down by a US gunboat; in the other, a South Korean airline had been shot down by a Soviet plane. (To fill in a bit of history here: the Iranians are traditionally US enemies, as were the Soviet Union until the 1990s; while the South Koreans have always been US allies.) As part of a broader framing analysis, Entman examined the attributions of blame that were made by quoted individuals in various news stories on US television and in prestigious newspapers and magazines. He found that some quotes talked of the shooting as 'deliberate', while others described it as a mistake. Typically, the Iranian disaster was seen as a military cock-up (with the US doing the shooting), while the South Korean disaster attracted screaming headlines of 'Murder In The Air!' (with the Soviets at fault). But the attributions in the articles varied according to the nature of the source. In the *Washington Post*, for example, all 16 instances of 'mistake' in the South Korean disaster were made by spokespersons for the Soviets; and most instances of 'deliberate' in the Iranian disaster were given by Iranians.

Making generalizations

One of the most important aspects of the framing process is the way in which single news items are joined up with longer running stories and themes. These may be issues that are directly related to the article. The bricks maniac story, for instance, mentions that three other brick attacks on motorists have taken place in the same area in recent weeks, leading police to conclude that the same individual is responsible.

However, generalizations may be less straightforward, and may be hinted at – allusions to other similar stories, or long-running issues that the news editors wish to use as interpretative **media templates**. For instance, many of our articles on older mothers tied the idea of delaying motherhood to 1960s' liberalism, a concept frequently cited in the conservative UK press to symbolize a turning point in British social history – typically, when 'things started to go downhill'.

Kitzinger (2000) has argued that media templates are useful devices for audiences to make sense of new information. Probably the most obvious example would be '9/11' or 'September 11', the mere mention of which generates a raft of shared ideas about security, terrorism, recent history and so on. It is therefore meaningful to talk about 'the world since 9/11', bringing into play a shared idea about increased security and anti-terrorism activity.

The generalization function of framing may just take the shape of juxtaposed reports, for example two stories of celebrities behaving badly placed side by side, leaving the reader to draw an obvious inference from one to the other.

Final analysis

Once you've gone through all the stages, you will be able to bring your analysis to a conclusion. Probably the best way of doing this is to identify a frame for each item in the analysis, build up an overall list of frames and try to reduce this to a manageable number for interpretative purposes.

For our voluntary childlessness (VC) study (Giles et al., 2009), we identified four dominant frames that captured most of the articles in the dataset. These were:

1 *Individual rights frame* (n = 50): VC presented as, fundamentally, a choice, often based on career interests or feminist ideals.

2 *Resistance frame* (n = 28): VC portrayed as resistance to social pressures to have children, characterized by disputes in the workplace (over leave for parenting activities and so on).

3 *Social change frame* (n = 24): VC framed as symbolic of broader changes in society, typically a move towards a more 'individualist' perspective.

4 *Personal frame* (n = 14): VC framed as a choice but primarily in the context of an individual life history, so not drawing on broader ideas of rights or social change.

Further analysis is, of course, possible, for example comparing different story sources, but this will depend on the specific research question. What, for example, is the psychological relevance of showing that some frames apply to some media outlets and not others?

While Media Framing Analysis is still in its infancy as a method, I hope that the ideas presented in this chapter will inspire readers to consider ways they might use media material as data for answering psychological questions.

⦿ Further reading

Reese, S.D., Gandy, O. and Grant, A. (eds) (2001). *Framing public life: Perspectives on media and our understanding of the social world.* Mahwah, NJ: Lawrence Erlbaum.

Chapter 10

Developmental psychology and the media

Introduction

This chapter concerns the role that media might play in developmental psychology and vice versa. Much of the research has been rather negative in assuming that children are incapable of understanding the complexities of television, and a key area of research concerns the age at which children are able to distinguish fantasy from reality. However, this is not a straightforward matter, and there are many instances of adult failure to apply logic and rationality to everyday life, while children's explanations of televisual phenomena may be sorely underestimated. I end the chapter with a brief discussion of how television may actually help to socialize children rather than simply teach them formal information like numeracy and literacy.

Traditional and contemporary approaches to children and media

We have already encountered a number of studies about children and media in this book, notably in Chapters 2–5, where children were seen as the passive victims of various negative media effects, from violence to advertising to 'thin media'. Much of the concern about negative media effects is driven by fears about the vulnerability of children to media effects in general, but, as discussed in Chapter 3, these derive from confusion about how these effects are realized. It is argued that, up to a certain ('magic') age, children are too young to understand media, to tell the difference between fantasy and reality, to realize when they are being sold to and so on. But does this make them more or less vulnerable to media effects?

One argument is that the media acts as a 'window on the world', so that when children watch, let's say, a Bugs Bunny cartoon, they believe that somewhere there really *is* a talking rabbit that munches carrots while being relentlessly pursued by a funny little man with a shotgun called Elmer Fudd, or perhaps that the characters inhabit the interior of the television set. This seems to be the position adopted by many media violence researchers in assuming that children imitate cartoon violence in the same way that Bandura's child participants imitated adult models in the laboratory (Chapter 2). But when children 'realize' that Bugs Bunny is a make-believe character, do they become invulnerable to its influence? If so, millions of dollars have been unwisely invested in media violence research on undergraduate subjects.

Generally speaking, most psychological research has been based on the assumption that traditional media, such as television, can only have harmful effects on children, from which children should be sheltered, or at least have a parent on hand to 'mediate' the effects. The one exception is the research on *Sesame Street*, which acknowledges that television may have a role in educating children, if only in areas like literacy and numeracy. However, research on new media has generally been much more positive; indeed, there is reason to believe that educationalists have placed too much faith in the educational potential of the Internet. But might media have beneficial social effects as well?

In this chapter I will try to unravel these issues by looking at theories from developmental psychology, and discuss how, over time, children become fully competent media users or not.

The great fantasy–reality debate

One of the most contentious topics in developmental media psychology concerns the supposed ability of children – at some 'magic' age – to fully discriminate between fantasy and reality when it comes to media. This, it seems, is such an important skill to acquire that it underpins much of the thinking about the harmfulness of media effects and the kind of legal restrictions placed on media producers and advertisers. But how can we tell when this developmental stage has been passed? And how meaningful is the **fantasy–reality distinction** anyway?

Throughout the ages, children have been encouraged to inhabit fictitious worlds where they are entertained through fairy stories and fables full of unbelievable and preposterous characters and events. Animals that talk, wardrobes that lead into a fantasy world, mirrors that talk back, witches and magicians that transform people into pumpkins and frogs to princesses. Most cultures have rich traditions of children's literature or oral storytelling that passes from generation to generation, and ever since the birth of radio and television, a vast array of fantastic characters and shows have been created for children. As adults, we delight in the fascination and pleasure that children take in pretend play and make-believe.

One glance at the developmental psychology literature, however, and the bubble bursts. Children's love of pretence and fantasy is seen as a cognitive deficit, a juvenile stage that they pass through as their brains mature and they begin to base their thinking around hard rationalism. Fairy castles are left to crumble into ruins as fully operational adolescents organize their worlds according to reason and logic.

Much of the research on the fantasy–reality divide has relied on children's answers to researchers' questions about the nature of media. How do the little people get into the television set? They're lowered in on a rope, of course. What would happen to a box of popcorn if you turn the TV upside down? It will spill all over the floor (see Flavell et al., 1990). There is a long, rich tradition of developmental psychologists asking children absurd questions, such as 'Is milk bigger than water?', and then registering their answers as evidence of feeble logic (see Hughes and Grieve, 1980).

My point here is this: if *you* were asked to describe how we come to see little people in a television set, or how a computer-generated character somersaults across the screen, how close would *your* explanation come to the 'reality' of cathode ray tubes, electromagnetic waves and pixels? Where does an intelligent adult with limited understanding of physics begin, let alone a child? In one study (Dorr et al., 1980), 10–year-old children were assumed to believe in the reality of cartoons because they were unable to produce a sophisticated account of the mechanics of animation. An alternative argument is that many children's charmingly naive explanations of televisual phenomena actually display considerable ingenuity and are firmly rooted in rationalism.

Furthermore, as Woolley (1997) and others have argued, adults are equally prone to failing the fantasy–reality distinction as children. If, between ages 11 and 14, we all reach Piaget's formal operational stage, how come adults cry when they see a fictional character dying in a romantic film? Or send inappropriate letters to fictional characters on television? Or berate soap actors for the behaviour of the characters they play? Or cross their fingers when they hope for a good outcome? Or take a lucky mascot to a football game? Or refuse to sit in seat 13 on an aeroplane, despite the fact that the plane has 200 seats and their own bad luck is therefore responsible for the welfare of the other 199 passengers?

Real, really real, or just pretend?

Developmental psychologists have struggled for decades to find a valid means of assessing children's understanding of fantasy and reality. Increasingly, researchers have begun to examine language use, particularly in relation to terms like 'real' and 'pretend'. As Bunce and Harris (2008) explain, much of the time children confuse 'real' with 'authentic', rather than taking 'real' to imply the concrete existence of a phenomenon. So a child can fail to be a real fairy because she lacks the correct costume, but the question of whether fairies exist per se is not resolved by the use of the word 'real'. Of course, such linguistic ambiguities cause no end of difficulties when we come to consider media. Is Bugs Bunny a real rabbit? Of course he isn't, he's a cartoon rabbit. Does this make him any less real? (See Woolley, 1997, for more dilemmas of this kind.)

If Bugs Bunny were the only fantasy–reality puzzle for children to solve, we might conclude that children have difficulty separating a single fictional world from real life. But in any week a child might be invited through storybooks and television screens to enter dozens of fictional worlds. For example, do Batman and SpongeBob SquarePants inhabit the same fictional world? Does Batman think that SpongeBob SquarePants is real? Can Batman touch Robin? Skolnick and Bloom (2006) posed these questions to a group of adults and a group of 4- to 6-year-old children and found that, on some questions, both groups showed full understanding of the separateness of the Batman and SpongeBob SquarePants worlds. Imputing rational cognition to Batman is, however, not quite the same thing as separating fantasy from reality. Indeed, one might argue that granting an independent mind to Batman constitutes a failure to recognize the distinction; after all, Batman only 'thinks' what his scriptwriter provides him with.

In another study, Weisberg and Bloom (2009) demonstrated children's ability between ages three and five to manipulate and keep separate different pretend worlds: a wooden block represents a pillow to one puppet character but something else to a second character and so on. Other studies of **pretend play** (see Harris, 2000) have found that children are very good at switching between fantasy worlds, or, at least, fantasy roles, without hopelessly confusing them. This is just as well, since children's media demand an ability to manipulate symbols and process multiple layers of fantasy.

An example of how complex this can become is provided in two studies by Emmison and Goldman (1996, 1997), who produced a finely detailed analysis of *The Sooty Show*, a children's programme that for many decades was an institution within British television. Sooty is a yellow bear glove puppet who has never uttered a word in over 50 years; instead he appears to whisper into the ear of the show's presenter, who then relays his comments to the audience. Alternatively, one of Sooty's fellow puppets provides their own interpretation, most notably Sweep, a dog, who, like Sooty, cannot speak but communicates via a series of prosodic squeaks, that is, with the same rhythm as the intended speech. The only long-running puppet in the show that 'speaks' is Soo, a female panda.

Emmison and Goldman's analysis effectively dismantles the show into its fantasy and reality components. First, the bizarre interactional network is scrutinized in order to demonstrate how the non-speaking puppets enter into the conversation as perfectly competent communicators through the facilitative role of the presenter. Furthermore, the symbolism of the puppets is multilayered. On the one hand, the viewer has to believe they are animate, or 'alive', since they appear to move autonomously, even though we know a puppeteer has his hand up their bottoms; on the other hand, they are supposed to represent animals, so Sooty will occasionally do bear-like things and Sweep dog-like things. Thus they are neither real creatures nor are they real animals.

Just to complicate matters further, there are frequent moments in the show where Sooty and the others adopt roles that are fundamentally human; for instance in one series, they perform the duties of staff in a hotel, requiring them to carry out all kinds of professional activities. At the same time, they continue to slip in and out of their animal identities. In one scene, where, in a further transformation, they are pretending to be waiter and customer in a restaurant, Sweep orders sausages and attempts to eat them under the table. The fact that young children follow and enjoy such complicated role-switching suggests that they are capable of juggling the demands of different levels of pretence and symbolism.

Narrative and children's understanding of media

It would seem that the cognitive complexity of children's media should be out of all proportion to their immature neural architecture. So how do they juggle all these symbols, disguises, and imaginative twists and turns? One answer lies in the importance of narrative in children's (and adults') understanding of fictional worlds.

In *The Sooty Show*, no matter how many symbolic transformations the characters undergo, the action and dialogue are never anything less than *naturalistic*. Indeed, much of the interaction is highly reminiscent of the kinds of conversations held between adults and children. For this reason, Emmison and Goldman (1996, 1997) talk of the puppets being linguistically constituted as children: the presenter tells them off for messing around, while they conspire behind the presenter's back to carry out some mischievous prank. In many of the sequences, the presenter is teaching the puppets some new skill or activity (sport, music, or whatever), much in the way that a parent might.

The point here is that each episode of *The Sooty Show* falls back on a story, or narrative, that is familiar to the child audience, and the same is largely true of most children's television, even in its most bizarre manifestations. The fantasy figures may look like nothing on earth, but they all speak good English, or whatever language is shared by the audience, and are familiar with the cultural details of the viewers.

One of the most important skills for young children to acquire when using media is an understanding of its formal features. Early in life they are able to distinguish different programme genres in television – what the adverts are, what a news bulletin looks like, what segment of broadcasting 'belongs' to them (children's television) – along with the conventions of programming, such as theme tunes and title sequences. These, like repeatedly screened adverts, are often the most popular elements of children's programmes because they are predictable, and children often join in with the jingles and slogans (Palmer, 1986).

Likewise, certain programmes have repetitive sequences built in. An older example from British television is the 1960s' puppet drama *Thunderbirds*, in which the various rockets emerge from the bowels of Tracy Island as the superficial landscape of palm trees and swimming pools glides away, and the characters travel through various chutes and passageways in order to board the engines. These elongated sequences might seem tedious to an adult audience but are loved by children because they learn the order of events, bringing an element of control and assurance to the viewing situation.

◉ Theory of mind and socialization

The final part of this chapter concerns the possibility that media may teach children more than numbers and language and that they may have an important social function. It might seem surprising to claim that children are unable to attribute psychological qualities to television characters, but this was the conclusion reached by Bearison et al. (1982). Their study was based on **Piaget's stage theory of cognitive development** (Piaget and Inhelder, 1969), in which children are said to pass through four stages of cognitive sophistication as they move into adolescence.

Bearison et al. (1982) selected three age groups of participants, which roughly corresponded to Piaget's preoperational stage (5–6 years), concrete operational (7–10) and formal operational (11–14):

- in the preoperational stage, the child is entirely egocentric
- in the concrete operational stage, they reason only on the basis of personal experience
- only at the formal operational stage is abstract reasoning possible.

The authors showed the children a short clip from a daytime soap opera and then asked them to describe the sequence of events. In line with Piagetian theory, the youngest children described just the physical settings and superficial aspects of the behaviour; while the concrete and formal operational groups were able to go beyond these and discuss the thoughts and feelings of the characters. They also produced many more statements about the action, so it is likely that the younger participants were held back by their lack of vocabulary.

Nevertheless, in other studies, researchers have found young children performing quite extensive psychological analyses of fictional characters.

Babrow et al. (1988) found that they provided more abstract psychological descriptions of children appearing on television than they did of their own friends. It is true that the scripted nature of media material, and the privileged insight that viewers have into characters' interior worlds, makes it relatively easy for us.

One aspect of children's media that has been somewhat underexplored is the contribution it might make to the development of **theory of mind** (Premack and Woodruff, 1978). Theory of mind (ToM) is the ability to impute mental states to others and use this information to predict their behaviour; in other words, the ability to become a psychologist. It is said to be the fundamental deficit in autism, and has been widely studied, using ingenious experimental designs where children are asked questions about the thoughts of various puppets, itself a leap into the world of pretence, but one that seems to have been conveniently ignored by researchers. Several authors have argued that ToM is achieved earlier in children with more social opportunities, such as later-born siblings in large families (Perner et al., 1994), and others have argued that social and cultural factors are important influences (Feldman, 1992).

We still await the first study to explore ToM acquisition in relation to media, but one interesting twist on the standard experimental procedure was provided by Rosen et al. (1997). These authors chose to present children with a ToM scenario not in a laboratory construction using unfamiliar puppets and situations, but from an episode of *The Pink Panther* cartoon. In this sequence, a hunter is chasing a bird, which, having evaded the hunter, disappears into a cave. The children were then asked where the hunter will look for the bird. A child who has yet to acquire ToM might answer that he would look in the cave, because they fail to realize that the hunter could not know that that is where the bird has gone. Most (56%) of the three-year-olds in the study said that the hunter would look in the cave. This is to be expected, since the same children had already failed two traditional ToM tasks. But the percentage failure rate in those two tasks was much higher – 81 and 86%. By age five, half the children were still failing the traditional ToM tasks, but almost all (94%) passed *The Pink Panther* test.

There are several ways of interpreting this finding. One could argue that young children have better theory of mind skills than developmentalists have credited them with, and it just requires more meaningful material to bring these skills to the fore. It is also possible that children who partake in a lot of fictional media have encountered more and more

ToM-style situations like *The Pink Panther* one and have begun to under-stand the conventions – whether they apply them socially and spontane-ously is another matter. Either way, this study indicates that there is potentially much more research that could be carried out exploring chil-dren's socialization and their use of media.

Further reading

Hodge, B. and Tripp, D. (1986). *Children and television: A semiotic approach*. Cambridge: Blackwell.

New Media

Section summary

The last section of the book is dedicated to technological forms that have emerged during the past couple of decades (1990–2010), representing probably the biggest expansion of media in history. Lording it over them all is the Internet, introduced in Chapter 11, which has grown so rapidly and in such diverse ways that people have almost stopped referring to 'the Internet' per se and refer instead to its relevant constituent parts (social networking) or individual websites that constitute phenomena by themselves (*eBay* and so on). Chapter 12 looks in depth at several 'new media' phenomena that constitute subjects of study in their own right – social networking sites, online dating, and mobile phones.

Academia has a problem with new media, largely because the pace of change is so rapid that it becomes hard to keep up. Email looked like it was going to become the most important communication medium of the 21st century before SMS burst onto the scene and changed it all in a matter of months. Despite the pace of technological change, academic research continues to plod along at its old rate. It still takes years to conceive, plan, fund, conduct and publish a single study. While some online journals have speeded up the time it takes to report findings, the prestigious journals take as long as ever. Meanwhile, entire research projects might be devised one year and become redundant the next, as people simply stop using the technology.

Not surprisingly, then, research is still relatively thin on the ground when it comes to the psychological impact of new media. In these two chapters I will draw on academic research as and when relevant, but the phenomena themselves are just as interesting to psychologists as any presumed effects they might have on their users. It is through our use of the Internet that human nature is revealed, not the other way round.

Chapter 11

Psychology and the Internet

👁 Introduction

This chapter explores the impact that the Internet has made on psychological knowledge over the past couple of decades. It begins by discussing some of the social changes wrought by mass adoption of Internet technology and returns to some of the early concerns of psychologists to see how valid these are in modern online culture. In the second part of the chapter there is a discussion of several contemporary phenomena that have fascinated psychologists – Internet-based activity such as blogs, shopping and massive multiplayer games – and ends with an interesting study using 'avatars' as fake participants in a replication of the classic Milgram obedience studies.

👁 How the Internet has changed our lives

The following is a real-life conversation between my 79-year-old mother and a shop assistant:

> Assistant: Have you got one of our store cards?
> Mum: No, but it might be useful.
> Assistant: OK, I'll take down some details. Address? Telephone number? Email address?
> Mum: I don't have an email address. I don't own a computer.
> Assistant: Oh well, I'm afraid I can't issue a store card without that information.

UNIVERSITY OF WINCHESTER LIBRARY

It is already hard to imagine life without the Internet. So profoundly has it affected our lives that, like the car, it has become a vital component of everyday existence, to the point where we barely notice it as a separate entity. 'I'll just email you the documents.' 'We've run out of leaflets but all the info is on our website.' 'I'll load the photos onto my Facebook page.' 'Let's chat on Skype.' 'Can you tweet about your journey?' If the response to any of these statements/questions is 'Well, that's no good to me/I can't, I haven't got a computer', you run the risk of being ostracized from society.

What is more amazing than our helpless dependence on computers and their modems is the length of time it has taken for us to arrive at this situation. In 1995, very few people in the world had Internet access. Those of us in the academic world had office computers, and we were having fun sending one another emails and loading our photos onto university websites, but for most people the Internet belonged to the world of boffins and geeks. The majority did not even know how to turn a computer on.

A mere decade or two on, and we have all become boffins and geeks. And for those of us who are still struggling to locate the on switch, well, our two-year-olds can usually do the job for us. In historical terms, this transformation in society has taken place almost overnight. In 1999, every other news bulletin featured a story about someone who 'has just set up a website'. A year or so later, this was no longer news. Instead, there were endless stories about the revolution in online shopping, shortly to be followed by 'the bursting of the e-commerce bubble', as thousands of brand-new online businesses failed to compete with established retailers, who had, naturally, set up their own websites.

One of the earliest ideas about the Internet is that it would revolutionize food shopping because everyone would buy their food electronically. We would buy 'intelligent fridges' that automatically ordered a pint of milk when you started running low, and you would no longer need to pollute the atmosphere with car fumes every day and fight your way through crowds with your trolley in order to get your groceries. Contrary to all the predictions, in 2010 supermarkets have never been more crowded, at all times of the day and night. Instead of closing them down, they have made them bigger, selling far more than just food. They have opened up coffee shops. In 2009, market research company Mintel found that only 11% of the UK population regularly buys their groceries online. So what went wrong?

We might find the answer by returning to Marshall McLuhan, who we last met in Chapter 1, and his ideas of media creating their own needs rather than simply satisfying existing ones. While some old media phenomena simply updated themselves via the Internet, such as pornography, the real revolution in online shopping didn't involve groceries; instead, it took us back in time to the street market culture of bartering for goods in the form of *eBay*. Online shopping tended towards the exotic and the previously difficult to reach. Holidays used to have to be arranged either by endless telephoning or the help of a travel agent, but now we can search and book plane tickets, hotels and car hire with a few simple mouse clicks. The budget airline Ryanair now demands that all its passengers check in online before arriving at the airport. No computer? No seat.

👁 What is the Internet, anyway?

The Internet first emerged as a technology some time during the 1960s, when fears of nuclear war were at a peak, and the US military thought it would be useful to have some kind of communication system that would survive such a catastrophe. It was also felt important that this system was not under state control, which meant it could fall into the wrong hands. The first system was a network that linked together individual computers, known as ARPANET (Advanced Research Projects Agency Network), which was developed by the US military and then implemented in the university system – just four US universities in 1969, spreading to 37 by 1972.

Increasingly, the university network began to be used for interacademic communication. In the 1980s, a bulletin board called Usenet allowed people in different universities to post messages to each other. The year 1989 saw the birth of the **World Wide Web**, the system we use today to construct websites and communicate via cyberspace (hence the www at the start of website addresses). It formalized certain conventions, such as the use of **hypertext** (communication in the form of highlighted links). This was followed by the creation of browsers like *Netscape* and *Internet Explorer*, which enabled users to visit multiple websites, and search engines, like *Google*.

At the same time, email was developed as a separate function, and other means of communication became linked to the Web. These can be classified as either synchronous or asynchronous. **Synchronous communication** is instantaneous in the way that a telephone is – incorporating things like chat rooms, Skype and instant messaging. It can be verbal or written. **Asynchronous communication**, on the other hand, is always in the form of text, and there is a delay between posting a message and having others respond to it. This form of communication is most often seen on message boards or discussion forums linked to websites.

👁 Early research on the psychology of the Internet

It is hardly surprising that much of the research carried out in the 1990s about the Internet already seems ludicrously dated. But, as explained earlier, that is the price paid for such fast-moving changes in technology. It is interesting in its own right to see the sort of questions that troubled researchers in the early days of the uptake of a new medium.

Who uses the Internet?

Today, most of us have access to the Internet either through a workplace network or domestic computer with a modem. In 2006, it was estimated that 73% of Americans had an Internet connection that they used, rising to 89% among the 18–29 age group (Dittmar et al., 2007). Obviously, the question of who uses the Internet today no longer has the relevance of a couple of decades ago; instead, it is more instructive to ask why a small portion of the population doesn't use it – 'refuseniks' who choose to live their lives permanently offline. According to a 2009 survey by UK communications 'watchdog' Ofcom, 60% of UK homes and 61% of US households now have an Internet connection, while 42% of those that don't simply had no interest or failed to see a need for it.

What people use the Internet for has ceased to be a particularly interesting question, smacking as it does of the **functionalist** approach to media. This was, however, an approach taken by several early researchers, such as Ferguson and Perse (2000), who at least studied the Internet from a uses and gratifications perspective, albeit as an 'alternative' to television. Diary studies and questionnaires found that adolescents still preferred television as a way of relaxing and passing the time (after all, it requires less input from the user), but that the Internet had some entertainment purposes. Within a decade, however, the situation will have become unrecognizable, with teenagers using the Internet primarily as a social medium (see Chapter 12).

Internet addiction

During the 1990s in particular, there was a fear that people might become addicted to the Internet. Indeed, there were many stories in the media of relationships that had failed because one partner spent all night online, playing games or surfing the Web. Psychologists took this seriously enough to develop psychometric measures of Internet addiction. Young (1998) identified 400 users as 'internet dependent', with an average online time of 38 hours a week. Today, this might be a job requirement for some media researchers and other Web-based professions.

More recently, concern has switched from excessive use of the Internet per se towards preoccupation with specific types of website or network, such as social networking sites and multiplayer games. Generally speaking, there now seems to be far less concern about the actual hours spent online than on the nature of the activity; that is, what files people are downloading, what information people are communicating and so on.

Self and identity online

Perhaps the most interesting early Internet research was the most speculative. Entire books were devoted to the possibilities of the Internet for redefining the self, and using cyberspace as an 'identity laboratory' (Turkle, 1995; Wallace, 1999). What seemed most attractive about online identity was its non-visual quality. This seemed to imply that users would be liberated from their physical restrictions and free to select whatever kind of online identity they liked.

Today, this use of Internet technology is more likely to cause concern than celebration, after many news stories of paedophiles masquerading as adolescents in order to lure their online pals to offline meetings. Even in the early days, there was much concern about abuse of concealed identities, such as the well-known instance of the New York male psychiatrist who interacted online under the guise of a disabled woman and cultivated many online friends, who felt bitterly betrayed when he eventually chose to 'kill off' his alter ego (Bell, 2001).

Ironically, it is probably through the glorification of actual selves that the Internet has had its greatest successes, with the huge popularity of social networking and dating websites teeming with photographs of their users. These sites are dependent usually on users actually meeting offline before agreeing to award each other the status of 'friend' so they can gain access to their personal pages. Not much chance of any identity experimentation there.

However, there are ways in which the Internet has been beneficial for people with 'marginalized' identities. Many online communities have been developed whose primary goal is not social but informational, particularly in areas like mental health. The pro-ana community (see Chapter 5) relies largely on the fact that people with eating disorders cannot meet together offline, and it is probably the anonymity of the users that encourages many people to become involved.

One early study found that the anonymity of online interaction encouraged much more disclosure than would be possible in an offline situation (McKenna and Bargh, 1998). The researchers found that people often used online interaction as a way of rehearsing offline behaviour, for example gay users 'coming out' first online to cyberfriends, and this giving them the encouragement to come out offline too.

⊙ Contemporary Internet topics

As this century progresses, and the Internet has moved from a fascinating new social experiment to an indispensable tool for acquiring social competence, so academic interest has shifted away from earlier concerns towards more specialized fields of research. In 2010, the predominant topic of psychological interest is social networking sites, which will be dealt with at greater length in Chapter 12. In the remainder of this chapter, I will consider a few general topics of current interest.

Personality and Internet communication

While early studies of Internet users focused on what people used the Internet for, particularly as an alternative to old media (for entertainment purposes, information and so on), more recent research has focused on users' preference for online communication over offline social interaction. From the early days, psychologists have been interested in the way that the anonymity of online communication facilitates more personal disclosure compared, certainly, with face-to-face interaction (Joinson, 2003).

On the face of it, then, we might assume that the Internet has been a godsend for shy or socially awkward individuals. Some research on the personality of Internet users has partially supported this idea. In an adolescent sample, Peter et al. (2005) found that extravert individuals disclosed more and communicated more frequently, as one might expect, but that introverts were equally prone to disclose personal information if they were strongly motivated to use the Internet for communication purposes. In other words, if they had a preference for online communication due to shyness, they managed to overcome this once online. Nevertheless, the authors conceded that the Internet produces something of a 'Matthew effect' (as the rich get richer, the poor get poorer) in relation to social confidence. In the long run, the Internet may have rather been a godsend for socially skilled, highly disclosing extraverts, simply by offering them a means of interacting with more people, more frequently. In a study across several age ranges, Madell and Muncer (2006) found that use of the Internet for communication purposes was not correlated with social interaction anxiety or social phobia, although socially phobic individuals expressed a slight preference for using chat rooms.

Running slightly counter to these findings is Marcus et al.'s (2006) finding that personal website owners tended to be somewhat introverted. However, this study was conducted just before the explosion of social networking sites, and related to the creation of websites that were solely geared towards publicizing the individual owner (or their family), rather than being linked to a specific activity, field of interest or professional purpose.

Blogs

Towards the end of the 2000s, blogs (short for 'weblogs') had become a worldwide Internet phenomenon. A **blog** is typically defined as 'a website which contains a series of frequently updated, reverse chronologically ordered posts on a common web page, usually written by a single author' (Hookway, 2008, p. 92). However, the term has become used rather more widely, so that what a website owner might once have called an 'online diary' is now automatically referred to as a 'blog'. For this reason, it is impossible to estimate the number of blogs that exist at any one time in cyberspace, and global figures have been cited anywhere between 2.8 million and 100 million. Equally confusing is the term 'blogosphere', which is liberally bandied about by bloggers and cultural commentators but misleadingly conjures up the concept of an online community. In practice, the term 'blogosphere' tends to be used simply to describe that portion of cyberspace devoted to blogs, which may be why Hookway (2008) describes it as feeling like being in a 'black hole'.

If the term 'blogosphere' could be said to have any useful meaning, it is with respect to websites that exclusively host blogs, such as *Blogger* and *WordPress*. These blogs can deal with any topic, so they are usually categorized by subject – politics, music and so on. Some bloggers have become well known simply for their blogs, such as Salam Pax, 'the Baghdad blogger', who posted daily accounts of Iraqi life in the last days of Saddam Hussein's dictatorship. Most of the time they emanate from traditional sources – typically journalists, political commentators and so on, who have insider knowledge of their field and are paid to air their views. Today, even newspapers have blogs attached to their online editions that are authored by their staff. Even Salam Pax ended up becoming a journalist and writing for traditional newspapers.

For this reason, Chin and Hills (2008) are strongly critical of arguments that have been put forward to claim blogging as a form of political power that has been handed back to the people. Such claims include the idea that blogs have broken down the distinction between media users and producers (e.g. Marshall, 2004), and the distinction between media professionals and the public. Chin and Hills argue that most amateur bloggers are simply unable to devote the energy and commitment to their activities as professionals, and frequently abandon their blogs, while pro bloggers (celebrities, politicians and so on) are rarely influenced by amateurs.

Recently, the social gossip website *Twitter* has supplanted blogging for a lot of individuals, particularly media professionals, who can deliver instantaneous 'tweets' (brief comments about what the author is thinking or doing at that moment in time) rather than in-depth reflection. Psychological research on blogging or tweeting is sadly, at the time of writing, virtually non-existent.

Online buying

The world of **e-commerce** in 2010 is unrecognizable from that envisaged 10 years earlier, from online auction sites like *eBay* to specialist sites selling spare parts and obscure items, in addition to the giants of retailing and a handful of long-running online successes such as *Amazon*. Online retail sales for December 2009 in the UK reached £5.46 billion, a 17% rise from the previous year, although the proportion of total sales is still relatively small: in 2008 it was around 3.5% (Teather, 2009).

Initially, it was anticipated that the Internet would encourage people to shop more rationally, in that online buying would be largely instrumental – people targeting specific items, placing their order and then logging off. **Impulse buying** would be rare because Internet users would be less vulnerable to the kind of in-store sales techniques that persuade offline shoppers to part with their cash for unnecessary items (Burke, 1997). However, research on compulsive buying has found that its online incidence is broadly similar to that offline, between 10 and 17% of all online buyers compared with an offline figure of 13% (Dittmar et al., 2007).

Why have the supposedly more instrumental Internet shoppers yielded to temptation in the same way as those strolling down the high street? One argument is that the act of clicking a few buttons with a mouse does not feel like spending money in the same way as handing over cash or cards in a shop (Dittmar et al., 2004). However, this explanation could really only apply to the first generation of online shoppers – those whose buying habits have been formed offline. A more recent suggestion is that buying online satisfies the same psychological needs as offline: boosting self-confidence, enhancing mood, and making us feel good about ourselves (Dittmar et al., 2007). And, of course, marketing experts have got to work with links and pop-ups to tempt us down further avenues, so that the online environment recreates that same seductive store display as you would find in the local supermarket.

Games

I covered video games in Chapter 3, albeit largely in the context of their levels of violence and supposed effects on users. Games in general have become an increasingly important topic in media psychology, as much because of their global prevalence as anything. As discussed previously, the past decade or so has seen a revolution in the games industry, overtaking films and music in terms of revenue, but serious research on game playing is treated with suspicion, games being seen as essentially trivial and less worthy of consideration than entertainment in general.

All that has changed in the past decade, up to a point. There is now an academic discipline called game studies, or gaming studies, with its own journals and conferences (Gee, 2006). Many people call for games to be recognized as an art form in their own right; indeed, journalist Charlie Brooker (2009, p. 6) has described the video game as 'the most rapidly evolving creative medium in human history'. Concerns over children's use of games has tended to dwell on the antisocial implications of teenagers stuck in darkened bedrooms playing solo shoot–em–up games on a console, although in practice many video games require multiple players.

In addition to video games, there are now millions of Internet users worldwide who take part in what are called **MMORPGs** (Massively Multiplayer Online Role-Playing Games), which involve the participation of enormous numbers of contestants. By the end of 2006, *Second Life*, the most famous of these, had more than 1.7 million players (or 'inhabitants'), while *World of Warcraft*, a long-running fantasy world game, had a staggering 7.5 contestants (Utz, 2008), growing to 11 million by the end of 2009 (Walters, 2009). As with video games, the image of a computer user playing a fantasy online game conjures up an image of a lone figure in a bedroom late at night cut off from all social activity, whereas much of the enjoyment derived from MMORPGs comes from the social interaction with other participants, and many such games involve players operating in teams, 'guilds' or 'clans' (Klimmt and Hartmann, 2008). While some of these units are composed of offline friends, many involve the creation of new online relationships and so address social needs as well as entertainment ones.

◉ Relationships with virtual figures

Many scholars in areas like human–computer interaction, and, of course, the new discipline of game studies, have studied the relationship between Internet users and the figures that represent them in online environments. Many games require participants to design customized three-dimensional representations of human beings known as **avatars**, which then interact in the game according to the user's directions.

Some interesting studies have been conducted by communication experts on the similarities between avatar behaviour and interpersonal human behaviour. For instance, Yee et al. (2007) studied interaction between player representatives in *Second Life* and found that they mimicked many of the behavioural phenomena observed between humans. For instance, gender differences regarding interpersonal distance are replicated online, so that male avatars maintained longer distances from one another and maintained less eye contact. There was also, as in real life, a correlation between interpersonal distance and gaze avoidance for both sexes. This was measured by the researchers taking numerous snapshots or 'screen dumps' of the scenarios, which recorded information relating to the avatars and their users. They were then able to measure the angle of avatar eye gaze and relate this to the characteristics (gender and so on) of the players.

Is the player's relationship with their avatar a form of parasocial interaction? Not really, since because the player creates and controls the avatar, one cannot really be said to interact with an aspect of oneself. While it is perfectly reasonable to talk about parasocial interaction with other avatars and other figures in the game environment (Hartmann, 2008), a different concept is required to deal with player–avatar relationships. **Character attachment** describes the strength of connection felt between players and their avatars, and a measure of this has been found to predict both game enjoyment and the amount of time spent playing (Lewis et al., 2008).

One of the early theories about Internet communication was that the anonymity of online interaction would enable users to reinvent themselves to resemble anyone they liked – film stars, sports heroes, fantasy figures. On the contrary, it seems that we have an inbuilt predilection for seeing our own characteristics reflected. In one extraordinary study, Bailenson et al. (2006) conducted a survey of attitudes towards the rival candidates (George W. Bush and John Kerry) in the 2004 US presidential election, with Bush and Kerry's faces appearing at the top of the online questionnaire. In two-thirds of the questionnaires, the candidates' faces had been digitally morphed to resemble the respondents' faces (one-third with Bush, one-third with Kerry), although not to an extent that was noticed by the respondents themselves. When analysed, attitudes towards the candidates were significantly affected by this transformation, so if the picture of Bush looked a little bit like you, you were more likely to vote for him!

👁 Milgram revisited

The degree of affinity we have for digitally produced faces, and the equation of avatar behaviour with real-life behaviour, has opened up some fascinating possibilities for future psychological research. Slater et al. (2008) examined this by creating an online replication of the famous Milgram obedience study, in which human participants interacted with a female avatar. How much compassion, if any, would participants show towards a bunch of pixels masquerading as a human being?

As in the Milgram originals, participants were introduced to the 'learner', only of course this time they were not under the illusion that she was a fellow participant randomly allocated to the role. The procedure of the learning trials and the delivery of electric shocks were identical to the original experiment, conducted with the utmost seriousness by the researchers, and the onscreen avatar responded to the shocks in the same way as the Milgram confederates, crying out with pain and occasionally requesting the participant to stop. As one might expect, the majority (17 out of 23, or 74%) of participants delivered shocks to the avatar all the way to the highest level, compared to 62.5% in the Milgram studies (Milgram, 1974) . However, the general behaviour of participants demonstrated a remarkable similarity to those in the original experiments. Six of the participants who continued all the way to the highest shocks later said they had wanted to stop; several expressed concern for the participant, and delayed delivering the more powerful shocks. Electroencephalogram readings (of the electrical activity of the brain) indicated high stress levels in some participants. The very fact that six participants withdrew from the study before the end is itself a highly unusual occurrence in psychological research.

Some of the other Milgram phenomena were reproduced in the virtual study. For instance, the distance between 'teacher' and 'learner' was varied and closeness emerged as a significant factor in teachers' discomfort. In a second condition, the avatar was introduced onscreen at the outset but thereafter participants only heard her voice; more of these participants delivered high shocks, as had been the case when Milgram's human actor was out of sight. While several of the participants were familiar with the original studies, this did not have any significant impact on their behaviour in the experiment.

These findings provide convincing evidence for Hartmann's (2008) argument that we do indeed enter into parasocial interaction with avatars. The authors argue that the similarity with Milgram's findings indicates that the use of avatars can allow psychologists to return to the kinds of experimental designs that have long been outlawed, involving deception and other ethically dubious practices. Whether allowing participants to become distressed about the welfare of the avatar counts as ethically acceptable is another matter.

👁 Further reading

Joinson, A.N. (2003). *Understanding the psychology of internet behaviour: Virtual worlds, real lives*. Basingstoke: Palgrave Macmillan.

Chapter 12

Psychological issues in new media

⟨◉⟩ Introduction

This final chapter considers some of the issues explored by media psychologists in relation to three new media phenomena: online dating, social networking sites, and mobile phone communication.

⟨◉⟩ Online dating

Psychologists have long been interested in dating as a context for studying impression management and the construction of identity, for example in personal advertisements where individuals have limited space to present themselves. It is hardly surprising that traditional dating agencies quickly adopted the Internet in order to enhance advertisers' textual profiles, especially with the added benefit (or otherwise) of personal photographs. By the 21st century, exclusively online dating agencies had begun to appear, and these mushroomed rapidly in the following decade. By 2006, it was estimated that 74% of single Americans had used online sites as a means of finding a partner (Whitty, 2006).

Meanwhile, there has always been a tendency for Internet users to derive social benefits from online communication, and romantic liaisons have inevitably followed. Even in the 1980s era of bulletin boards, users met and dated following online communication, and chat rooms were frequently used for the same purpose (DeVoss, 2006). The early forms of MMORPGs (see Chapter 11), known as MUDs (multi-user domains), were hotbeds of social interaction; 77% of players had formed relationships through their participation, and a quarter of these were romantic in nature (Whitty, 2006).

Dating is one of those social phenomena that were envisaged as potentially liberating by early champions of the Internet because of the 'anonymity' that online communication offered its users. There may have been a brief period when individuals could have benefited from online relationships through constructing an online self that overcame the limitations of their offline selves, but early in the 21st century, the inclusion of pictures became almost obligatory for dating members and cyberspace was no longer a sanctuary for people who preferred to remain invisible yet benefit from online communication, except in specialized domains such as mental health communities.

Deception and betrayal in online dating

The two issues of most concern to online daters are honesty and fidelity. Although the inclusion of personal photographs has made it hard to lie about one's physical attributes, there are many other details that we might advertise that have only a fleeting connection with reality. For instance, we may credit ourselves with rather more educational or professional achievements than we have, or elaborate fantastically those that we have. Some half-truths may never be discovered, even in long-lasting relationships. Would your partner really check up to see if you own a copy of the highbrow novel you were claiming to be 'currently reading' when you first created your dating profile?

According to Gibbs et al. (2006), 80% of online daters are concerned that potential partners have misrepresented themselves to some extent. No doubt many of these concerns can be attributed to media reports of paedophile **grooming**, and occasional stories of couples communicating long distance for months and finally meeting only to discover that they look nothing like their pictures. However, in most cases, the deception involved is relatively minor, like name-dropping a cool book or film that you've actually not read or understood, or 'tweaking' certain vital statistics – a couple of inches on a man's height, a couple of pounds off a woman's weight and so on (Ellison et al., 2006).

Of course, it's difficult to establish whether people really are lying until you've seen the evidence in the flesh (as it were). New York-based researchers Hancock and Toma (2009) did just this, bringing 54 online daters into their laboratory and taking their photographs, and then getting a group of independent participants to rate the similarities between their 'actual' pictures and the photos posted on their dating profiles. They found at least one discrepancy in 47 of the dating site pictures, and that female pictures contained three times as many discrepancies as male pictures.

Raters based their similarity judgements on criteria ranging from age (is the person in the dating photo noticeably older than in the lab photo?) to physical attributes like skin and hair (presence of spots and so on), and photographic manipulations such as cropping and airbrushing. Age showed particular discrepancies for women; indeed, on further questioning, the female dating photos were on average 17 months old, compared with an average of 6 months for male photos. The authors interpret their findings in the light of evolutionary theories that claim that physical appearance and youthfulness are fundamental demands in heterosexual men's sexual selection (all the study participants were heterosexual).

Some caution should be exercised when interpreting these results, since participants were not instructed to scrub up specially for the study, and students tend not to spend too much time on hair and makeup prior to participating in psychology experiments. Dating photos, on the other hand, may reflect hours of painstaking preparation. Judges in the study were specifically instructed to ignore makeup and clothing, but to what extent is this feasible?

Cyberstalking

Although, of course, not restricted to dating sites, the prospect of being stalked in cyberspace by an undesired individual is something that must linger in the minds of anyone posting their picture and personal details on a website aimed at lovelorn singles. Finn (2004, p. 469) has defined **cyberstalking** as 'repeated threats or harassment by any kind of electronic communication that would make "a reasonable person" fear for their safety'.

While there is clearly a lot of this kind of activity taking place among close acquaintances in younger age groups, particularly by SMS or text (see the later section on mobile phones), dating website users are more likely to experience stalking from more remote unwanted suitors – either chancers trying their luck, or rejected dates bent on revenge. Sometimes this unwanted attention can escalate into highly unpleasant or even criminal behaviour, with victims being deluged with spam or junk email, abused (known as 'flaming'), being deliberately infected with an electronic virus, or even being subject to identity theft (Jerin and Dolinsky, 2006).

Social networking sites

Undoubtedly the online phenomenon of the late 2000s was the explosion of interest in **social networking sites** (SNS) across the world. It was a largely unforeseen trend, although in the early part of the decade, there were a number of websites with broadly similar aims, notably *Friends Reunited*, which hooked people up with former classmates. The site was blamed for splitting up several marriages before its broad appeal began to wear off; reminiscing about pranks in the back row of the biology class can only sustain a relationship for so long.

As mentioned previously, websites with mass usage have always fulfilled a social function of some sort – whether bulletin boards, multi-user games, or special interest websites of all kinds. However, it was assumed in the early days that online relationships would generally remain online, except for the odd burgeoning romance. The idea of a website that connected people living in the same geographical community took a long time to take root, and even in the early days the function of SNS was envisaged more remotely, as a means of connecting new people with shared interests, or connecting friends and relatives who were unable to meet face to face.

The rise of *MySpace* and *Facebook*

The two SNS that have come to dominate the Web are *Facebook* and *MySpace*, sites that enable users to construct a profile page with photographs galore, links to favourite media, personalized message boards with a host of interactive features, and various games and competitions that enable further communication. Perhaps most noteworthy of all is the **friending** feature that – particularly in *Facebook* – allows the user to restrict access to their profile to a select few (or many, in some cases) to whom the user has granted the status of 'friend'. The profile page records the current number of friends pertaining to each member, thereby introducing a further element of competition among some users.

By 2006, *MySpace* (which started in 2003) had acquired 20 million members and *Facebook* (which began in 2004) almost 10 million. The popularity of SNS among US students, and the dominance of the market by these two particular sites by 2007, can be seen in the fact that 87% of students in the study by Raacke and Bonds-Raacke (2008) had profiles on one or the other. In the UK, in 2007, 42% of young people aged 8–17 had a profile page on a site, rising to 55% for the older age group (Livingstone and Brake, 2010). Being a member of *Facebook* is no minor commitment: 60% of users in Gosling et al.'s (2008) study logged on to the site on a daily basis.

The Raacke and Bonds-Raacke (2008) study found that the vast majority (91%) of SNS members use the sites for maintaining existing social relationships, although over half said that they used them for making new friends (56%) or for locating old friends (54%). Livingstone and Brake (2010) obtained similar findings with their sample of British children and adolescents. One particularly appealing feature of *MySpace* was the members' ability to customize their home page and therefore exert considerable control over self-presentation, with 'pink candy stripes, glitter, angels, flowers, butterflies, hearts and more' (p. 2).

The friending feature of SNS has been the subject of some psychological interest, not least because there seems to be an element of competitiveness between members in relation to how many friends an individual can acquire. US research on this topic found large discrepancies between the number of *MySpace* friends teenage members claimed to have (a mean of 75) and the actual numbers recorded on the site (a mean of 27), although numbers over 100 are by no means uncommon (Livingstone and Brake, 2010).

How accurate are members' profiles? Given the distortion found in dating profiles by various researchers, one might expect a degree of fabrication in SNS profiles, albeit to a lesser extent since members are not out to attract an ideal partner so much as genuine friends; they are also handicapped by the fact that they already know most of their online 'friends' and can be easily 'outed' if they attempt to portray a false front. By comparing the 'Big Five' personality measures with the same measures estimated by a set of independent observers, Gosling et al. (2008) found that *Facebook* profiles were a pretty accurate representation of their owners' personalities. Extraversion in particular showed high concordance with raters' estimates.

Mobile phone communication

The final part of this chapter breaks away from the Internet itself to consider another highly successful 'new' medium, the mobile phone. **Cell phones** have a long history in telecommunications, but until the mid-1990s, they resembled house bricks, were prohibitively expensive and used largely in big business. Until the late 1990s, it would hardly be worth considering them within the scope of media psychology at all, since they differed little from ordinary **fixed-line (landline) telephones** in terms of their communicative function. Then, almost overnight, the whole communication field changed beyond recognition.

Mobile phones are, above all else, small – eventually pocket-sized – and priced within the reach of ordinary users. Initially, they were seen as useful additional devices for people away on business or in transit somewhere. Gradually, other features became popular, most notably the use of **SMS** (Short Message Service) or texting. By 2006, in the UK, **texting** had become a more popular means of communicating for young adults than speaking on a mobile phone (Devitt and Roker, 2009). Other features became popular, such as built-in cameras, which have themselves exerted enormous cultural influence, and the absorption of other new media such as email and World Wide Web access. Customized ringtones seemed to have appeared, utterly unforeseen, in the first half of the 2000s (Chesher, 2007). Increasingly, mobile phones have merged with the Internet, although they have evolved their own separate culture; the Internet connection is merely a hardware issue.

Unusually for a mass medium, mobile phones seemed to take off in Asia and Europe before they really established a presence among young Americans. In the rest of the world, they spread like wildfire. As early as 2002, global subscriptions to mobile phone companies had overtaken those for fixed lines, and each country was developing its own unique mobile phone culture. While British youngsters were busy texting one another to arrange a night out on the town, Indians were sending SMS prayers, Moroccan pilgrims were using their mobiles as an electronic compass to orientate themselves in the direction of Mecca, and Irish and Italian Catholics were receiving a daily 'thought' from the Pope's own Vatican texting service (Srivastava, 2005).

The culture around mobile phones is often hard to recognize, so caught up are we in the rituals and behaviours around them. Chesher

(2007) makes this point from an anthropological perspective while heading for a U2 gig in Australia. He describes how the interactional patterns of fans form a regular pattern – an exchange of 'where are yous?' and 'over heres' that constitute a form of 'recognition dance', culminating in the friends locating each other and displaying a gesture of greeting. In this way, media are incorporated seamlessly into our social worlds and help to create new forms of behaviour.

Social and emotional impact of mobiles

From a technological perspective, mobile phones and fixed-line phones should have too much in common to trouble the media psychologist. OK, so we have extra features in mobiles, but essentially the function is the same: you pick up the phone, dial a friend and, if you're lucky, speak to them. Conversations on the mobile differ very little in terms of structural organization from those on a landline, apart from obvious discussions about location ('I'm on a train right now' and so on) (Hutchby and Barnett, 2005).

However, there is much more psychologically to the mobile phone than the technology. First of all, while fixed-line telephones are by their nature bound to the geographical confines of a dwelling, mobiles belong uniquely (in most cases) to their owners. They are personal items rather than part of the furniture. And like other personal belongings, we can acquire sentimental and emotional attachments to them. Indeed, through the ingenuity of technological and marketing developments, mobiles have acquired more personal salience than almost any other single object, given the number of ways we can customize them – ringtones, backgrounds, headsets, not to mention the personalized and highly significant list of named, and sometimes pictured, contacts in the address book. It is not surprising, then, to find that mobile users report strong emotional attachments to their sets (Vincent, 2005).

Relatively little research has explored the effects of mobile use on the social environment, although it has been a major concern since their mass adoption. In a survey in 2003 conducted by Nokia, 89% of mobile users believed that other users needed better mobile phone etiquette, particularly with regard to intrusive ringtones and loud, animated conversations (Srivastava, 2005). This might be a spectacular instance of the third person effect, or simply a reflection of the general population's despair at inconsiderate users. As far as I can tell, mobile phone etiquette does not seem to have improved enormously over the rest of the decade either.

Children and mobiles: threats and hazards

In addition to noise pollution, mobile phones have been associated from the outset with various hazards. Fears of brain cancer and radioactive masts have subsided somewhat as the 2000s progressed, as society managed to function perfectly well despite half of the population's ears being permanently glued to their favourite personal items, and the mobile became seen as a necessity rather than a luxury (Contarello et al., 2007). Nevertheless, there are always concerns linked to any new medium, and these have mutated over the past decade from potential physical risks to social hazards.

Inevitably, much concern has focused on the effects of mobile phone use on children, particularly in the generations growing up with **txtspk** (use of SMS abbreviations), for whom the landline in their parents' house is an antique piece of rather unattractive furniture. As long ago as 2005, 97% of British females and 92% of males between 11 and 21 owned a mobile (Haste, 2005), and it has had a particular impact on the communication between young people and their parents.

Both of these groups say that the main advantage of mobiles is the security they offer, although while children envisage the safety advantage in terms of a parent coming to fetch them on a dark night, for parents it is the knowledge that they will be contacted immediately in case of an emergency (Devitt and Roker, 2009). In this way, mobiles have made young people more independent; as Devitt and Roker's participants explain, they are now able to stay out later and make last-minutes changes of plan because they can request permission from parents, or simply inform them of the updated arrangements.

Undoubtedly, where parents and children diverge, though, is on youngsters' preference for texting over talking. This is a repeated finding in the literature, and reflects the difference between synchronous and asynchronous communication discussed in Chapter 11. Asynchronous communication gives users more control over the interaction, since they have time to weigh up (and maybe discuss) their responses in a way that is difficult when put on the spot in a face-to-face or phone conversation (Madell and Muncer, 2007). Particularly difficult for parents is their children's preference for communicating sensitive information by text rather than talk, such as announcing a pregnancy or concerns about bullying (Devitt and Roker, 2009). Parents much prefer to learn about this kind of detail through face–to–face interaction.

One of the biggest concerns over children's use of mobiles relates specifically to the use of phones as cameras. The first camera phone was launched in Japan in 2000, but by the end of the decade, picture and video capture had become a universal feature of nearly all new mobile phone models, with the same electronic storage and transfer options as any basic digital camera. By the mid–2000s, lurid media reports abounded of young people attacking innocent bystanders and posting the video on *YouTube*, evolving into a phenomenon known as 'happy slapping', due to the delight expressed by the apparently sadistic assailants at having surprised an unwitting victim. Before long, tales of school children bullying one another in the same fashion had also made headlines (Nightingale, 2007).

Mobiles and children's literacy

One popular fear about mobile phones is that the use of text abbreviations will interfere with the acquisition of formal English spelling. It is often cited as yet further evidence of the 'dumbing down' of society, with generations of children coming to believe that 'later' is spelled *l8r*, 'tonight' is spelled *tonite*, 'to' *2* and 'for' *4*. As mentioned before, texting is more popular than talking for young people, and txtspk has evolved to a stage where many messages easily understood by teenagers appear almost unintelligible to adults.

One study that has explored the relationship between the frequency of texting and proficiency in English is Plester et al. (2008). The researchers asked British children between the ages of 10 and 12 to translate short passages from standard English into txtspk and vice versa. They found that the children with the highest scores on a spelling test were also best at translating to and from txtspk, and that the number of errors in the translation was unrelated to the amount of time the children had been using a mobile phone. Successfully switching between formal English and txtspk appears, ironically, to demand a higher level of literacy. You need to know that later is spelt *later* in order to be able to spell it *l8r*. The authors also found that the abbreviations children used in their translations were not consistent. Far from all the children spelling night *nite*, having been corrupted by the whims of texting, they also found it spelt *nt*, *nigt* and *nght*. There is a substantial element of creative wordplay involved.

Plester et al.'s findings are supported by a US study by Drouin and Davis (2009), who compared undergraduate texters and non-texters (texting has never taken off in quite the same way in the US as in the UK), and found no significant differences in literacy between the groups. However, they did find that 65% of the sample was unnecessarily worried that the use of txtspk would have a deleterious effect on their spelling, so anxiety due to popular fears seems to have filtered down to the students themselves.

Mobiles and driving

One final area where mobile phones have been associated with environmental hazard is in their ability to interfere with driving. Some research on this topic has been carried out by David Strayer and colleagues at the University of Utah in the US, where participants are placed in a driving simulator (a construction with an all-round screen that captures the experience of being in a car) and tested on their driving performance and other cognitive phenomena.

Generally speaking, driving simulator performance is worse when participants are distracted by a conversation on a mobile phone, even a hands-free version, compared to trials when the participant was carrying on a conversation with a passenger alongside (Strayer and Drews, 2007). Memory for objects displayed on the screen was substantially worse (50% accuracy compared with 88%), and driving manoeuvres were also poorer, such as braking time and distance. Strayer and Drews argue that this is due to a 'central processing bottleneck' (p. 131) that places too much demand on the driver's ability to think about the next conversational turn while also giving full attention to the road. Perhaps the most important advantage of speaking to a passenger is that they can orientate to the driving situation by reminding the driver about directions, pointing out potential hazards and so on, while the person on the other end of the mobile is fully focused on the conversation, unless they are also driving a car at the same time, thereby doubling the chances of an accident.

Final thoughts on new media

As with the Internet, mobile phones are best understood with reference to Marshall McLuhan's theory of media. Both technologies have opened up undreamt-of possibilities for human behaviour: if studied in terms of their dependency, one would wonder what 'old' media functions many of the phenomena are replacing. In the same way as nobody thought of going to the shops to buy a week's groceries until the car was invented, so nobody would have imagined that a corridor of students would be spending the night sitting at individual terminals mailing each other wacky videos. Whether these technologically driven changes are 'good for society' is not really the issue.

What does the future hold for new media? If you or I knew the answer, it probably wouldn't happen. At the end of the last century, one leading media expert claimed that the only 'information revolution' likely to take place was in pornography (Winston, 1998). He may yet be proved right. The speed of change in this century has been so rapid that many of the technological aspects we hold dear today, from blogging to *Facebook*, could disappear by the year 2015. What is particularly important to remember is that they won't necessarily be replaced with anything else. Throughout history, humans have always thought of new things to do with their time.

◉ Further reading

Whitty, M.T. and Joinson, A.N. (2008). *Truth, lies and trust on the internet*. London: Routledge.

Glossary

A-B-A (pre/post-test intervention) Type of experimental design where participants are compared on the same measure taken before and after some kind of intervention, for example body dissatisfaction measures before and after the participant has viewed a series of adverts.

active audience theory A cultural studies approach that considers the audience to have a certain degree of ownership of media texts, leaving them free to be creative.

attitude change Demonstrable change in an attitude towards an object (in advertising research, changing your mind about whether or not to buy a product).

audience participation media Umbrella term covering any media production that includes footage involving members of the public, although, for obvious reasons, it is largely restricted to broadcast media such as radio and TV.

avatars Three-dimensional computer graphic humans that act as players' representatives of the player in an online game.

blog Short for 'weblog', a blog is a personal website, usually carried by a specialist blogging site or an established site such as a newspaper, on which users produce a personal journal – it can be as simple as a day-to-day diary or as complex as a magazine website, with multiple contributors and themed sections.

body dissatisfaction General dissatisfaction with your own body.

catharsis hypothesis The argument that media violence has a 'cathartic' effect on the viewer, based on Freud's theory that humans have fundamental destructive instincts that they strive to rid themselves of. So the viewing of violence effectively 'purges' the viewer's own aggressive instinct (they act it out through identifying with the violent actor).

celebrity A condition experienced by famous individuals in cultures with mass communication, but may also be used to describe a famous individual in contemporary society.

celebrity involvement More specific than a parasocial relationship, it describes the extent to which an individual follows and is absorbed by a specific celebrity.

celebrity worship Similar to celebrity involvement, but implies an element of idolization that may go beyond mere admiration and take on pathological elements.

cell phones Technically, mobile phones that are connected to a cellular network (as opposed to cordless telephone sets connected to a fixed line). Until the mid-1990s, this was the common term in use in the UK, but gradually 'mobile' or 'mobile phone' took over. In the US, however, it is still used to refer to the same technology.

character attachment Players' attachment to their own avatars. Not to be confused with parasocial relationships, which occur with *other* characters, avatars included.

cognitive dissonance theory Festinger's theory explains how we try and resolve the cognitive discomfort caused by two opposing ideas.

cognitive priming Where certain thoughts are generated ('primed') by a stimulus, for example repeated watching of violence primes violent thoughts.

content analysis A research method that involves counting instances of certain things on a predesigned checklist, for example fight scenes in films.

cyberstalking Persistent attempts to contact people electronically, usually unreciprocated, that is, the other person ignores them, which sometimes escalatesing into mountains of spam emails or identity theft.

desensitization The argument that people become immune to the effects of a stimulus, for example violence, through repeated exposure.

docudramas Dramatic reconstruction of real-life events. Not to be confused with reality TV.

Drive For Muscularity (DFM) A psychometric scale measuring the attempts that people, typically young men, make to acquire a more muscular body.

ecological validity The extent to which a study's findings can be generalized to the 'real world'.

e-commerce Refers to online retail activity online.

Elaboration Likelihood Model Petty and Cacioppo's theory is based on the idea that some people will 'elaborate', that is, pay more attention, to some adverts than others and this will determine how they process the message.

eureka moment Named after the Ancient Greek mathematician Archimedes' discovery of water displacement as a way of measuring irregular objects while taking a bath. According to the story, Archimedes then ran naked through the streets shouting 'Eureka!' (I have found it!).

excitation transfer The idea that increased aggression results from the excitation generated by increased adrenaline, typically as the result of watching a violent movie.

fame A process by which individuals become recognized by a significant number of people outside their predictable social and professional networks.

fantasy–reality distinction The idea that children reach a certain 'magic' age at which they can then begin to tell the difference between what is real on television and what is fictional, or fantastic – based on the idea that adults can do this, and that the distinction is always that simple anyway.

field experiments An experiment conducted outside the laboratory, in a real-world setting.

fixed-line/landline telephone Two different terms referring to the same thing, that is, a telephone connected to the operating system by a wire, therefore limited in terms of coverage (as opposed to a mobile phone linked to a cellular network).

friending The act of adding new 'friends' to your social network profile.

functionalist With reference to media, this refers to the assumption that each new medium simply replaces an old one. When TV first appeared, people thought radio would immediately die out because TV replaced its audio function and added pictures. Since the arrival of the Internet, many commentators have predicted the 'death' of various old media.

grooming The use of chat rooms, SMS and other technologies to cultivate an online relationship with a younger, more vulnerable person, in order to trap them into an offline rendezvous (often with disastrous consequences).

hypertext Text that references other texts; for example, if you type http://www/ into a Word document, it will immediately start to activate a hyperlink to enable you to connect your current document to another one.

hypodermic needle theory The idea that media 'inject' ideas and beliefs directly into the viewer or listener's brain.

iconic memory The fleeting memory of a brief visual stimulus, recorded on the retina, which fades within seconds.

identification The extent to which we come to adopt another person's point of view, whether through our similarity to them (they are like us), or our wish to be like them, or perhaps simply because we have got caught up in the narrative.

implicit persuasion Where people are persuaded without realizing it.

impulse buying Purchases that are unplanned, usually triggered by marketing strategies such as appealing in-store displays or discounts.

Interest in Fame Psychological measure of one's interest in becoming famous, as opposed to emotionally charged terms like desire or wish to become famous.

internalization The idea that people come to 'internalize' or take on board certain ideas and beliefs.

Internet Global system of computers connected via various electronic and optical networking technologies. Carries the World Wide Web and email.

lifestyle show TV programme based around some aspect of viewers' everyday lives, typically cooking, gardening, DIY, fashion.

longitudinal study Takes a group of individuals and follows their progress over several months or years, analysing changes across the period.

makeover show Lifestyle show in which each episode follows members of the public who are undergoing some kind of transformation, either to themselves or their property.

Marshall McLuhan Key figure in media history and theory.

meaning transfer The way in which certain meanings transfer to associated media, for example a celebrity's image 'rubs off on' the product they are endorsing.

media dependency The idea that we come to rely on certain media sources for information, for example weather forecasts on the BBC rather than on commercial channels.

media effects tradition Research on media and their effects carried out usually in the form of laboratory experiments, typically with artificial stimuli representing media.

media figure Any human or animated persona encountered in the media – can be a real person, a fictional character, or a cartoon.

media framing The process by which media sources present a topic from a particular angle, through the use of headlines, pictures, captions, language use, source of quotes, and various other textual devices.

Media Framing Analysis (MFA) A relatively recent technique, based on long-standing traditions in the social sciences, for studying the processes involved in framing a news topic; mainly applied to health psychology so far.

media literacy Term based on the idea that audiences learn to 'read' media in the same way as we learn to read a language.

media literate Capable of 'reading' and understanding media in the same way (psychologically speaking) as one reads and understands written language.

media templates A concept used by media outlets as a convenient reference point that is understood by the audience, to the point where, say, Hillsborough comes to mean not a district of Sheffield, or even the name of Sheffield Wednesday's stadium, but the 1989 disaster involving the deaths of 96 Liverpool fans. Thus, 'another Hillsborough' is understood as a potential crowd crush, and 'another 9/11' as a terrorist attack, and not a recurrence of the mere date.

mere exposure effect The idea that we only have to be exposed to a piece of information for it to change our thinking or behaviour.

message A piece of information that travels from a sender to a receiver. At its most basic, a news item (the king has arrived at Southampton) carried by a specially appointed messenger to a specified hearer (someone who will be interested in the king's whereabouts). What constitutes a message, indeed what constitutes information, and whether it is possible to identify clearly senders and receivers are all important questions at the heart of communication study.

message framing The process by which an unspecified 'message' presents a topic from a particular angle, usually in terms of the losses or gains that the reader can experience through acting on it. Typically studied by changing one or two words in an experimental text and measuring the degree of readers' subsequent change in attitude.

MMORPGs (Massively Multiplayer Online Role-Playing Games) *Second Life* and *World of Warcraft* are two well-known examples, where up to several million contestants take part in continuous games.

mobile phones Those were developed in the 1990s, where digital technology allowed them to be pocket-sized rather than brick-sized.

modelling Developmental theory stating that children 'model' or copy the behaviour of others, whether adults, children, or even cartoon characters.

muscle dysmorphia The belief that your body is less muscular than it really is – largely applies to males, at least in existing research.

narrative context Used for understanding a piece of media content, for example a fight scene, in the context of the story or plot.

natural experiments Where naturally occurring behaviour is analysed as if an independent variable has been manipulated by the researcher.

negative relationship A negative correlation between two variables, meaning that as one goes up, the other goes down.

news peg The source of a particular story in the news media, effectively the reason for running a particular story, usually identified by some statement or quote in the article.

paradigm In psychology, this usually refers to a particular model for carrying out research – a type of experimental design, or some other research tradition.

parasocial interaction Concept from communication that describes behaving towards a figure on-screen (or in any kind of media) as if they are a real person in the same room as you.

parasocial relationships Usually taken to mean the attachment that develops over time with a media figure with whom we have interacted parasocially.

parental mediation Where a parent watches TV with their child and explains difficult or troubling material.

persuasion Field of research in psychology exploring the factors that enable people to persuade others, usually to bring about some kind of change in attitude or behaviour.

phenomenology The study of human experience, typically through first-person accounts or interviews that attempt to capture the individual's 'lifeworld'.

Piaget's stage theory of cognitive development Swiss psychologist Jean Piaget claimed (largely on the basis of observing his own son) that he could identify four discrete stages of cognitive development that represented the biological maturation of the human brain. Debate has raged since over the timing of these particular stages, to what extent the stages overlap, and whether it is necessary for a human to successfully complete each stage in order to reach full adult intelligence.

possible selves The idea that we each have certain possible future selves that we can entertain, be they good or bad.

pretend play Children playing at 'pretend', usually with the utmost seriousness.

pro-ana websites Websites set up by people with an eating disorder such as anorexia or bulimia that are fundamentally opposed to the idea of 'recovery' or treatment.

product placement Where a company gets a film or TV producer to insert one of its products in a scene in a film or series.

psychometric scales Questionnaires, typically in the form of a Likert-type scale, where respondents are asked to what extent they agree or disagree with a series of statements.

reality TV Programme in which a group of people compete against each other over several weeks while viewers vote for successive contestants to be removed until one is left. May take the form of a talent contest, or live footage of interaction in a confined setting.

revelation The key moment in an audience participation show where a transformation or piece of information is revealed to the (typically public) participants, triggering an authentic emotional response.

single factor construct A measurement scale in which all the items (or questions) are related to a single underlying construct or concept, determined using the statistical technique of factor analysis.

sleeper effect Some attitude change takes place slowly (you 'sleep on it').

SMS Short Message Service, the communication service that allows mobile phone users to send text messages to any other phone owner.

social networking sites Websites, like *Facebook*, *MySpace* and so on, that allow individuals to create profiles and post messages and other material for social purposes.

source credibility Whether or not you believe the source of a claim about a particular product.

stalking Pursuing or contacting an individual over a period of time to such an extent that they experience distress and discomfort, usually because they feel there is a threat to their safety.

subliminal perception The idea that people can process information, such as an advertising slogan, without being consciously aware of doing so.

synchronous/asynchronous communication Refers to communication (of any type) that can either occur in the same time frame, for example a telephone conversation is synchronous, or where there is a delay between turns, for example an email is asynchronous.

talk show TV programme where a celebrity host interacts with a studio audience. Not to be confused with chat show.

texting The act of sending a text message. Note that SMS and texting are usually used to refer to the same thing in different countries.

theory of mind (ToM) The awareness that each person has their own unique mental perspective on the world, and a mental life broadly similar to that of the perceiver. As with Piaget's early 'egocentric' stage, needs to be 'passed' in order for the child to fully develop social skills (empathy and so on). Is generally recognized as the key intellectual deficit in autism.

thin ideal The idea that the ideal body shape is a thin one.

third person effect The belief that other people are more strongly influenced by the media than you.

turning point A standard narrative device used for dramatic effect, such as a chance finding or flash of inspiration, often not quite reflecting the painstaking and methodical way that most scientific discoveries usually come about.

txtspk Use of extensive abbreviation in SMS or texting. Variously referred to as textspeak, txt spk, txtese.

typology A formal system for classifying a phenomenon into various types.

uses and gratifications (U&G) theory Research tradition that considers the audience to be composed of media users who have some control over what media they select, based on personal preferences and choices.

voyeurism Prurient interest in an individual's private business.

Web 1.0/Web 2.0 Used to distinguish earlier Internet phenomena, such as multi-user domains, from more recent ones like social networking.

World Wide Web Global network of documents connected via hypertext links.

References

Addley, E. (2009). Big Brother contestant Sree Dasari slashes his wrists. *The Guardian*, 30 July.

Alperstein, N. (1991). Imaginary social relationships with celebrities appearing in television commercials. *Journal of Broadcasting and Electronic Media*, 35, 43–58.

Ambler, T. (2008). Who's messing with whose mind? Debating the Nairn and Fine argument. *International Journal of Advertising*, 27, 885–95.

Amos, C., Holmes, G. and Strutton, D. (2008). Exploring the relationship between celebrity endorser effects and advertising effectiveness: A quantitative synthesis of effect size. *International Journal of Advertising*, 27, 209–34.

Anderson, C.A. and Bushman, B.J. (2002). Human aggression. *Annual Review of Psychology*, 53, 27–51.

Anderson, C.A. and Murphy, C.R. (2003). Violent video games and aggressive behaviour in young women. *Aggressive Behaviour*, 29, 423–29.

Anderson, C.A., Carnagey, D.L., Flanagan, M. et al. (2004). Violent video games: Specific effects of violent content on aggressive thoughts and behaviour. *Advances in Experimental Social Psychology*, 36, 199–249.

Anderson, C.A., Gentile, D.A. and Buckley, K.E. (2007). *Violent video game effects on children and adolescents: Theory, research, and public policy.* New York: Oxford University Press.

Anderson, D.R., Bryant, J., Murray, J.P. et al. (2006). Brain imaging: An introduction to a new approach to studying media processes and effects. *Media Psychology*, 8, 1–6.

Anderson, D.R., Fite, K.V., Petrovich, N. and Hirsch, J. (2006). Cortical activation while watching video montage: An fMRI study. *Media Psychology*, 8, 7–24.

Anderson, R.C. and Pichert, J.W. (1978). Recall of previously unrecallable information following a shift in perspective. *Journal of Verbal Learning and Verbal Behaviour*, 17, 1–12.

Aubrey, J.S. (2006). Effects of sexually objectifying media on self-objectification and body surveillance in undergraduates: Results of a 2-year panel study. *Journal of Communication*, 56, 366–86.

Babrow, A.S., O'Keefe, B.J., Swanson, D.L. et al. (1988). Person perception and children's impressions of television and real peers. *Communication Research*, 15, 680–98.

Bailenson, J.N., Garland, P., Iyengar, S. and Yee, N. (2006). Transformed facial similarity as a political cue: A preliminary investigation. *Political Psychology*, 27, 373–86.

Baker, C. (2004). Membership categorization and interview accounts. In Silverman, D. (ed.) *Qualitative research: Theory, method and practice* (2nd edn, pp. 162–76). London: Sage.

Ball, S. and Bogatz, G.A. (1970). *The first year of Sesame Street: An evaluation.* Princeton, NJ: Educational Testing Service.

Ball-Rokeach, S.J. and DeFleur, M.L. (1976). A dependency model of mass media effects. *Communication Research*, 3, 3–21.

Bandura, A., Ross, D. and Ross, S.A. (1961). Transmission of aggression through imitation of aggressive models. *Journal of Abnormal and Social Psychology*, 63, 575–82.

Baran, S.J., Chase, L.J. and Courtright, J.A. (1979). Television drama as a facilitator of prosocial behaviour: *The Waltons. Journal of Broadcasting*, 23, 265–76.

Barker, M. and Petley, J. (eds) (2001). *Ill effects: The media/violence debate* (2nd edn). London: Routledge.

BBC (British Broadcasting Corporation) (2002). Springer sued over murdered guest. Downloaded 22 January 2010 from http://news.bbc.co.uk/1/hi/entertainment/tv_and_radio/2121700.stm.

BBC (British Broadcasting Corporation) (2009). Reality TV star Jade Goody dies. Downloaded 22 January 2010 from http://news.bbc.co.uk/1/hi/entertainment/7925719.stm.

Bearison, D.J., Bain, J.M. and Daniele, R. (1982). Developmental changes in how children understand television. *Social Behaviour and Personality*, 10, 133–44.

Bearman, S.K., Presnell, K. and Martinez, E. (2006). The skinny on body dissatisfaction: A longitudinal study of adolescent girls and boys. *Journal of Adolescence*, 35, 217–29.

Bell, D. (2001). *An introduction to cybercultures*. New York: Routledge.

Bem, D.J. (1967). Self-perception: An alternative interpretation of cognitive dissonance phenomena. *Psychological Review*, 74, 183–200.

Bergstrom, R.L., Neighbors, C. and Lewis, M.A. (2004). Do men find 'bony' women attractive? Consequences of misperceiving opposite sex perceptions of attractive body image. *Body Image*, 1, 183–91.

Berkowitz, L. (1984). Some effects of thoughts on anti- and prosocial influences of media events: A cognitive-neoassociation analysis. *Psychological Bulletin*, 95, 410–27.

Birkeland, R., Thompson, J.K., Herbozo, S. et al. (2005). Media exposure, mood, and body image dissatisfaction: An experimental test of person versus product priming. *Body Image*, 2, 53–61.

Bjurström, E. (1994). *Barn och TV-reklam: En introduction till forskningen om TV-reklamens påverkan på barn* [Children and television advertising: An introduction to the research on the effects TV commercials have on children]. Stockholm: Konsumentverket (Rapport 29).

Bolls, P., Lang, A. and Potter, R. (2001). The use of facial EMG to measure emotional responses to radio. *Communication Research*, 28, 627–51.

Bransford, J.D. and Johnson, M.K. (1973). Considerations of some problems of comprehension. In W. Chase (ed.) *Visual information processing* (pp. 383–438). New York: Academic Press.

Braudy, L. (1997). *The frenzy of renown: Fame and its history* (2nd edn). New York: Vintage Books.

Brooker, C. (2009). Now press play. *The Guardian*, 11 December, Games special (pp. 6–9).

Brotsky, S.R. and Giles, D.C. (2007). Inside the 'pro-ana' community: A covert online participant observation. *Eating Disorders: The Journal of Treatment and Prevention*, 19, 93–109.

Brown, J.D. and L'Engle, K.L. (2009). X-rated: Sexual attitudes and behaviours associated with U.S. early adolescents' exposure to sexually explicit media. *Communication Research*, 36, 129–51.

Brown, W.J., Basil, M.D. and Bocarnea, M.C. (2003). Social influence of an international celebrity: Responses to the death of Princess Diana. *Journal of Communication*, 53, 587–605.

Brownell, K.D. and Napolitano, M.A. (1995). Distorting reality for children: Body size proportions of Barbie and Ken dolls. *International Journal of Eating Disorders*, 18, 295–8.

Buckley, K.E. and Anderson, C.A. (2006). A theoretical model of the effects and consequences of playing video games. In P. Vorderer and J. Bryant (eds) *Playing video games: Motives, responses, and consequences* (pp. 363–78). Mahwah, NJ: Lawrence Erlbaum.

Buijzen, M. (2007). Reducing children's susceptibility to commercials: Mechanisms of factual and evaluative advertising interventions. *Media Psychology*, 9, 411–30.

Buijzen, M. (2009). The effectiveness of parental communication in modifying the relation between food advertising and children's consumption behaviour. *British Journal of Developmental Psychology*, 27, 105–22.

Buijzen, M. and Valkenburg, P.M. (2005). Parental mediation of undesired advertising effects. *Journal of Broadcasting and Electronic Media*, 49, 153–65.

Buijzen, M., Rozendaal, E., Moorman, M. and Tanis, M. (2008). Parent vs. child reports of parental advertising mediation: Exploring the meaning of agreement. *Journal of Broadcasting & Electronic Media*, 52, 509–25.

Bunce, L. and Harris, M. (2008) 'I saw the real Father Christmas!' Children's everyday uses of the words real, really, and pretend. *British Journal of Developmental Psychology*, 26, 445–55.

Burke, R.R. (1997). Do you see what I see? The future of virtual shopping. *Journal of the Academy of Marketing Sciences*, 25, 352–360.

Bushman, B.J. (1995). Moderating role of trait aggressiveness in the effects of violent media on aggression. *Journal of Personality and Social Psychology*, 69, 950–60.

Bushman, B.J. and Anderson, C.A. (2001). Media violence and the American public. *American Psychologist*, 56, 477–89.

Bushman, B.J. and Geen, R.G. (1990). Role of cognitive-emotional mediators and individual differences in the effects of media violence on aggression. *Journal of Personality and Social Psychology*, 58, 156–63.

Button, E.J., Benson, E., Nollett, C. and Palmer, R.L. (2005). Don't forget EDNOS (Eating Disorder Not Otherwise Specified): Patterns of service use in an eating disorders service. *Psychiatric Bulletin*, 29, 134–6.

Cafri, G., Strauss, J. and Thompson, J.K. (2002). Male body image: Satisfaction and its relationship to well-being using the somatomorphic matrix. *International Journal of Men's Health*, 1, 215–31.

Cafri, G., Thompson, J.K., Ricciardelli, L. et al. (2005). Pursuit of the muscular ideal: Physical and psychological consequences and putative risk factors. *Clinical Psychology Review*, 25, 215–39.

Cantor, J. and Sparks, G.G. (1984). Children's fear responses to mass media: Testing some Piagetian predictions. *Journal of Communication*, 34, 90–103.

Cantril, H. (1940). *The invasion from Mars: A study in the psychology of panic*. Princeton, NJ: Princeton University Press.

Caraher, M., Landon, J. and Dalmeny, K. (2006). Television advertising and children: Lessons from policy development. *Public Health Nutrition*, 9, 596–605.

Cashmore, E. (2006). *Celebrity/Culture*. Abingdon: Routledge.

Centerwall, B.S. (1993). Television and violent crime. *The Public Interest*, 111, 56–71.

Chesher, C. (2007). Becoming the Milky Way: Mobile phone and actor networks at a U2 concert. *Continuum: Journal of Media & Cultural Studies*, 21, 217–25.

Chesley, E.B., Alberts, J.D., Klein, J.D. and Kreipe, R.E. (2003). Pro or con? Anorexia nervosa and the Internet. *Journal of Adolescent Health*, 32, 123–4.

Cheung, C.K. and Yue, X.D. (2004). Adolescent modeling after luminary and star idols and development of self-efficacy. *Journal of Adolescence and Youth*, 11, 251–67.

Chin, B. and Hills, M. (2008). Restricted confessions? Blogging, subcultural activity and the management of producer-fan proximity. *Social Semiotics*, 18, 253–72.

Clarke, C.E. (2008). A question of balance: The autism–vaccine controversy in the British and American elite press. *Science Communication*, 30, 77–107.

Cohen, J. (1999). Favourite characters of teenage viewers of Israeli serials. *Journal of Broadcasting and Electronic Media*, 43, 327–45.

Cole, C., Arafat, C., Tidhar, C. et al. (2003). The educational impact of Rechov Sumsum/Shara's Simsim: A *Sesame Street* television series to promote respect and understanding among children living in Israel, the West Bank, and Gaza. *International Journal of Behavioral Development*, 27, 409–22.

Contarello, A., Fortunati, L. and Sarrica, M. (2007). Social thinking and the mobile phone: A study of social change with the diffusion of mobile phones, using a social representations framework. *Continuum: Journal of Media & Cultural Studies*, 21, 149–63.

Courbet, D., Fourquet-Courbet, M. and Intartaglia, J. (2008). Publicité sur Internet: Que reste-t-il des mots, que reste-t-il des images, trois mois après en mémoire implicite? [E-advertising: What images and words remain in implicit memory after three months?] *Revue des Interactions Humaines Médiatiseés*, 9, 1–22.

Cowley, E. and Barron, C. (2008) When product placement goes wrong. *Journal of Advertising*, 37, 89–98.

Coyne, S.M. and Archer, J. (2004). Indirect aggression in the media: A content analysis of British television programmes. *Aggressive Behaviour*, 30, 254–71.

Culpeper, J. (2001). *Language and characterisation: People in plays and other texts*. Harlow: Longman.

De Backer, C., Nelissen, M., Vyncke, P. et al. (2007). Celebrities – from teachers to friends: A test of two hypotheses on the adaptiveness of celebrity gossip. *Human Nature*, 18, 334–54.

Devitt, K. and Roker, D. (2009). The role of mobile phones in family communication. *Children & Society*, 23, 189–202.

DeVoss, D.N. (2006). From the BBS to the Web: Tracing the spaces of online romance. In M.T. Whitty, A.J. Baker and J.A. Inman (eds) *Online matchmaking* (pp. 17–30). Basingstoke: Palgrave Macmillan.

Dhoest, A. (2006). Everybody liked it: Collective memories of early Flemish television fiction. *Particip@tions*, *3*. Downloaded 18 January 2010 from http://www.participations.org/volume%203/issue%20 1/3_01_contents.htm.

Dias, K. (2003). The ANA sanctuary: Women's proanorexia narratives in cyberspace. *Journal of International Women's Studies*, 4, 32–45.

Diddi, A. and LaRose, R. (2006). Getting hooked on news: Uses and gratifications and the formation of news habits among college students in an Internet environment. *Journal of Broadcasting & Electronic Media*, 50, 193–210.

Dietz, P.E., Matthews, D.B., Van Duyne, C. et al. (1991). Threatening and otherwise inappropriate letters to Hollywood celebrities. *Journal of Forensic Sciences*, 36, 185–209.

Dittmar, H. and Howard, S. (2004). Ideal-body internalization and social comparison tendency as moderators of thin media models' impact on women's body focused anxiety. *Journal of Social and Clinical Psychology*, 23, 768–91.

Dittmar, H., Halliwell, E. and Stirling, E. (2009). Understanding the impact of thin media models on women's body-focused affect: The roles of thin-ideal internalisation and weight-related self-discrepancy activation in experimental exposure effects. *Journal of Social and Clinical Psychology*, 28, 43–72.

Dittmar, H., Lloyd, B., Dugan, S. et al. (2000). The 'body beautiful': English adolescents' images of ideal bodies. *Sex Roles*, 42, 887–913.

Dittmar, H., Long, K. and Bond, R. (2007). When a better self is only a button click away: Associations between materialistic values, emotional and identity-related buying motives, and compulsive buying tendency online. *Journal of Social and Clinical Psychology*, 26, 334–61.

Dittmar, H., Long, K. and Meek, R. (2004). Buying on the Internet: Gender differences in online and conventional buying motivations. *Sex Roles*, 50, 423–44.

Dohnt, H.K. and Tiggemann, M. (2006). Body image concerns in young girls: The role of peers and media prior to adolescence. *Journal of Youth and Adolescence*, 35, 141–51.

Donnerstein, E. (1984). Pornography: Its effect on violence against women. In N.M. Malamuth and E. Donnerstein (eds) *Pornography and sexual aggression* (pp. 53–81). Orlando, FL: Academic Press.

Dorr, A., Graves, S.B. and Phelps, E. (1980). Television literacy for young children. *Journal of Communication*, 30, 71–83.

Drouin, M. and Davis, C. (2009). R u texting? Is the use of text speak hurting your literacy? *Journal of Literacy Research*, 41, 46–67.

Eagle, M., Wolitzky, D.L. and Klein, G.S. (1966). Imagery: Effect of a concealed figure in a stimulus. *Science*, 151, 837–9.

Ellison, N., Heino, R. and Gibbs, J. (2006). Managing impressions online: Self-presentation processes in the online dating environment. *Journal of Computer-Mediated Communication*, 11, article 2. Downloaded 20 January 2010 from http://jcmc.indiana.edu/vol11/issue2/ellison.html.

Emmison, M. and Goldman, L. (1996). 'What's that you said Sooty?' Puppets, parlance and pretence. *Language and Communication*, 16, 17–35.

Emmison, M. and Goldman, L. (1997). The Sooty Show laid bear: Children, puppets and make-believe. *Childhood*, 4, 325–42.

Entman, R.M. (1991). Framing U.S. coverage of international news: Contrasts in narratives of the KAL and Iran Air incidents. *Journal of Communication*, 41, 6–27.

Entman, R.M. (2007). Framing bias: Media in the distribution of power. *Journal of Communication*, 57, 163–73.

Eron, L.D. (1993). *The problem of media violence and children's behaviour*. New York: Henry Frank Guggenheim.

Eyal, K. and Cohen, J. (2006). When good *Friends* say goodbye: A parasocial breakup study. *Journal of Broadcasting and Electronic Media*, 50, 502–23.

Feilitzen, C. and Linne, O. (1975). Identifying with television characters. *Journal of Communication*, 25, 51–5.

Feldman, C.F. (1992). The new theory of theory of mind. *Human Development*, 35, 107–17.

Ferguson, D.A. and Perse, E.M. (2000). The world wide web as a functional alternative to television. *Journal of Broadcasting and Electronic Media*, 44, 155–74.

Ferguson, E. and Gallagher, L. (2007). Message framing with respect to decisions about vaccination: The roles of frame valence, frame method and perceived risk. *British Journal of Psychology*, 98, 667–680.

Fernbach, M. (2002). The impact of a media campaign on cervical screening knowledge and self-efficacy. *Journal of Health Psychology*, 7, 85–97.

Feshbach, S. and Singer, R.D. (1971). *Television and aggression*. San Francisco: Jossey-Bass.

Festinger, L. (1957). *A theory of cognitive dissonance*. Evanston, IL: Row, Peterson.

Festinger, L. and Carlsmith, J.M. (1959). Cognitive consequences of forced compliance. *Journal of Social and Abnormal Psychology*, 58, 203–10.

Finn, J. (2004). A survey of online harassment at a university campus. *Journal of Interpersonal Violence*, 19, 468–83.

Fisch, S., Truglio, R.T. and Cole, C.F. (1999). The impact of *Sesame Street* on preschool children: A review and synthesis of 30 years' research. *Media Psychology*, 1, 165–90.

Fiske, J. (1989). Moments of television: Neither the text nor the audience. In E. Seiter, H. Borchers, M. Kreutzner and E.-M. Warth (eds) *Remote control television: Audiences and cultural power*. London: Routledge.

Flavell, J.H., Flavell, E.R., Green, F.L. and Korfmacher, J.E. (1990). Do young children think of television images as pictures or real objects? *Journal of Broadcasting and Electronic Media*, 34, 399–419.

Fowles, J. (1996). *Advertising and popular culture*. Thousand Oaks, CA: Sage.

Fowles, J. (1999). *The case for television violence*. Thousand Oaks, CA: Sage.

Fox, N., Ward, K. and O'Rourke, A. (2005). Pro-anorexia, weight-loss drugs and the internet: An 'anti-recovery' explanatory model of anorexia. *Sociology of Health & Illness*, 27, 944–71.

Franzini, L.R. and Grossberg, J.M. (1995). *Eccentric and bizarre behaviours*. New York: John Wiley.

Fraser, B.P. and Brown, W.J. (2002). Media, celebrities, and social influence: Identification with Elvis Presley. *Mass Communication & Society*, 5, 183–206.

Freedman, J.L. (2002). *Media violence and its effects on aggression: Assessing the scientific evidence*. Toronto: University of Toronto Press.

Gamson, J. (1994). *Claims to fame: Celebrity in contemporary America*. New York: Columbia University Press.

Gamson, W.A. and Modigliani, A. (1989). Media discourse and public opinion on nuclear power: A constructionist approach. *American Journal of Sociology*, 95, 1–37.

Garner, D.M., Garfinkel, P.E., Schwartz, D. and Thompson, M. (1980). Cultural expectations of thinness in women. *Psychological Reports*, 47, 483–91.

Gauntlett, D. (2005). *Moving experiences: Media effects and beyond* (2nd edn). New Barnet: John Libbey.

Gauntlett, D. (2007). *Media studies 2.0*. Downloaded 20 January 2010 from http://www.theory.org.uk/mediastudies2.htm.

Gee, J.P. (2006). Why game studies now? Video games: A new art form. *Games and Culture*, 1, 58–61.

Gentile, D.A., Anderson, C.A., Yukawa, S. et al. (2009). The effects of prosocial video games on prosocial behaviours: International evidence from correlational, longitudinal, and experimental studies. *Personality and Social Psychology Bulletin*, 35, 752–63.

Gerbner, G. (1994). The politics of media violence: Some reflections. In O. Linné and C.J. Hamelink (eds) *Mass communication research: On problems and policies: The art of asking the right questions*. Norwood, NJ: Ablex.

Gerbner, G., Gross, L., Eleey, M. et al. (1978). Cultural indicators: Violence profile #9. *Journal of Communication*, 26, 173–99.

Gerbner, G., Gross, L., Morgan, M. et al. (2002). Growing up with television: Cultivation processes. In J. Bryant and D. Zillmann (eds) *Media effects: advances in theory and research* (2nd edn, pp. 43–67). Hillsdale, NJ: Lawrence Erlbaum.

Gibbs, J.L., Ellison, N.B. and Heino, R.D. (2006). Self-presentation in online personals: The role of anticipated future interaction, self-disclosure, and perceived success in Internet dating. *Communication Research*, 33, 1–26.

Giles, D.C. (2000). *Illusions of immortality: A psychology of fame and celebrity*. Basingstoke: Macmillan – now Palgrave Macmillan.

Giles, D.C. (2002a). Parasocial interaction: A review of the literature and a model for future research. *Media Psychology*, 4, 279–302.

Giles, D.C. (2002b). Keeping the public in their place: Audience participation in lifestyle television programming. *Discourse & Society*, 13, 603–28.

Giles, D.C. (2006). Constructing identities in cyberspace: The case of eating disorders. *British Journal of Social Psychology*, 45, 463–77.

Giles, D.C. (2008). Parasocial interaction: current directions in theory and method. Paper presented as part of the symposium With stars in their eyes: Investigating star-audience relations, ECREA 2nd European Communication Conference, November, Barcelona.

Giles, D.C. and Close, J. (2008). Exposure to 'lad magazines' and drive for muscularity in dating and non-dating young men. *Personality and Individual Differences*, 44, 1610–16.

Giles, D.C. and Maltby, J. (2004). The role of media in adolescent development: Relations between autonomy, attachment, and interest in celebrities. *Personality and Individual Differences*, 36, 813–22.

Giles, D.C. and Shaw, R.L. (2009). The psychology of news influence and the development of media framing analysis. *Social and Personality Psychology Compass*, 3/4, 375–93.

Giles, D.C., Shaw, R.L. and Morgan, W. (2009). Representations of voluntary childlessness in the UK press, 1990–2008. *Journal of Health Psychology*, 14, 1218–28.

Goedkoop, R. (1985). The game show. In B.G. Rose (ed.) *TV genres: A handbook and reference guide* (pp. 287–306). Westport, CT: Greenwood.

Gosling, J. (2009). *Waging the war of the worlds: A history of the 1938 radio broadcast and resulting panic, including the original script*. Jefferson, NC: McFarland.

Gosling, S.D., Gaddis, S. and Vazire, S. (2008). First impressions from the environments that we create and inhabit. In J. Skowronski and N. Ambady (eds) *First Impressions* (pp. 334–56). New York: Guilford.

Grabe, S., Ward, L.M. and Hyde, J.S. (2008). The role of the media in body image concerns among women: A meta-analysis of experimental and correlation studies. *Psychological Bulletin*, 134, 460–76.

Greenberg, B.S. (1980). *Life on television: Content analysis of U.S. TV drama*. Norwood, NJ: Ablex.

Greenwald, A.G., Spangenberg, E.R., Pratkanis, A.R. and Eskenazi, J. (1991). Double-blind tests of subliminal self-help audiotapes. *Psychological Science*, 2, 119–22.

Greenwood, D.N., Pietromonaco, P.R. and Long, C.R. (2008). Young women's attachment style and interpersonal engagement with female TV stars. *Journal of Social and Personal Relationships*, 25, 387–407.

Greitemeyer, T. (2009). Effects of songs with prosocial lyrics on prosocial thoughts, affect, and behaviour. *Journal of Experimental Social Psychology*, 45, 186–90.

Grimes, T. and Bergen, L. (2008). The epistemological argument against a causal relationship between media violence and sociopathic behaviour among psychologically well viewers. *American Behavioural Scientist*, 51, 1137–54.

Gunter, B. (1981). Measuring television violence: A review and suggestions for a new analytical perspective. *Current Psychological Reviews*, 1, 91–112.

Gunter, B. (1985). *Dimensions of television violence*. Aldershot: Gower.

Gunter, B. (2008). Media violence: Is there a case for causality? *American Behavioral Scientist*, 51, 1061–122.

Gunter, B., Panting, C., Charlton, T. and Coles, D. (2002). Relationships between children's viewing patterns and social behavior. In T. Charlton, B. Gunter and A. Hannan (eds) *Broadcast television effects in a remote community* (pp. 83–106). Mahwah, NJ: Lawrence Erlbaum.

Habermas, J. (1989). *The structural transformation of the public sphere: An inquiry into a category of bourgeois society* (T. Bruger with F. Lawrence trans.). Cambridge, MA: MIT Press.

Hagell, A. and Newburn, T. (1994). *Young offenders and the media: Viewing habits and preferences*. London: Policy Studies Institute.

Halliwell, E. and Dittmar, H. (2006). Associations between appearance-related self-discrepancies and young women's and men's affect, body image, and emotional eating: A comparison of fixed-item and respondent-generated self-discrepancy measures. *Personality and Social Psychology Bulletin*, 32, 447–58.

Hancock, J.T. and Toma, C.L. (2009). Putting your best face forward: The accuracy of online dating photographs. *Journal of Communication*, 59, 367–86.

Haney, C., Banks, W.C. and Zimbardo, P.G. (1973). Interpersonal dynamics in a simulated prison. *International Journal of Criminology and Penology*, 1, 69–97.

Hargreaves, D.A. and Tiggemann, M. (2009). Muscular ideal media images and men's body image: Social comparison processing and individual vulnerability. *Psychology of Men & Masculinity*, 10, 109–19.

Hargreaves, I., Lewis, J. and Spears, T. (2002). *Towards a better map: science, the public and the media*. Swindon: ESRC.

Harris, A. (2001). Revisiting bedroom culture: new spaces for young women's politics. *Hecate*, 27, 128–38.

Harris, J.L., Bargh, J.A. and Brownell, K.D. (2009). Priming effects of television food advertising on eating behaviour. *Health Psychology*, 28, 404–13.

Harris, P.L. (2000). *The work of the imagination*. Oxford: Blackwell.

Hartmann, D., Stuke, D. and Daschmann, G. (2008). Positive parasocial relationships with drivers affect suspense in racing sport spectators. *Journal of Media Psychology*, 20, 24–34.

Hartmann, T. (2008). Parasocial interactions and telecommunication with new media characters. In E.A. Konijn, S. Utz, M. Tanis and S.B. Barnes (eds) *Mediated interpersonal communication* (pp. 177–99). New York: Routledge.

Haste, H. (2005). *Joined-up texting: The role of mobile phones in young people's lives*. NSRP: London.

Hatoum, I.J. and Belle, D. (2004). Mags and abs: Media consumption and bodily concerns in men. *Sex Roles*, 51, 397–407.

Hawkins, N., Richards, P.S., Granley, H. and Stein, D.M. (2004). The impact of exposure to the thin-ideal media images on women. *Eating Disorders: The Journal of Treatment & Prevention*, 12, 35–50.

Hearold, S. (1986). A synthesis of 1043 effects of television on social behavior. In G. Comstock (ed.) *Public communications and behavior* (vol. 1, pp. 65–113). New York: Academic Press.

Heath, R. and Feldwick, P. (2007). Fifty years using the wrong model of advertising. *International Journal of Market Research*, 50, 29–58.

Heinberg, L.J. and Thompson, J.K. (1995). Body image and televised images of thinness and attractiveness: A controlled laboratory investigation. *Journal of Social and Clinical Psychology*, 14, 325–8.

Heinberg, L.J., Thompson, J.K. and Stormer, S. (1995). Development and validation of the sociocultural attitudes to appearance questionnaire. *International Journal of Eating Disorders*, 17, 81–9.

Hill, A. (1997). *Shocking entertainment: Viewer response to violent movies*. Luton: University of Luton Press.

Hill, A. (2001). Media risks: The social amplification of risk and the media violence debate. *Journal of Risk Research*, 4, 209–25.

Hills, M. (2002). *Fan cultures*. London: Routledge.

Holmes, S. (2005). 'Reality goes pop!' Reality TV, popular music, and narratives of stardom in *Pop Idol*. *Television & New Media*, 5, 147–72.

Holmes, S. (2008). 'The viewers have ... taken over the airwaves?' Participation, reality TV, and approaching the audience-in-the-text. *Screen*, 49, 13–31.

Holmes, S. and Jermyn, D. (2004). Introduction: Understanding reality TV. In S. Holmes and D. Jermyn (eds) *Understanding reality television* (pp. 1–32). London: Routledge.

Holmwood, L. (2009). Media companies back MPs on BBC Worldwide curbs. *The Guardian*, 7 April. Downloaded 11 January 2010 from http://www.guardian.co.uk/media/2009/apr/07/bbc-worldwide-channel-41.

Hookway, N. (2008). 'Entering the blogosphere': Some strategies for using blogs in social research. *Qualitative Research*, 8, 91–113.

Hoorens, V. and Nuttin, J.M. (1993). Overvaluation of own attributes: mere ownership or subjective frequency? *Social Cognition*, 11, 177–200.

Horton, D. and Wohl, R.R. (1956). Mass communication and para-social interaction: Observation on intimacy at a distance. *Psychiatry*, 19, 185–206.

Hovland, C.I. and Weiss, W. (1951). The influence of source credibility on communication effectiveness. *Public Opinion Quarterly*, 15, 635–50.

Hovland, C.I., Lumsdale, A.A. and Sheffield, F.D. (1949). *Experiments on mass communication: Studies in social psychology in World War II* (vol. 3). Princeton: Princeton University Press.

Huesmann, L.R. and Eron, L.D. (1986). *Television and the aggressive child: A cross-national comparison*. Hillsdale, NJ: Lawrence Erlbaum.

Huesmann, L.R., Moise-Titus, J., Podolski, C. and Eron, L.D. (2003). Longitudinal relation between children's exposure to TV violence and their aggressive and violent behaviour in young adulthood. *Developmental Psychology*, 39, 201–21.

Hughes, M. and Grieve, R. (1980). On asking children bizarre questions. *First Language*, 1, 149–60.

Huston, A.C. and Wright, J.C. (1998). Television and the informational and educational needs of children. *Annals of the American Academy of Political and Social Science*, 557, 9–23.

Hutchby, I. and Barnett, S. (2005). Aspects of the sequential organisation of mobile phone conversation. *Discourse Studies*, 7, 147–71.

Ivory, J.D. and Kalyanaraman, S. (2007). The effects of technological advancement and violent content in video games on players' feelings of presence, involvement, physiological arousal, and aggression. *Journal of Communication*, 57, 532–55.

Jenkins, H. (1992). *Textual Poachers: Television Fans and Participatory Culture*. New York: Routledge.

Jerin, R. and Dolinsky, B. (2006). Cyber-victimisation and online dating. In M.T. Whitty, A.J. Baker and J.A. Inman (eds) *Online matchmaking* (pp. 147–58). Basingstoke: Palgrave Macmillan.

John, D.R. (1999). Consumer socialization of children: a retrospective look at twenty-five years of research. *Journal of Consumer Research*, 26, 183–213.

Joinson, A.N. (2003). *Understanding the psychology of internet behaviour: Virtual worlds, real lives*. Basingstoke: Palgrave Macmillan.

Jones, J. (2002). *Let me take you down: Inside the mind of Mark David Chapman, the man who killed John Lennon*. New York: Villard.

Josephson, W. (1987). Television violence and children's aggression: Testing the priming, social script and disinhibition predictors. *Journal of Personality and Social Psychology*, 53, 882–90.

Kanazawa, S. (2002). Bowling with our imaginary friends. *Evolution and Human Behaviour*, 23, 167–71.

Karson E.J. and Korgaonkar, P.K. (2001). An empirical investigation of Internet advertising and the elaboration likelihood model. *Journal of Current Issues & Research in Advertising*, 23, 53–72.

Katz, E., Blumler, J.G. and Gurevitch, M. (1974). Uses of mass communication by the individual. In W.P. Davison and F.T. Yu (eds) *Mass communication research: Major issues and future directions* (pp. 11–35). New York: Praeger.

Kellow, C.L. and Steeves, H.L. (1998). The role of radio in the Rwandan genocide. *Journal of Communication*, 48, 107–28.

Kitzinger, J. (2000). Media templates: Patterns of association and the (re) construction of meaning over time. *Media, Culture & Society*, 22, 61–84.

Klimmt, C. and Hartmann, T. (2008). Mediated interpersonal communication in multiplayer video games: Implications for entertainment and relationship management. In E.A. Konijn, S. Utz, M. Tanis and S.B. Barnes (eds) *Mediated interpersonal communication* (pp. 309–30). New York: Routledge.

Lang, A. (1994). What can the heart tell us about thinking? In A. Lang (ed.) *Measuring psychological responses to media messages* (pp. 99–111). Mahwah, NJ: Lawrence Erlbaum.

Lasswell, H.D. (1935). *World politics and personal insecurity*. New York: Free Press.

Law, C. and Labre, M.P. (2002). Cultural standards of attractiveness: A thirty-year look at changes in male image in magazines. *Journalism & Mass Communication Quarterly*, 79, 697–713.

Leit, R.A., Gray, J.J. and Pope, H.G. (2002). The media's representation of the ideal male body: A cause for muscle dysmorphia? *International Journal of Eating Disorders*, 31, 334–8.

Levy, M.R. (1979). Watching TV news as para-social interaction. *Journal of Broadcasting*, 23, 69–80.

Lewis, M. (1994). Good news, bad news. *The Psychologist*, 7, 157–9.

Lewis, M.L., Weber, R. and Bowman, N.D. (2008). 'They may be pixels, but they're MY pixels': Developing a metric of character attachment in role-playing video games. *CyberPsychology & Behaviour*, 11, 515–18.

Leyens, J., Camino, L., Parke, R.D. and Berkowitz, L. (1975). Effects of movie violence on aggression in a field setting as a function of group dominance and cohesion. *Journal of Personality and Social Psychology*, 32, 346–60.

Lister, M., Dovey, J., Giddings, S. et al. (2009). *New media: A critical introduction* (2nd edn). Abingdon: Routledge.

Livingstone, S. (2009). Debating children's susceptibility to persuasion – where does fairness come in? A commentary on the Nairn and Fine versus Ambler debate. *International Journal of Advertising*, 28, 170–4.

Livingstone, S. and Brake, D.R. (2010). On the rapid rise of social networking sites: New findings and policy implications. *Children & Society*, 24, 75–83.

Livingstone, S. and Helsper, E.J. (2006). Relating advertising literacy to the effects of advertising on children. *Journal of Communication*, 56, 560–84.

McCaul, K.D., Jacobson, K. and Martinson, B. (1988). The effects of a state-wide media campaign on mammography screening. *Journal of Applied Social Psychology*, 28, 504–15.

McCracken, G. (1986). Culture and consumption: a theoretical account of the structure and movement of the cultural meaning of consumer goods. *Journal of Consumer Research*, 13, 71–85.

McCreary, D.R. and Sasse, D.K. (2000). An exploration of the drive for muscularity in adolescent boys and girls. *Journal of American College Health*, 48, 297–304.

McCutcheon, L.E., Lange, R. and Houran, J. (2002). Conceptualisation and measurement of celebrity worship. *British Journal of Psychology*, 93, 67–87.

McGuire, W.J. (1974). Psychological motives and communication gratification. In J.G. Blumler and E. Katz (eds) *The uses of mass communications*. Beverly Hills, CA: Sage.

Mackay, T., Ewing, M., Newton, F. and Windisch, L. (2009). The effect of product placement in computer games on brand attitude and recall. *International Journal of Advertising*, 28, 423–38.

McKenna, K.Y. and Bargh, J.A. (1998). Coming out in the age of the Internet: Identity 'demarginalisation' through virtual group participation. *Journal of Personality and Social Psychology*, 75, 681–94.

McLuhan, M.D. (1964/2001). *Understanding media: The extensions of man*. London: Routledge Classics.

McManus, J. (2009). The dream she dreamed: Cheers for a voice to silence the cynics. *Washington Post*, 17 April.

McQuail, D. (2005). *McQuail's Mass Communication Theory* (5th edn). Thousand Oaks, CA: Sage.

Madell, D.E. and Muncer, S.J. (2006). Internet communication: An activity that appeals to shy and socially phobic people? *CyberPsychology & Behaviour*, 9, 618–22.

Madell, D.E. and Muncer, S.J. (2007). Control over social interactions: An important reason for young people's use of the Internet and mobile phones for communication? *CyberPsychology & Behaviour*, 10, 137–40.

Maltby, J. (2010, in press). An interest in fame: Confirming the measurement and empirical conceptualization of fame interest. *British Journal of Psychology*.

Maltby, J. and Giles, D.C. (2008). Toward the measurement and profiling of celebrity worship. In J.R. Meloy, L. Sheridan and J. Hoffman (eds) *Stalking, threatening, and attacking public figures* (pp. 271–86). New York: Oxford University Press.

Maltby, J., Day, L., McCutcheon, L.E. et al. (2004). Celebrity worship using an adaptational-continuum model of personality and coping. *British Journal of Psychology*, 95, 411–28.

Maltby, J., Day, L., McCutcheon, L.E. et al. (2006). Extreme celebrity worship, fantasy proneness and dissociation: Developing the measurement and understanding of celebrity worship within a clinical personality context. *Personality and Individual Differences*, 40, 273–83.

Maltby, J., Houran, J., Lange, R. et al. (2002). Thou shalt worship no other gods – unless they are celebrities: The relationship between celebrity worship and religious orientation. *Personality and Individual Differences*, 32, 1157–72.

Maltby, J., Houran, M.A. and McCutcheon, L.E. (2003). A clinical interpretation of attitudes and behaviours associated with celebrity worship. *Journal of Nervous and Mental Disease*, 191, 25–9.

Marcus, B., Machilek, F. and Schütz, A. (2006). Personality in cyberspace: Personal web sites as media for personality expressions and impressions. *Journal of Personality and Social Psychology*, 90, 1014–31.

Mares, M. and Woodard, E. (2005). Positive effects of television on children's social interactions: A meta-analysis. *Media Psychology*, 7, 301–22.

Markus, H.R. and Nurius, P. (1986). Possible selves. *American Psychologist*, 41, 954–69.

Marshall, P.D. (2004). *New media cultures*. London: Arnold.

Marshall, R., Woonbong, N.A., State, G. and Deuskar, S. (2008). Endorsement theory: How consumers relate to celebrity models. *Journal of Advertising Research*, 48, 564–72.

Martin, K.D. and Smith, N.C. (2008). Commercializing social interaction: The ethics of stealth marketing. *Journal of Public Policy and Marketing*, 27, 45–56.

Martin, S. (2005). What does Heathcliff look like? Performance in Peter Kosminsky's version of Emily Brontë's *Wuthering Heights*. In M. Aragay (ed.) *Books in motion: Adaptation, intertextuality, authorship* (pp. 51–68). Amsterdam: Rodopi Press.

Maslow, A. (1943). A theory of human motivation. *Psychological Review*, 50, 370–96.

UNIVERSITY OF WINCHESTER
LIBRARY

Matthes, J., Schemer, C. and Wirth, W. (2007). More than meets the eye: Investigating the hidden impact of brand placements in television magazines. *International Journal of Advertising*, 26, 477–503.

Meloy, J.R., Sheridan, L. and Hoffmann, J. (2008). Public figure stalking, threats and attacks: The state of the science. In J.R. Meloy, L. Sheridan and J. Hoffman (eds) *Stalking, threatening, and attacking public figures* (pp. 3–36). New York: Oxford University Press.

Milgram, S. (1974). *Obedience to authority; An experimental view*. New York: HarperCollins.

Mooney, A. (2008). Boys will be boys: Men's magazines and the normalisation of pornography. *Feminist Media Studies*, 8, 247–65.

Morrison, D.E. (1999). *Defining violence: The search for understanding*. Luton: University of Luton Press.

Morry, M.M. and Staska, S.L. (2001). Magazine exposure: Internalization, self-objectification, eating attitudes, and body satisfaction in male and female university students. *Canadian Journal of Behavioural Science*, 33, 269–79.

Moseley, R. (2000). Makeover takeover on British television. *Screen*, 41, 299–314.

Mrowicki, J. and Giles, D.C. (2005). Desire and motivation for fame in a group of aspiring musicians: A qualitative study. Paper presented at the annual conference of the International Communication Association, New York.

Murray, J.P. (2008). Media violence: The effects are both real and strong. *American Behavioural Scientist*, 51, 1212–30.

Nairn, A. and Fine, C. (2008). Who's messing with my mind? The implications of dual-process models for the ethics of advertising to children. *International Journal of Advertising*, 27, 447–70.

Nash, A.S., Pine, K.J. and Messer, D.J. (2009). Television alcohol advertising: Do children really mean what they say? *British Journal of Developmental Psychology*, 27, 85–104.

Neumark-Sztainer, D., Paxton, S., Hannan, P. et al. (2006). Does body satisfaction matter? Five-year longitudinal associations between body satisfaction and health behaviours in adolescent females and males. *Journal of Adolescent Health*, 39, 244–51.

Newson, E. (1994). Video violence and the protection of children. *The Psychologist*, 7, 272–4.

Nightingale, V. (2007). The cameraphone and online image sharing. *Continuum: Journal of Media & Cultural Studies*, 21, 289–301.

North, A.C., Bland, V. and Ellis, N. (2005). Distinguishing heroes from celebrities. *British Journal of Psychology*, 96, 39–52.

Ofcom (2009). The consumer experience 2009: research report. Downloaded 13 April 2010 from http://www.ofcom.org.uk/research/tce/ce09/research09.pdf.

Olson, C.K., Kutner, L.A. and Warner, D.E. (2008). The role of violent video game content in adolescent development. *Journal of Adolescent Research*, 23, 55–75.

Ostrov, J.M., Gentile, D.A. and Crick, N.R. (2006). Media exposure, aggression and prosocial behaviour during early childhood: A longitudinal study. *Social Development*, 15, 612–27.

Owen, L., Auty, S., Lewis, C. and Berridge, D. (2008). Children's understanding of advertising: An investigation using verbal and pictorially cued methods. *Infant and Child Development*, 16, 617–28.

Paik, H. and Comstock, G. (1994). The effects of television violence on antisocial behavior: A meta-analysis.*Communication Research*, 21, 516–46.

Palmer, P. (1986). *The lively audience: A study of children around the television set.* Sydney: Allen & Unwin.

Palmgreen, P. and Rayburn, J.D. (1985). An expectancy-value approach to media gratification. In K.E. Rosengren, L.A. Wenner and P. Palmgreen (eds) *Media gratifications research: Current perspectives* (pp. 61–72). Beverly Hills, CA: Sage.

Parker, I. (1992). *Discourse dynamics: Critical analysis for social and individual psychology.* London: Routledge.

Pearson, J. (1972). *The profession of violence: The rise and fall of the Kray Twins.* London: Weidenfeld & Nicholson.

Penner, L.A., Dovidio, J.F., Pilavin, J.A. and Schroeder, D.A. (2005). Prosocial behaviour: Multilevel perspectives. *Annual Review of Psychology*, 56, 365–92.

Perloff, R.M. (1999). The third-person effect: A critical review and synthesis. *Media Psychology*, 1, 353–78.

Perner, J., Ruffman, T. and Leekam, S.R. (1994). Theory of mind is contagious: You catch it from your sibs. *Child Development*, 65, 1228–38.

Perse, E.M. and Rubin, R.B. (1989). Attribution in social and parasocial relationships. *Communication Research*, 16, 59–77.

Peter, J. and Valkenburg, P.M. (2009). Adolescents' exposure to sexually explicit internet material, sexual uncertainty, and attitudes toward uncommitted sexual exploration: Is there a link? *Communication Research*, 35, 579–601.

Peter, J., Valkenburg, P.M. and Schouten, A.P. (2005). Developing a model of adolescent friendship formation on the Internet. *CyberPsychology & Behaviour*, 8, 423–30.

Peters, D.P. and Ceci, S.J. (1982). Peer-review practices of psychological journals: The fate of published articles, submitted again. *Behavioural and Brain Sciences*, 5, 187–255.

Petty, R.E. and Cacioppo, J.T. (1981). *Attitudes and persuasion: Classic and contemporary approaches.* Dubuque, IA: Brown.

Petty, R.E. and Cacioppo, J.T. (1986). *Communication and persuasion: Central and peripheral routes to attitude change.* New York: Springer-Verlag.

Phillips, D.P. (1983). The impact of mass media violence on US homicides. *American Sociological Review*, 48, 560–68.

Phillips, D.P. and Hensley, J.E. (1984). When violence is rewarded or punished: The impact of mass media stories on homicide. *Journal of Communication*, 34, 101–16.

Piaget, J. and Inhelder, B. (1969). *The psychology of the child.* New York: Basic.

Plester, B., Wood, C. and Bell, V. (2008). Txt msg n school literacy: Does texting and knowledge of text abbreviations adversely affect children's literacy attainment? *Literacy*, 42, 137–44.

Pope, H.G., Olivardia, R., Gruber, A.J. and Borowiecki, J. (1999). Evolving ideals of male body image as seen through action toys. *International Journal of Eating Disorders*, 26, 65–72.

Pope, H.G., Phillips, K.A. and Olivardia, R. (2000). *The Adonis complex: The secret crisis of male body obsession.* New York: Free Press.

Premack, D.G. and Woodruff, G. (1978). Does the chimpanzee have a theory of mind? *Behavioral and Brain Sciences*, 1, 515–26.

Propp, V.J. (1958). *Morphology of the folktale.* Bloomington, IN: Indiana University. (Originally published 1928.)

Raacke, J. and Bonds-Raacke, J. (2008). MySpace and Facebook: Applying the uses and gratifications theory to exploring friend-networking sites. *CyberPsychology & Behaviour*, 11, 169–74.

Raney, A.A. (2004). Expanding disposition theory: Reconsidering character liking, moral evaluations, and enjoyment. *Communication Theory*, 14, 348–69.

Reeves, B. and Nass, C. (1996). *The media equation: How people treat computers, television and new media like real people and places.* Stanford University: Cambridge University Press.

Rockwell, D. and Giles, D.C. (2009). Being-in-the-world of celebrity: The phenomenology of fame. *Journal of Phenomenological Psychology*, 40, 178–210.

Rosen, C.S., Schwebel, D.C. and Singer, J.L. (1997). Preschoolers' attribution of mental states to pretence. *Child Development*, 68, 1133–42.

Royal College of Psychiatrists (2009). Position paper on pro-eating disorder websites. Downloaded 15 January 2010 from http://www.rcpsych.ac.uk/pressparliament/pressreleases2009/proanawebsites.aspx.

Rubin, A.M., Perse, E.M. and Powell, R.A. (1985). Loneliness, parasocial interaction, and local television news viewing. *Human Communication Research*, 12, 155–80.

Ruddock, A. (2001). *Understanding audiences: Theory and method.* London: Sage.

SanJosé-Cabezudo, R., Gutiérrez-Aranz, A.M. and Gutiérrez-Cillán, J. (2009). The combined influence of central and peripheral routes in the online persuasion process. *CyberPsychology & Behaviour*, 12, 299–308.

Savage, J. and Yancey, C. (2008). The effects of media violence exposure on criminal aggression: A meta-analysis. *Criminal Justice and Behaviour*, 35, 772–91.

Scheufele. D.A. (1999). Framing as a theory of media effects. *Journal of Communication*, 49, 103–22.

Schlesinger, P., Dobash, E., Dobash, R.P. and Weaver, K.C. (1992). *Women viewing violence.* London: British Film Institute.

Schlesinger, P., Haynes, R., Boyle, R. et al. (1998). *Men viewing violence.* London: Broadcasting Standards Council.

Schooler, D. and Ward, M. (2006). Average Joes: Men's relationships with media, real bodies, and sexuality. *Psychology of Men & Masculinity*, 7, 27–41.

Shaw, R. (2004). Making sense of violence: A study of narrative meaning. *Qualitative Research in Psychology*, 1, 131–52.

Shaw, R.L. and Giles, D.C. (2009). Motherhood on ice? A media framing analysis of older mothers in the UK news. *Psychology & Health*, 24, 221–36.

Shoemaker, P.J. (1996). Hardwired for news: Using biological and cultural evolution to explain the surveillance function. *Journal of Communication*, 46, 32–47.

Signorielli, N. (1990). Television's mean and dangerous world: A continuation of the cultural indicators perspective. In N. Signorielli and M. Morgan (eds) *Cultivation analysis: New directions in media effects research*. Newbury Park, CA: Sage.

Simonton, D.K. (1994). *Greatness: Who makes history and why*. New York: Guilford Press.

Skolnick, D. and Bloom, P. (2006). What does Batman think about SpongeBob? Children's understanding of the fantasy/fantasy distinction. *Cognition*, 101, B9–18.

Slater, M., Antley, A., Davison, A. et al. (2006). A virtual reprise of the Stanley Milgram obedience experiments. *PLoS ONE*, *1*, e39. Downloaded 17 January 2010 from http://www.plosone.org/article/info:doi%2F10.1371%2Fjournal.pone.0000039.

Snyder, M. and de Bono, K.G. (1985). Appeals to image and claims about quality: Understanding the psychology of advertising. *Journal of Personality and Social Psychology*, 49, 586–97.

Sood, S. (2002). Audience involvement and entertainment–education. *Communication Theory*, 12, 153–72.

Sperling, G. (1960). The information available in brief visual presentations. *Psychological Monographs*, 74 (11, Whole no. 498).

Srivastava, L. (2005). Mobile phones and the evolution of social behaviour. *Behaviour & Information Technology*, 24, 111–29.

Stevenson, N., Jackson, P. and Brooks, K. (2000). The politics of 'new' men's lifestyle magazines. *European Journal of Cultural Studies*, 3, 266–85.

Stever, G.S. (2009). Parasocial and social interaction with celebrities: Classification of media fans. *Journal of Media Psychology*, 14. Downloaded 22 January 2010 from http://www.calstatela.edu/faculty/sfischo/.

Stice, E., Schupak-Neuberg, E., Shaw, H. and Stein, R. (1994). Relation of media exposure to eating disorder symptomatology: An examination of mediating mechanisms. *Journal of Abnormal Psychology*, 103, 836–40.

Strayer, D.L. and Drews, F.A. (2007). Cell-phone-induced driver distraction. *Current Directions in Psychological Science*, 16, 128–31.

Sullivan, D.B. (1991). Commentary and viewer perception of player hostility: Adding punch to televised sports. *Journal of Broadcasting & Electronic Media*, 35, 487–504.

Tal-Or, N. and Papirman, Y. (2007). The fundamental attribution error in attributing fictional figures' characteristics to the actors. *Media Psychology*, 9, 331–45.

Taylor, L. (2005). It was beautiful before you changed it all: Class, taste and the transformative aesthetics of the garden lifestyle media. In D. Bell and J. Hollows (eds) *Ordinary lifestyles: Popular media, consumption and taste* (pp. 113–27). Maidenhead: Open University Press.

Taylor, L.D. (2006). College men, their magazines, and sex. *Sex Roles*, 55, 693–702.

Teather, D. (2009). Amazon gets set for cyber Monday as Christmas shopping online clicks. *The Guardian*, 23 November.

Thompson, G. (2009). *Measles and MMR statistics*. Social and General statistics, Parliamentary Research Briefings, House of Commons. Downloaded 25 January 2010 from http://www.parliament.uk/commons/lib/research/briefings/snsg-2581.pdf.

Tiggemann, M. (2005). Television and adolescent body image: The role of program content and viewing motivation. *Journal of Social and Clinical Psychology*, 24, 361–81.

Tiggemann, M. and Slater, A. (2003). Thin ideals in music television: A source of social comparison and body dissatisfaction. *International Journal of Eating Disorders*, 35, 48–58.

Tiggemann, M., Polivy, J. and Hargreaves, D. (2009). The processing of thin ideals in fashion magazines: A source of social comparison or fantasy? *Journal of Social and Clinical Psychology*, 28, 73–93.

Time (1982). Dividends: How sweet it is. *Time*, 26 July. Downloaded 13 January 2010 from http://www.time.com/time/magazine/article/0,9171,922960,00.html.

Toffler, A. (1970). *The third wave*. New York: Bantam.

Tudor, A. (1974). *Image and influence: Studies in the sociology of film*. London: George Allen & Unwin.

Turkle, S. (1995). *Life on screen: Identity in the age of the internet*. New York: Simon & Schuster.

Tversky, A. and Kahneman, D. (1981). The framing of decisions and the psychology of choice. *Science*, 211, 453–8.

Twemlow, S.W. and Bennett, T. (2008). Psychic plasticity, resilience, and reactions to media violence: What is the right question? *American Behavioural Scientist*, 51, 1155–83.

Utz, S. (2008). Social identification with virtual communities. In E.A. Konijn, S. Utz, M. Tanis and S.B. Barnes (eds) *Mediated interpersonal communication* (pp. 252–70). New York: Routledge.

Valkenburg, P.M. and Cantor, J. (2001). The development of a child into a consumer. *Journal of Applied Developmental Psychology*, 22, 61–72.

Vincent, J. (2005). Emotional attachment to mobile phones: An extraordinary relationship. In L. Hamill and A. Lasen (eds) *Mobile world: Past, present and future* (pp. 95–104). New York: Springer.

Vincent, R.C. and Basil, M.D. (1997). College students' news gratifications, media use, and current events knowledge. *Journal of Broadcasting & Electronic Media*, 41, 380–92.

Wallace, M. (2006). Big Brother: Worse than bear baiting. *Daily Mail*, 2 June.

Wallace, P. (1999). *The psychology of the Internet*. Cambridge: Cambridge University Press.

Walters, A. (2009). Virtual reality is coming of age. *The Guardian*, 31 December.

Weber, R., Behr, K., Tamborini, R. et al. (2009). What do we really know about first-person-shooter games? An event-related, high-resolution content analysis. *Journal of Computer-Mediated Communication*, 14, 1016–37.

Weber, R., Ritterfeld, U. and Mathiak, K. (2006). Does playing violent video games induce aggression? Empirical evidence of a functional magnetic resonance imaging study. *Media Psychology*, 8, 39–60.

Weisberg, D.S. and Bloom, P. (2009). Young children separate multiple pretend worlds. *Developmental Science*, 12, 699–705.

Whitty, M.T. (2006). Introduction. In M.T. Whitty, A.J. Baker and J.A. Inman (eds) *Online matchmaking* (pp. 1–16). Basingstoke: Palgrave Macmillan.

Wilson, B.J., Smith, S.L., Potter, W.J. et al. (2002). Violence in children's television programming: Assessing the risks. *Journal of Communication*, 52, 5–35.

Winston, B. (1998). *Media, technology and society – a history: From the telegraph to the Internet*. London: Routledge.

Wiseman, C.V., Gray, J.J., Mosimann, J.E. and Ahrens, A.H. (1990). Cultural expectations of thinness in women: An update. *International Journal of Eating Disorders*, 11, 85–9.

Wood, W., Wong, F.Y. and Chachere, J.G. (1991). Effects of media violence on viewers' aggression in unconstrained social interaction. *Psychological Bulletin*, 109, 371–83.

Woolley, J.D. (1997). Thinking about fantasy: Are children fundamentally different thinkers and believers from adults? *Child Development*, 68, 991–1011.

Yee, N., Bailenson, J.N., Urbanek, M., Chang, F., and Merget, D. (2007). The unbearable likeness of being digital: The persistence of nonverbal social norms in online virtual environments. *CyberPsychology & Behaviour*, 10, 115–21.

Young, B. (1990). *Children and television advertising*. Oxford: Clarendon.

Young, K. (1998). *Caught in the net*. Chichester: Wiley.

Zajonc, R.B. (1968). Attitudinal effects of mere exposure. *Journal of Personality and Social Psychology*, 9, Monograph supplement 2.

Zillmann, D. (1971). Excitation transfer in communication-mediated aggressive behaviour. *Journal of Experimental Social Psychology*, 7, 419–34.

Index

Entries in **bold** refer to glossary definitions

Reading guide

This table identifies where in the book you'll find relevant information for those of you studying or teaching A-level. You should also, of course, refer to the Index and the Glossary, but navigating a book for a particular set of items can be awkward and we found this table a useful tool when editing the book and so include it here for your convenience.

Topic	Page
Attitude change	56
Attraction of 'celebrity' – evolutionary explanations	112
Attraction of 'celebrity' – social psychological explanations	106
Celebrity worship	102, 106, 115–16, 190
Cognitive consitency	58–9
Cognitive dissonance	58–9
Effectiveness of television in persuasion	53, 55
Effects of computers	167
Effects of media on antisocial behaviour	31–48
Effects of media on prosocial behaviour	31–48
Effects of video games	38
Elaboration likelihood	60–1
Hovland Yale	56–8
Influence of attitude on decision–making	62, 64, 72
Persuasion	54
Self-perception	59–60
Stalking	117, 195

UNIVERSITY OF WINCHESTER
LIBRARY